Energy Law in Slovenia

Energy Law in Slovenia

Second Edition

Aleš Ferčič
Nataša Samec Berghaus

This book was originally published as a monograph in the International Encyclopaedia of Laws/Energy Law.

Founding Editor: Roger Blanpain
General Editor: Frank Hendrickx
Volume Editors: Kurt Deketelaere & Bram Delvaux

Wolters Kluwer

Published by:
Kluwer Law International B.V.
PO Box 316
2400 AH Alphen aan den Rijn
The Netherlands
E-mail: international-sales@wolterskluwer.com
Website: lrus.wolterskluwer.com

Sold and distributed by:
Wolters Kluwer Legal & Regulatory U.S.
7201 McKinney Circle
Frederick, MD 21704
United States of America
Email: customer.service@wolterskluwer.com

ISBN 978-94-035-2994-3

e-Book: ISBN 978-94-035-2943-1
web-PDF: ISBN 978-94-035-2944-8

The Authors

Dr Aleš Ferčič is an associate professor, a holder of the Jean Monnet Chair of Energy Law and Policy, and the head of the Institute of Public Law at the Faculty of Law of the University of Maribor, Slovenia, where he holds several courses within bachelor, master and doctoral study programmes which are directly or indirectly related to the field of energy law, i.e. energy law and policy of the European Union (EU); public economic law; liberalization of infrastructure sectors, public services and competition; constitutional and administrative law of the EU; European competition law (Erasmus programme); administrative law; public administration; and constitutional and administrative law, and EU legal system: selected issues. Moreover, he has hold invited lectures at several foreign universities as well as speeches at international conferences. His recent research work is mostly associated with public economic law, particularly with energy market regulation, competition and public services, as well as with environmental law. For example, his recent bilateral international projects analysed the existing Slovenian and Croatian energy legislation in the context of the new energy legislative package Clean Energy for all Europeans, and the role of non-governmental organizations in energy infrastructure projects. What is more, he is author or co-author of several monographs (e.g., *Public Services and Related Concepts in the European Union: Understanding the European Union's Legal Framework for Services of General Economic Interest*; *Genesis of Liberalized Sectors*; *Energy Law in Slovenia*; *State Aids: Theory, Practice and Legislation*; and *Introduction to European Union Law*) as well as scientific and expert papers. His research work is published by credible publishers, such as Kluwer Law International (Wolters Kluwer); Springer; Oxford University Press; Nova Science Publishers; C. H. Beck Verlag; and C. F. Müller Verlag. In addition to the said theoretical work, he is also engaged in legal practice providing public administration, undertakings and law firms with expert opinions and consulting services. Moreover, he is on the list of arbitrators of the Ljubljana Arbitration Centre at the Chamber of Commerce and Industry of Slovenia. And last but not least, he is also a member of several professional associations, including European Law Institute in Vienna.

The Authors

Dr Nataša Samec Berghaus is an associate professor at the Faculty of Law, University of Maribor, teaching the following subjects: Law of Obligations, Substantive Civil Law and Capital Market and Securities Law. She is also a permanent arbiter at the Central Securities Clearing Corporation of Slovenia. She received two awards: the Chancellor's Award for Best Law Student of the Generation by the University of Maribor and Young lawyer award for remarkable achievements by the Association of Slovenian Lawyers' Societies for her Master's thesis. She passed the bar exam in 2003. Under the mentorship of her professor at the Faculty of Law, University of Ljubljana, Slovenia, she got her Ph.D. She has been an active researcher for over twenty years. The subject of her research was initially focused on corporate law (analysing good corporate governance), capital market and securities law, commercial law and law of obligations (with particular emphasis on the issues of compensation claims in various fields). Since 2013, she has been working actively on medical law and the issues related to environmental and energy law. She has participated in six research projects and four research programmes in her research fields. Along with her two scientific monographs (*Corporate Takeover Defence: Preventive and Curative Defence Mechanisms* and *Stock Options: Aspects of Law of Obligations, Corporate Law, Labour Law, Insiders Perspective, and Tax Aspects*) and co-authorship of the monograph *Energy Law in Slovenia*, she has published twenty-three original scientific articles in Slovenia and abroad so far.

Table of Contents

Table of Contents

List of Abbreviations

ACER	Agency for the Cooperation of Energy Regulators
AEE	Act on Energy Economy
AN OVE	(Slovenian) RES Action Plan
AN-URE	(Slovenian) Energy Efficiency Action Plan
BA	Building Act of 2017
BOAL	Basic Organizations of Associated Labour
CHP	Combined Heat and Power
CO_2	Carbon Dioxide
DSO	Distribution System Operator
DSO	Distribution System Operator
EA	(Slovenian) Energy Act of 1999
EA-1	(Slovenian) Energy Act of 2014
EEU	Efficient Energy Use (Energy Efficiency)
EIA	Environmental Impact Assessment
EPA-1	Environmental Protection Act of 2004
EU	European Union
EU-ETS	EU Emission Trading System
GDP	Gross Domestic Product
GHG	Greenhouse Gas
GWh	Gigawatt-Hour
HECU	Heat and Electricity Coproducing Units
ICSID	International Centre for Settlement of Investment Disputes
IPPC	Integrated Pollution Prevention and Control
ITO	Independent Transmission Operator
km	Kilometre
Kt	Kiloton
kV	Kilovolt
kW	Kilowatt
kWh	Kilowatt-hour

List of Abbreviations

LNG	Liquefied Natural Gas
m^2	Square Metre
Mm	Millimetre
MW	Megawatt
NCA	Nature Conservation Act (1999)
NNP	National Normative Provisions
OECD	Organisation for Economic Co-operation and Development
PCA	Protection of Competition Act
PRCA	Prevention of Restriction of Competition Act (1999)
PRCA-1	Prevention of Restriction of Competition Act (2008)
RES	Renewable Energy Sources
SFRY	Socialist Federal Republic of Yugoslavia
(s)m^3	(Standard) Cubic Metre
t	Ton
TFEU	Treaty on the Functioning of the European Union
toe	Tonne of Oil Equivalent
TSO	Transmission System Operator
TWh	Terawatt-Hour
UN	United Nations
VAT	Value Added Tax
WA	Waters Act
Wh	Watt-Hour
ZRud-1	(Slovenian) Mining Act

Preface to the First Edition

This monograph discusses the energy legislation applicable in the Republic of Slovenia, which has been subject to significant change in the recent years. Although most of the changes were the result of adapting to European Union energy law, we have also highlighted changes (that occurred) as a result of a shift in the economic model. Social market economy was only introduced to the Republic of Slovenia a quarter of a century ago, which may, at first glance, seem a long time ago. However, in reality that is not long ago, especially considering the complexity of making the transition from a state plan (administrative) economy to a social market economy. The circumstances in which the authors wrote this monograph also represented an additional challenge. In 2014, after a significant delay, the new Energy Act of 2014 (EA-1) was adopted, which brought numerous novelties and modifications at the system level. At the same time, it abrogated dozens of regulations, most of which were only replaced with new regulations as the writing of this monograph came to an end (or even later; some of them are listed because of greater clarity).

Due to the aforementioned, in writing this monograph, the authors were only able to rely on the new legal framework without the adequate or sufficient support in Slovenian legal theory and jurisprudence concerning this new framework. The authors are aware of the relative nature of their positions or arguments concerning pending issues or open questions (which are their personal positions and arguments and do not necessarily reflect the official positions of the institutions they are employed by or are involved with in any other way), which will be clarified only gradually through jurisprudence and legal theory. Thus, the authors wish to already express their gratitude for any constructive criticism, notes or proposals for any potential improvements.

The information provided in this monograph has been verified with high accuracy. However, the information cannot substitute any legal or practical advice in a particular case.

Despite the pioneering nature of this monograph, both authors hope that it provides a comprehensive insight into the (emerging) energy law and policy of the Republic of Slovenia and that as such it will be of interest to those in scientific and professional circumstances interested in this evermore important economic sector.

The authors would like to take this opportunity to thank their families for all assistance, understanding and patience they received.

Preface to the Second Edition

Since 2016, when the first edition of this monograph was published, the Slovenian core legislative act in the field of energy, i.e. the Energy Act of 2014, was amended twice; namely in 2019 and 2020.[1] The 2019 amendment was relatively extensive since around sixty provisions were modified, mostly in order to, first, eliminate inconsistencies with the European Union legislation, second, to eliminate inconsistency with the Constitution of the Republic of Slovenia, and third, to enable new trends in the field of renewable energy. On the other hand, the 2020 amendment was less extensive and it was not adopted in order to eliminate past shortcomings but rather in order to accomplish the transposition of Directive (EU) 2019/692 of the European Parliament and of the Council of 17 April 2019 amending Directive 2009/73/EC concerning common rules for the internal market in natural gas in the Slovenian legal system.[2] In addition, numerous regulations and general acts, which further concretize the Energy Act of 2014, were adopted. Furthermore, let us not forget the case law since few judgments were issued which can be used as an interpretative tool. The latter is highly welcome since after four years from the first edition of this monograph the support offered by the Slovenian legal theory and case law remains modest. As a consequence, also this time we often stayed alone with the legislative acts.

Since the field of energy law is not an island but rather an integral part of the bigger system, at least some attention must be paid to other fields of law, e.g. environmental law, construction law, tax law, competition law, etc. As one might anticipate, there was a development also in these fields since 2016. Therefore, where appropriate, we pointed out also the modifications of legislative acts regulating the said fields of law, yet, at basic level only since the main focus is the currently valid Energy Act.

Moreover, we would like to emphasize that we are well aware of the fourth legislative package Clean Energy for all Europeans and of its anticipated impact on the Slovenian energy law. Indeed, it will bring significant legislative changes, but we have reasonable doubts whether the transposition in question will be achieved in due time. For illustration, the third legislative package was transposed with the delay which exceeded three years while more than an additional year was needed

1. Before that the Energy Act of 2014 was amended at the end of 2015, when the first edition was already in the print stage. The amendment in question was a minor one since it only modified four provisions on out-of-court settlement of disputes with household customers regarding the supply of natural gas as discussed in this edition.
2. Official Journal of the European Union, L 117, 3.5.2019, 1–7.

for the adoption of regulations and other general acts concretizing the Energy Act of 2014. After careful consideration of all relevant facts with the editor, we jointly decided to prepare the second edition of this monograph already in the second half of 2020 while future legislative acts needed for a transposition of the fourth legislative package will be discussed in the third edition.

The second edition of this monograph can be considered as both an update and upgrade of the first edition. Namely, more or less all legislative amendments of the Energy Act of 2014 are included in the second edition, and some parts of the text used in the first edition are further discussed or supplemented with relevant comments and facts.

As in the first edition of this monograph, the authors would like to explicitly point out that the information provided in this monograph has been verified with high accuracy; however, the information cannot substitute any legal or practical advice in a particular case. Moreover, not all issues are discussed in detail. At the same time, the authors wish to already express their gratitude for any constructive criticism, notes or proposals for any potential improvements.

And last but certainly not least, the authors would like to use this opportunity to thank once more their families for all assistance, understanding and patience they received when working on the second edition of this monograph.

General Introduction

1. The aim of the introduction to this monograph is to briefly examine the Republic of Slovenia and its subsystems, most notably those of particular significance from the perspective of energy sector and energy law and policy. It contains selected highlights and information of greater or lesser relevance to the discussion of all energy-related themes covered later in this monograph in substantively comprehensive sections and the corresponding chapters. The primary aim of the introduction is to facilitate a proper understanding of the complex energy challenges facing Slovenia's current energy law and policy.

2. Chapter 1 (General Background) presents general information about the Republic of Slovenia, its energy sector, the structure of the Government and the political arrangements, and its legal system.

3. Chapter 2 (Basic Principles of Slovenian Energy Law) deals with basic features and principles of energy law within the Slovenian legislation. In addition, it explains the relation between energy law and energy policy in Slovenia.

4. Chapter 3 (Historical Background and Development of Slovenian Energy Law) deals with some basic features of the development of the energy sector and energy legislation in Slovenia, which actually started on the territory of the Republic of Slovenia before the country declared its independence.

5. Chapter 4 (Role of Government Institutions in the Shaping and Administration of Slovenian Energy Law and Policy) presents the main players in Slovenian energy law and policy, with a particular focus on the executive branch of public authority (government), i.e., on the ministries and the bodies under the aegis of the ministries, and on public agencies that have a direct or indirect influence on the Slovenian energy sector. The bodies discussed are, inside the Ministry of Infrastructure, the Energy Directorate and the Infrastructure Inspectorate of the Republic of Slovenia (and its inspection departments), and inside the Ministry of the Environment and Spatial Planning, the Slovenian Nuclear Safety Administration and the Environment Agency. The Energy Agency and the Slovenian Competition Protection Agency are examined later, as extra-governmental institutions.

6. Chapter 5 (Legal Sources of Slovenian Energy Law) presents some of the key sources forming general Slovenian energy law, and certain other sources that are of significance to the energy sector despite not relating exclusively to it.

Chapter 1. General Background

7. This chapter contains general information about the Republic of Slovenia, including population and location, its energy capacities, and its political and (constitutional) legal system. It should be noted that this chapter consciously does not touch on any issues of Slovenian energy policy and law, as these are dealt with in the other chapters of the introductory section (Chapters 2–5), and comprehensively and in detail in other parts of the monograph (Parts I–VI).

§1. General Information about Slovenia

8. Slovenia became an independent country on 26 June 1991, having previously been one of the constituent republics of the Socialist Federal Republic of Yugoslavia (SFRY) as of 1945.[3] The country covers an area of 20,273 km^2, has the third-highest level of forestation in Europe and some of the richest water resources in the European continent. Its geography includes Alpine, Pannonian, Karst / Dinaric Alps and Mediterranean areas. It lies in the heart of Europe, and borders other European Union (EU) Member States, namely Italy, Austria, Hungary and Croatia.

9. It has a population of approximately 2.06 million, and the capital is Ljubljana, which is the biggest city with the highest number of inhabitants located in the central region. More or less all parts of the country are inhabited; yet, there is a clear 'gravitation' towards cities or urban centres. This is confirmed by significant differences in terms of density of population between individual parts or areas of the country. However, the average density of population is relatively low since it amounts 1,031 inhabitants per km^2.

10. The official language in Slovenia is Slovene or Slovenian language. In those municipalities where Italian or Hungarian national communities reside, Italian or Hungarian is also recognized as an official language.

11. The country joined the EU in 2004, and three years later joined the Eurozone. Of course, it is also a member of numerous other international organizations, both economic and non-economic, such as the United Nations (UN), the Council of Europe, the North Atlantic Treaty Organization, the World Trade Organization, and the Organisation for Economic Co-operation and Development (OECD).[4]

3. Between WWI and WWII it had been part of the State of Slovenes, Croats and Serbs, then joining the Kingdom of Serbs, Croats and Slovenes, which became the Kingdom of Yugoslavia. Before this it had been part of the Hapsburg monarchy and Austria-Hungary. Here there is a conscious decision not to go into earlier periods.
4. Since large investments in infrastructure, concessions, etc. often contain environmental dimension, here shall be also pointed out the Slovenia's membership in the ICSID.

12. Slovenia's economy is organized along the lines of the social market model. Protection of private property, freedom of economic enterprise and market competition are defined in the Constitution. It is ranked in the middle of EU Member States in terms of wealth (per capita Gross Domestic Product (GDP) stood at 22,083 EUR in 2018). Services account for by far the largest proportion of Slovenia's economy, the figure having strongly exceeded a half for some time now, while manufacturing accounts for approximately a quarter, construction for approximately a tenth, and agriculture for approximately two percent of the output. The economy is highly export-oriented, but is also heavily dependent on imports; imports and exports are close to three-quarters of GDP.

§2. General Information about the Slovenian Energy Sector

13. The Slovenian energy sector was – as a part of the then Yugoslavian energy sector – for decades after WWII organized according to the model of state-planned economy. Not surprisingly, exclusive and special rights lead to monopolistic or oligopolistic market structures in which public undertakings were not subject to genuine competition pressure.[5] In other words, there was a clear lack of classical market mechanisms. Things started to change after the country's independence, i.e. at the beginning of the nineties, since it introduced the social market economy. But of course, this shift from one to another kind of economic system cannot be done overnight. It is a long-term process which was largely accelerated by the then (European) Community law. In fact, already the first wave of energy sector liberalization as demanded by the first energy legislative package in the second half of the nineties affected the Slovenian energy law. Although the country was not formally obliged to transpose the supranational rules as contained in the first energy legislative package in its legal system, this was done largely since the country strived to join the then Community. Yet, already the second energy legislative package was a must for the country since the deadline for its transposition into national legal system expired after the country already joined the then Community. It is needless to discuss in detail that the same goes for the third and fourth energy legislative package and more generally, for the acquis communautaire.

14. Hence, it is possible credibly to form a thesis that the Slovenian energy sector was liberalized under the influence of EU law. This applies particularly to the energy and natural gas sectors, where the legal obstacles (i.e., exclusive or special rights) to enter onto those markets have been removed in advance, which we could call pro-competitive deregulation. However, such deregulation (in combination with general rules of competition, which serve to protect competition rather than to establish it) would not suffice for the transformation of previously closed and uncompetitive markets into (more) competitive markets, since companies that wish to enter this market would not be able to effectively provide use of a network infrastructure, which by its nature is a *conditio sine qua non* for selling energy, either in the form

5. Yet, similar can be said for the 'old' Member States of the then (European) Community; *see infra* note 47.

of electricity or natural gas. The next logical step is pro-competitive (*ex ante*) regulation, through which actual and not merely formal conditions would be created for the establishing of (desired) competition. It was precisely the problem of infrastructure that had to be solved, which is characterized by a combination of a natural monopoly and the economic irreversibility of fixed costs, which is known as a monopolistic bottleneck. This was done in such a way that the obligation of the former monopolist (incumbent), which owns and operates the (network) infrastructure, was defined such that it had to provide interested companies with access to it, and at a price which it did not set itself, but was set by the national sectoral regulator, which was established as an independent public agency precisely in order to implement price and other *ex ante* regulation of the energy sector. Since the simultaneous presence of the former vertically integrated monopolist on the markets both above and below the network infrastructure proved to be problematic, and also since it led it to the temptation of flexing its muscle, which stems from ownership and operation of the infrastructure, on the upstream or downstream markets, this led to disintegration or the separation of business activities, and this in most cases, as is discussed in the following parts of this monograph, at the most intensive level, i.e., to the owner's separating of the management of the transmission network from the other business activities on the upstream and downstream markets (this *ex ante* measure of regulation is known as ownership unbundling or separation). Similar situation and regulatory challenges (but not exactly the same) are characteristic of the distribution network, where, however, unbundling or separation has not reached the highest level. Namely, no ownership unbundling has occurred, although legal unbundling has, meaning that the economic entity managing the distribution network (or a part thereof) may not provide activities on either the upstream or downstream market, although a linked or related person can (e.g., a subsidiary or sister company). Of course, all just mentioned should be treated as a kind of a simplification only. Precise information for electricity, natural gas, coal and oil are contained in specific parts of this monograph.

15. Today, the Slovenian energy sector is an integral part of the internal market, and the consequences of this are examined in separate chapters. This chapter merely gives a rough illustration using selected figures for 2019.[6] Selected figures from Slovenia's energy balance are first presented, followed for practical reasons by selected figures which enable insight into the Slovenian energy sector.

16. The annual energy balance predicts the total annual consumption of individual energy sources and the methods of ensuring energy supply in the country. The anticipated energy balance for 2019, prepared according to the OECD/IEA

6. *See* Report of the Slovenian Energy Agency on the Situation in the Slovenian Energy Sector in 2019 [Poročilo o stanju na področju energetike v Sloveniji v letu 2019], 2020;
Report of the Slovenian Energy Agency, Important Indicators of the Electricity and Natural Gas Supply in 2014 [Pomembnejši kazalniki na področju oskrbe z električno energijo in zemeljskim plinom za leto 2014], May 2015; Energetska bilanca Republike Slovenije za leto 2014 [Energy Balance of Republic of Slovenia], August 2014; Report of the Slovenian Energy Agency on the Situation in the Slovenian Energy Sector in 2015 [Poročilo o stanju na področju energetike v Sloveniji v letu 2013], June 2014.

methodology, reveals the dominance of the petroleum products in various spheres. For example, the share of petroleum products in the structure of final energy consumption stands out with a share of 46.6%, followed by electricity (23.5%), renewable energy sources (RES) (12.6%), natural gas (11.9%), heat (3.6%), solid fuels (0.8%) and non-renewable industrial waste (1.0%).[7] Since Slovenia depends on import of petroleum products and natural gas,[8] whose share exceeds half of final energy consumption, it is only logical that the country depends on import of energy. The country's energy import dependence in 2019 amounts 49.2%.[9,10]

17. Electricity, as the second largest source in the final energy consumption, is produced from numerous power plants. The Slovenian electricity mix is structured as follows: nuclear fuel amounts 37.6%, renewable sources of energy amount 33.6%[11] and fossil fuels amount 28.8%. This relatively favourable structure, however, has a drawback. Namely, the operation of two important power plants, which produce more than 60%[12] of the produced energy in Slovenia, is relatively uncertain. Nuclear power plant in Krško, which is the only nuclear power plant in Slovenia,[13] started to operate in 1983. According to the original plan, it shall operate forty years, i.e. until 2023. But at the moment the procedure for prolongation of its operation for an additional twenty years, i.e. until 2043, is in progress. In this regard, the administrative body of first instance, i.e. the Slovenian Environment Agency, issued the decision in 2017 according to which there is no need to assess the environmental impact and to obtain an environmental consent.[14] In principle, the Slovenian Environment Agency decided this way since all annual safety inspections were positive, since the last operation permit issued in 2013 defined strict preventive measures, and since the anticipated impacts shall remain unchanged. However, several Slovenian NGOs, i.e. Focus, Pravno-informacijski center nevladnih organizacij, Umanotera and E-forum, lodged an appeal against the decision in question.

---

7. *See* Energy Balance of the Republic of Slovenija for the year 2019 [Energetska bilanca Republike Slovenije za leto 2019], Republic of Slovenia, Ministry of Infrastructure, 2019, p. 7.
8. In 2019, almost all natural gas and petroleum products were imported; *see* Energy Balance of the Republic of Slovenija for the year 2019 [Energetska bilanca Republike Slovenije za leto 2019], Republic of Slovenia, Ministry of Infrastructure, 2019, p. 13.
9. *See* Energy Balance of the Republic of Slovenija for the year 2019 [Energetska bilanca Republike Slovenije za leto 2019], Republic of Slovenia, Ministry of Infrastructure, 2019, p. 12.
10. In order to get a broader picture about the Slovenia's dependence on imported energy, the following data shall be considered: 47% in 2018; 48% in 2017; 46% in 2016; 48% in 2015; 44% in 2014; 46.9% in 2013; 50.9% in 2012; 47.5% in 2011; 48.7% in 2010; 47.5% in 2009; 54.8% in 2008; 52.0% in 2007; 51.4% in 2006; 51.8% in 2005; 51.3% in 2004; 52.6% in 2003; 49.7 in 2002. Moreover, it shall be pointed out that oil (petroleum) was fully imported while almost all natural gas was imported.
11. Within this share of the renewable sources of energy the hydro power contributed 92.4%, sun power contributed 4.8%, biomass contributed 2.7% and wind power contributed 0.1%.
12. *See* Report on Situation in the field of Energy Sector in Slovenia [Poročilo o stanju na področju energetike v Sloveniji], Agency for energy, 2019, p. 11.
13. But it is not the only object which falls under Council Directive 2009/71/Euratom of 25 Jun. 2009 establishing a Community framework for the nuclear safety of nuclear installations, Official Journal of the European Union, L 172, 2.7.2009, 18–22. The second object is the Research Centre TRIGA Mark II located in Podgorica near Ljubljana. Moreover, the central storage of radioactive waste is located in Brinje while two storages of tailings are located in Jazbec and Boršt.
14. *See* the Slovenian Environment Agency's decision, No. 35405-286/2016-16, 17.2.2017.

On the basis of this appeal, the Ministry of the Environment and Spatial Planning abolished the discussed decision.[15] It pointed out, *inter alia*, Case C-127/02,[16] according to which any plan or project not directly connected with or necessary to the management of the site is to be subject to an appropriate assessment of its implications for the site in view of the site's conservation objectives if it cannot be excluded, on the basis of objective information, that it will have a significant effect on that site, either individually or in combination with other plans or projects.[17] The Nuclear Power Plant Krško lodged an action against the Ministry's decision, and the Administrative Court of the Republic of Slovenia abolished the Ministry's decision due to relevant uncertainties which shall be cleared in the new decision.[18] In its new decision,[19] the Ministry followed the Agency's position and, as a consequence, the above-mentioned NGOs lodged an action against this decision which was upheld by the Administrative Court of the Republic of Slovenia.[20] The latter has, *inter alia*, considered several judgments of the Court of Justice of the European Union, e.g. Case C-137/14,[21] Case C-411/17,[22] Case C-121/11,[23] and Case C-2/07.[24] As a consequence, the Slovenian Environment Agency was bound to decide again about the necessity of the environmental impact assessment regarding the planned prolongation of operation period of the nuclear power plant (for additional twenty years, i.e. from 2023 to 2043). This time the Agency decided that for the discussed prolongation of operation the environmental impact assessment must be carried out and environmental consent must be acquired.[25] Considering the complexity, duration and uncertainty of the discussed assessment and related procedure, there is a real chance that the conditions for the prolongation of the operation will not be fulfilled until 2023, that is to say, until the expiration of the existing environmental consent. If this will be the case, a logical question arises: namely, how will the Republic of Slovenia fill a huge gap in the electricity supply, considering the importance of the nuclear power plant for the Slovenian electric-energy system. Moreover, also the operation of Thermal Power Plant Šoštanj is relatively uncertain. Namely, according to the original plan it shall operate until 2054, but there are constant calls for its premature closure mainly from environmental NGOs and some politicians. At the end of the day, however, due to the fact that Slovenia is dependent on imported energy, including electricity,[26] as well as that both power plants together produce more than 60% of the produced electricity in Slovenia, i.e. Nuclear Power Plant Krško 37.45% and Thermal Power Plant Šoštanj 24.84%, it is highly likely that at

15. *See* the Ministry's decision, No. 35402-10/2017/5, 14.7.2017.
16. ECLI:EU:C:2004:482.
17. It seems the most important issue is the seismic turning point in Libna.
18. *See* the Administrative Court's judgment, No. I U 1729/2017-18, 5.6.2018 (ECLI:SI:UPRS:2018:I.U.1729.2017.18).
19. *See* the Ministry's decision, No. 35402-10/2017/13, 11.9.2018.
20. *See* the Administrative Court's judgment, No. I U 2135/2018-17, 16.1.2020 (ECLI:SI:UPRS:2020:I.U.2135.2018.17).
21. ECLI:EU:C:2015:683.
22. ECLI:EU:C:2019:622.
23. ECLI:EU:C:2012:225.
24. ECLI:EU:C:2008:133.
25. *See* the Slovenian Environment Agency's decision, No. 35405-286/2016-42, 2. 10. 2020.
26. In 2019, the share of imported energy for households and industry was 16.5%.

least one or even both of them will continue to operate for a while.[27] This is even more so because several projects for new hydroelectric power plants were rejected due to the environmental concerns.[28] In this regard, we think that we need a broad public discussion or even a debate in Slovenia about the future development of the energy sector. This debate shall not be isolated or focused on individual energy projects, i.e. one-by-one, but shall rather include all energy projects. In other words, it seems there will be always a majority against each individual energy infrastructure project; however, we need a robust and sustainable energy sector and energy supply. Only this way, we believe, majority of people will realize some of the planned energy infrastructure projects are necessary in case they want to retain the present way of living. And here comes the ugly truth, the 'business as usual' demands energy, and at this level of development we simply need energy infrastructure which is never totally neutral from the environmental perspective.

18. Electricity production was 16,095 GWh,[29] of which nuclear accounted for 5,821 GWh, thermal power plants for 5,282 GWh, and hydro for 4,682 GWh. The transmission network is managed by a single company, i.e. ELES, and covers 2,859 km, of which 669 km is at 400 kV, 328 km is at 220 kV, 1,866 km is at 110 kV and 13 km is power cables. Slovenia is connected with the transmission networks with all neighbouring countries (Italy,[30] Austria[31] and Croatia)[32] except with Hungary.[33] The distribution network is formally managed by a single company, i.e. SODO, who contracts the direct provision of this service out to five companies, i.e. Elektro Ljubljana, Elektro Maribor, Elektro Celje, Elektro Gorenjska and Elektro Primorska.[34] The distribution network measures 64,714 km in length, of which 898 km is at 110 kV, 17,504 km is at 35 kV, 20 kV and 10 kV, and 44,312 km is at 0.4 kV. Electricity consumption amounted to 13,819 GWh, of which households accounted for 3,368 GWh, and the corporate sector, including the one pumped hydro station, for 10,415 GWh. Electricity imports amounted to 9,021 GWh, while exports amounted to 9,340 GWh. The market shares of the five largest suppliers on the retail electricity market are as follows: (a) for all final electricity users 18.0%, 17.3%, 12.9%, 10.8% and 8.8%; (b) in the electricity distribution system: no data for 2019;

27. This can be also deduced from the Slovenian National Energy and Climate Plan (*see infra*, Part I, Chapter 1) since it does not provide for immediate closure of the discussed power plant but it rather provides for gradual (long-term) process of its closure. For illustration, it provides for 30% decrease of lignite use. Moreover, the plan for the gradual closure shall be prepared until 2021 in the document called National Strategy for decrease of use of coal and restructuring of mining areas.
28. And similar can be said for wind turbines.
29. 1 toe = 0.01163 GWh.
30. One 400 kV and one 220 kV transmission networks.
31. *Ibid.*
32. Two 400 kV, two 220 kV and three 110 kV transmission networks.
33. At the moment, one 400 kV transmission network is under construction and shall be operative in the best case scenario in 2021.
34. In addition, there are few operators of closed distribution systems, i.e. SIJ Acroni, Petrol Energetika d.o.o., ZDS Jesenice, and Talum d.o.o.

(c) for corporate consumers of electricity: 17.4%, 15.9%, 12.7%, 9.8% and 9.3%; (d) for household consumers of electricity: 24.6%, 16.8%, 15.4%, 13.9% and 13.4%.[35]

19. Natural gas production was around 6,917,00 sm^3 which is less than 1% of whole gas consumption, which means almost all consumed natural gas was imported. The gas transmission network was managed by a single company, and covers 1,174 km, of which 963 km comprised the transmission of natural gas at above 16 bar and 211 km was transmission at 16 bar or below. The gas distribution network (at 16 bar or below) was managed by thirteen companies according to the local principle, and was 4,532 km in length.[36] Natural gas consumption amounted to 742 sm^3, of which 136 sm^3 went to household consumers and 606 sm^3 went to non-household consumers. Gas imports amounted to 885 sm^3 and its export was insignificant. This only confirms the finding that Slovenian users of natural gas almost fully depend on imported gas,[37] which is mainly[38] imported from Austria. The market shares of the five largest suppliers on the natural gas retail network were: 79.4%, 13.5%, 4.4%, 2.6% and 0.1%.[39]

20. In the Slovenian coal industry there was mining during the observation period; however, a real production is more or less limited to Premogovnik Velenje d.d. In Slovenia, there were numerous mines where brown and black coal as well as minerals and 'metals' were mined but they are closed or in the process of closure (e.g., in Trbovlje, Hrastnik, and Senovo). As a consequence, only lignite was mined in 2019, i.e. 3,142.8 t. It is also worthy to point out that the mining company Premogovnik Velenje d.d. is essentially dependent on the consumption of the Thermal Power Plant Šoštanj which still plays, as already explained above, a relatively important role in the Slovenian energy system.

§3. General Information about Government Structure and Political Arrangements in Slovenia

21. With regard to the governmental or public authorities arrangements in Slovenia, by way of introduction, it should be noted that the Constitution states that[40] Slovenia is organized as a democratic republic in which political power is vested in the people, who are primary in this sense, and who exercise their power directly and

35. In comparison, five years ago the shares of the five largest suppliers on the retail electricity market were as follows: (a) for all final electricity users: 23.0%, 18.2%, 12.7%, 11.8% and 9.5%; (b) in the electricity distribution system: 26.6%, 22.2%, 14.5%, 14.3% and 8.7%; (c) for corporate consumers of electricity: 25.3%, 16.0%, 12.6%, 11.6% and 9.4%; (d) for household consumers of electricity: 24.7%, 19.2%, 16.2%, 16.1% and 10.4%.
36. In addition, four companies are operators of closed distribution system.
37. While, as already pointed out, all used or consumed oil (petroleum) is imported.
38. The share of imported natural gas from Austria amounts 88%.
39. In comparison, five years ago the shares of five biggest natural gas suppliers on the retail natural gas markets were as follows: 56.8%, 10.4%, 7.8%, 5.7% and 5.2%.
40. The English version of the Constitution is available on the website of the Constitutional Court of the Republic of Slovenia http://www.us-rs.si/en/about-the-court/legal-basis/constitution/.

through elections, consistent with the principle of the separation of the legislative, executive and judicial branches of power.[41] Not surprisingly, most of political activities and public matters are carried out in the form of indirect democracy, i.e. through public authorities, yet, in some cases a referendum as a form of direct democracy is possible.[42] In last thirty years, there were twenty-three referendums in Slovenia while only one of them had a direct energy and environmental component.[43] In the same period, there were twenty-two peoples' initiatives and none of them had a direct effect in the field of energy and environment.

22. It is also worth to point out that the Slovenian Constitution defines the Republic of Slovenia as a legal and social state. Both concepts, i.e. the principles of legal and social state, can affect energy and environmental issues. For example, a connection between the principle of social state and energy is particularly obvious in case of energy poverty and its management while almost each energy and environmental issue sooner or later depends on the concept of legal state which demands, broadly speaking, a strict implementation of the rule of law, and it works like a kind of umbrella principle covering numerous legal principles such as legality, proportionality, protection of human rights and fundamental freedoms,[44] protection of vested rights and legitimate expectations, legal certainty and security, etc. Moreover, the public authority organs and other persons of public law may only act in the cases and in the manner set out by law, while persons of private law may do anything that is not prohibited by law. In this regard already the Slovenian Constitution stipulates several limitations for individuals in favour of the environment which affects, *inter alia*, energy issues such as energy infrastructure. For example, according to Article 67(1) of the Slovenian Constitution, the manner in which property is acquired and enjoyed shall be established by law so as to ensure its economic, social, and environmental function. Moreover, there are several other constitutional provisions which are important from the environmental (and energy) perspective, e.g. Article 70 (public good and natural resources), Article 70a (right to drinking water), Article 71 (protection of land), Article 72 (healthy living environment), Article 73 (protection of natural and cultural heritage).

---

41. It is a kind of a principal (people)–agent (politicians) relationship.
42. The Slovenian Constitution stipulates the possibility of referendum in case of the country's accession to international organizations as well as for confirmation of constitutional changes and for confirmation of legislative acts, and for establishment of municipality; *see* Arts 3a, 90, and 139 of the Slovenian Constitution. The constitutional provisions are concretized by the Referendum and Popular Initiative Act (Official Gazette of the Republic of Slovenia, No. 26/07 – official consolidated text, and 6/18). Moreover, a referendum on municipality acts is possible. Another form of direct democracy is peoples' initiative; a proposal to initiate the procedure for amending the Constitution may be made by at least thirty thousand voters, while at least five thousand voters may submit a draft act to the National Assembly; *see* Art. 88 of the Slovenian Constitution and Arts 57 and 58 of the Referendum and Popular Initiative Act.
43. Namely, in 1996, people largely rejected the legislative act on (public) financing of a new block for the thermal power plant in Trbovlje (TET 3).
44. It is important to underline that constitutional provisions on human rights and fundamental freedoms are directly applicable.

23. Since Slovenia joined the EU supranational rules of the latter, i.e. acquis communautaire, must be considered as well. Article 3a of the Slovenian Constitution stipulates, *inter alia*, that legal acts and decisions adopted within international organizations to which Slovenia has transferred the exercise of part of its sovereign rights shall be applied in Slovenia in accordance with the legal regulation of these organizations. To put it simply, EU law must be applied in accordance with EU law starting with fundamental principles, such as autonomy, primacy and effectiveness of the EU law, its direct effect and beyond. It is the EU law which defines conditions for its own penetration in the Member States' legal system, the relationship between supranational and national rules in case of their collision, the conditions when individuals can directly claim rights established by supranational rules before national organs, etc. The sources of EU law which penetrate into the Slovenian legal system become its integral part; moreover, they have a constitutional character.[45] This is very important since EU environmental law is a huge corpus of law. The EU law is not a kind of a foreign law but rather law of Member States. Namely, primary EU law is created by Member States while secondary EU law is created by institutions of the EU which are composed by national representatives.[46]

24. The institutions of the EU must be considered as a part of the Member States' authorities or Member State's governance structure; in other words, Member States 'share' EU institutions.

I. Legislative Branch

25. The National Assembly and the National Council perform the function of a bicameral parliament,[47] although it should be noted that the legislative function is centred on the National Assembly. The latter alone is a purely representative body,[48] which has the exclusive right to pass laws, while the National Council, which represents certain precisely defined interest groups (representatives of employers, employees, farmers, craftsmen, freelancers, non-economic sector and local authorities), has limited powers, as it can merely propose laws to the National Assembly for adoption, provides it with (non-binding) opinions, or requests a parliamentary investigation or a revote on a particular law.

45. *See* §4 of this chapter.
46. For example, the European Parliament is consisted of representatives elected directly by EU citizens; the European Council is consisted of prime ministers and of presidents of Member States; the Council of the EU is consisted of competent ministers of Member States and so forth.
47. In the formal sense it is not a bicameral parliament, as the National Council is defined (merely) as a separate body and is not a part of the parliament in formal organizational terms, although it does have certain powers that are customary of an upper house, for which reason the National Council can be labelled the second chamber of the Slovenian parliament in substantive terms.
48. It consists of members who are directly elected by eligible voters.

II. Executive Branch

26. The Government exercises the executive function,[49] and consists of the prime minister and ministers (heading ministries). The Government and the ministers are independent and accountable to the National Assembly within the framework of their powers. The ministries are each established for performing administrative tasks in one or several administrative areas, including energy and environmental issues. Expert or professional support for the ministries is provided by the civil service or administration, who perform the administrative tasks set out by law.

27. Bodies within a ministry are established for performing specific expert tasks, executive and developmental administrative tasks, tasks in connection with inspections and other types of supervision, and tasks in the area of public services, where this ensures greater efficiency and quality in the performance of the tasks or where the nature of the tasks or the area of work requires a greater level of professional independence in the performance of tasks, while administrative units are established for performing state administration tasks that need to be organized and provided on a territorial basis.[50] It is common to all of these bodies that in the formal organizational sense they fall within the remit of the state administration, although it should be noted that administrative tasks can be delegated to bodies outside the state administration in the legal organizational sense, i.e., to holders of public authorizations. A public authorization to perform specific administrative tasks can be obtained by a legal person under public or private law or a natural person, by law or pursuant to law. In exercising these public authorizations, the holders have the rights and obligations of administration as set out by law or other regulations.

28. Among the holders of public authorizations, certain public agencies are worthy of note: they are persons under public law that are established for performing regulatory, developmental or expert tasks in the public interest, insofar as any other status is not envisaged by law. In general, it can be said that they are established when doing so makes the performance of administrative tasks more effective and more efficient than it would be at an administrative body, in particular when the performance of administrative tasks can be fully or primarily financed by means of administrative fees or user payments, or when, given the nature or type of the (administrative) tasks, continual direct political control of the performance of the delegated (administrative) tasks is neither needed nor appropriate. Put simply, it could be said that the essence of a public agency is its specialization, its expertise and its autonomy and independence from politicians, political pressures and lobbying in general, which ought to be a key attribute of the regulator of the sector.[51]

49. The executive branch also includes the administration and the president of the Republic of Slovenia (the latter has very limited operational powers).
50. The Constitution also envisages local self-government, whereby the powers of the municipalities are set out by law. In principle it can be said that the powers of the municipalities are relatively modest.
51. For more on the regulator of the energy sector, *see infra*; Introduction, §4 General Information about Slovenian Legal System.

29. The Ministry of Infrastructure covers, *inter alia*, the field of energy infrastructure and energy sector in general. It is consisted of several organizational units, namely, Minister's Office, Energy Directorate, Land Traffic Directorate, Air and Maritime Traffic Directorate, Sustainable Mobility and Traffic Policy Directorate, etc. Moreover, there are few public bodies within the discussed ministry; namely, the Slovenian Infrastructure Agency, the Infrastructure Inspectorate of the Republic of Slovenia, and the Slovenian Maritime Inspectorate. At the end of the day, however, the most important organizational unit in the field of energy is the Energy Directorate (which ensures the performance of administrative tasks and measures to ensure a reliable energy supply, increase energy efficiency and savings, and boost the use of energy from renewable sources, and it also carries out the implementation of administrative tasks and measures related to mining).

30. The Ministry of the Environment and Spatial Planning is currently consisted of several organizational units, i.e. Minister's Office, Environment Directorate, Water and Investments Directorate, Spatial Planning, Construction and Housing Directorate, Public Relations Office, Internal Audit Service, EU Coordination and International Affairs Service, Environmental and Spatial System Service, Integrity and Transparency Service, Secretariat. Moreover, there are several public bodies within the discussed ministry; namely, Slovenian Environment Agency, Inspectorate of the Republic of Slovenia for the Environment and Spatial Planning, Surveying and Mapping Authority of the Republic of Slovenia, Slovenian Nuclear Safety Administration, and Slovenian Water Agency.

III. Judicial Branch

31. The courts exercise the judicial function, and judges are independent in their work, bound solely by the Constitution and the legislative acts. The arrangements and powers of the courts in Slovenia are set out by the law. General courts, specialist courts and the Constitutional Court of the Republic of Slovenia are distinguished.

32. General courts decide on all matters other than those reserved for the specialist courts. The Courts of First Instance are local courts and district courts; in simple terms it could be said that the district courts have jurisdiction over cases where the value in dispute or the size of the potential fine is above a value stipulated by law (in cases of criminal law departments), or, in short, in more complex cases. There are (four) higher Courts of Second Instance, which are primarily responsible for deciding on appeals, which are an ordinary legal remedy. The court of third instance is the Supreme Court of the Republic of Slovenia, which is primarily responsible for deciding on extraordinary legal remedies.

33. The specialist courts decide on matters of labour law and social law (the Labour and Social Court of the Republic of Slovenia) and administrative law (the Administrative Court of the Republic of Slovenia). It is mainly the Administrative Court that is of importance from the energy perspective. It rules on administrative disputes, while judicial control is exercised by the Supreme Court. There are merely two instances in these cases, not three as elsewhere.

34. Mention should also be made of the Constitutional Court, which is entirely independent of the other bodies, is the most senior judicial body for the protection of constitutionality and legality, human rights and fundamental freedoms, and is *inter alia* responsible for ruling on: the constitutional compliance of laws; the compliance of laws and other regulations with ratified international treaties and the general principles of international law; the compliance of secondary legislation with the Constitution and with laws; the compliance of general (legal) acts issued for the exercise of public authorizations with the Constitution, laws and secondary legislation; and constitutional appeals against violations of human rights and fundamental freedoms by individual acts.

§4. General Information about Slovenian Legal System

35. The Slovenian legal system consists of formal legal acts of domestic origin and of transposed formal legal acts. Under the principle of primacy, EU law generally takes precedence over all other acts that are part of the Slovenian legal system. The Slovenian Constitution stipulates that legal acts and decisions adopted within the framework of the EU are applied in Slovenia in accordance with the EU legal system, which in simple terms means that it is EU law and not the Slovenian Constitution that determines the manner and the conditions for the former's penetration into the Slovenian legal system, its position within the Slovenian legal system and the conditions that must be met for an individual to be able to exercise the rights set out in EU law in proceedings before the national authority. In the event of a collision between any EU rules and any (other) rules of Slovenia, in principle the EU rules take precedence and are applied in the specific case, while any national rule that contravenes a supranational rule is simply ignored. By contrast, the situation is different with regard to classical international law, which consists of (traditional) international treaties, general legal principles and international customary law, as all the aspects mentioned previously are determined by the Constitution. Namely, the latter stipulates that international treaties penetrate the Slovenian legal system upon ratification and publication, while by contrast this condition is not stipulated for general legal principles recognized by civilized nations and international customary law. In the hierarchical sense, the Constitution stipulates that international treaties ratified by parliament via a law, general legal principles and international customary law are directly below the Constitution and above laws and secondary legislation, while international treaties ratified by the Government via a decree rank below laws but above secondary legislation.

36. In the hierarchical sense it could thus be said in rather simplified terms that the apex of the Slovenian legal system consists of EU law and the Slovenian Constitution; the second rank consists of international treaties by which Slovenia is bound that have been ratified by the National Assembly via a law (the legislator), and the general principles recognized by civilized nations and international customary law; the third rank consists of laws or acts; the fourth rank consists of international treaties by which Slovenia is bound that have been ratified by the Government via a decree; and the fifth rank consists of secondary legislation and other general acts.

37. Slovenian law has the traditional division into public law and private law. In slightly simple terms, it could be said that public law regulates relations in which central government bodies, local government bodies or holders of public authorizations act as the executive *(iure imperii).* By contrast, private law applies to civil and commercial relations *(iure gestionis)*, including also commercial relations between public entities and private persons.

38. Both public law and private law are important to the energy sector, although it should be noted that the former is prevalent when there is any consideration of the bodies presented in Chapter 4 of this introductory part. Namely, these bodies may adopt both general and individual acts, whereby in the context of the issues under discussion it should be noted that individual acts via which rulings are made in administrative (or public) law on the rights, obligations or legal benefits of persons under private law are adopted within the framework of administrative proceedings. Administrative proceedings are regulated by several laws, one of which is general and regulates all aspects of administrative proceedings, and as such is applied in rulings on all administrative matters (and *mutatis mutandis* in other public law matters), unless stipulated otherwise for the individual case by a specific law (in this case the law governing general administrative proceedings is applied on a subsidiary basis, which means that it only applies to those aspects not regulated by the specific law). An administrative dispute is allowed in principle against (substantive) rulings adopted in administrative proceedings, and is heard before the specialist Administrative Court or before the Supreme Court. A constitutional appeal is allowed in the case of violations of human rights and fundamental freedoms, and is ruled on by the Constitutional Court.

Chapter 2. Basic Features, Objectives and Principles of Slovenian Energy Law

39. This chapter deals with basic features, objectives and principles of Slovenian energy law.

§1. Basic Features of Slovenian Energy Law

40. Energy law, being conceived as a system of rules and principles governing energy sources management,[52] is a relatively young legal branch. In the territory of Slovenia, the genuine energy law was developed after WWII. This post-war period can be divided into several parts as discussed latter in this monograph,[53] but for practical reasons we are focusing only on time period after Slovenia became an independent country with social market economy. As of the nineties, the Slovenian energy law was essentially influenced by the EU law. First, the Energy Act of 1999 (EA) was adopted; however, this act was modified in accordance with the EU law. In 2014, the EA was abrogated by the Energy Act-1 of 2014 (EA-1). The latter constitutes the very core of the Slovenian energy law (for a more detailed overview of the distribution of the sources of the Slovenian energy law *see* Chapter 5 Sources of the Slovenian Energy Law), but it seems after the transposition of the legislative package Clean Energy for all Europeans, the EA-1 will be substituted by several legislative acts.[54] However, due to the considerations pointed out in the preface to the second edition of this monograph, in this edition we deal with the latest version of the EA-1.

41. The framework of the energy law in Slovenia, which has been set within Article 1 EA-1, includes the rules that define the following:

- energy policy principles;
- energy market operation rules;
- methods and practices of the performance of commercial public services in the energy sector;
- principles and measures to achieve security of energy supply, improve energy efficiency and energy conservation, and boost renewable energy use;
- operating conditions for energy equipment;
- powers, organization, and operations of the Energy Agency and powers of other authorities that perform their functions in accordance with the EA-1.

52. Cf. R.J. Heffron, *Energy Law: An Introduction*, SpringerBriefs in Law, 1.
53. *See* Chapter 3.
54. For example, with at least three legislative acts, namely, on energy efficiency, renewable energy, and energy market regulation.

42. The EA-1 shall in principle[55] apply to:

(1) all performers of energy sector activities (legal entities of public and private law and natural persons) in processing of oil and petroleum products; storing of gaseous, liquid and solid fuels; transmission of energy and fuels through networks; production, trading and distribution of liquid fuels; electricity generation; production and distribution of heat for district heating and cooling; operation of electricity market; trading, representation and intermediation in electricity and natural gas markets; and
(2) other parties (other legal entities under public and private law and natural persons), including:
   - economic operators who perform the activities of coal, petroleum, and natural gas extraction;
   - providers of energy services, energy consulting, and energy audits;
   - fitters of installations using RES;
   - producers or their authorized agents or importers that place energy-related products on the market;
   - producers or their authorized agents or importers who place on the market installations for the production of heat from RES;
   - operators or owners of public car parks and car parks accessible to the public, and car parks within buildings of public sector entities;
   - public sector entities;
   - Eco Fund, Slovenian Environmental Public Fund;
   - owners of buildings;
   - users of buildings;
   - legal entities of public and private law and natural persons who are owners or users of energy installations, plants and lines; and
   - final customers of energy.

43. The EA-1 is supplemented by a number of sectoral acts (a particular part of energy law) and implementing regulations, which combined constitute Slovenian energy law (please find more on the energy legislation in the past and now in Chapters 3 and 5, respectively).

44. Energy law can be defined as intradisciplinary, as it is related to many other legal fields (e. g. competition law, environment protection law, tax law, consumer protection law, public procurement law, concessions law, administrative law, civil law) but it can also be considered interdisciplinary because of the influence of other disciplines (e.g., economy, electrical and mechanical engineering), which are its imperative constituent part.

45. Energy law can by large be regarded under the domain of the public law, both from the point of view of its authorities, presented in more detail in Chapter 4,

55. The EA-1 defines when its rules do not apply to a particular person liable from Art. 6 EA-1; For example, rules on functional separation of distribution system operators do not apply to distribution system operators having less than 1,000 customers connected (Art. 84(3) EA-1).

who are empowered to adopt general as well as individual acts, and the point of view of the legal nature of its norms. At the same time, energy law incorporates also some elements of private law, since both contractual and non-contractual (liability) relationships and other private law situations exist among the entities on the energy market. Whenever individual entities which are subject to special security/cogent norms enter into such (private law) relationships – which might (or not) be about carrying out public functions or acting under public authorization – their autonomy of the will in the conclusion of legal transactions is naturally restricted by public law rules (contracting obligation, safeguarding the principles of energy law, consumer protection, environmental protection). However, in the evaluation of civil law issues (assumptions in legal transactions, damage liability, refund claims, property law issues) general rules and principles of civil law or law of obligations will apply.

46. On the grounds that legal relations within energy law are largely influenced by rules pertaining to public law, a number of general principles that have been formed under the classical administrative law can also apply to this field of law. The definition and the use of rules under energy law are naturally to a large extent determined by EU law – both special rules pertaining to energy law and general EU rules.

47. Let us mention that even in 2020, energy law is still a rather relatively unknown field of law in Slovenia, which lacks basic academic literature, which is typical of other legal fields. Also, energy law is not included in curriculums as a special subject. Instead, individual segments covering energy law are incorporated into other subjects (competition protection law, environmental protection law, and the law of obligations in the segment dealing with consumer protection). However, at certain universities, Energy Law can be selected by faculty students as an elective course.

§2. Objectives and Principles of Energy Law

48. The purpose of the Slovenian energy law pursuant to Article 3 EA-1 is to ensure a competitive, secure, reliable and accessible supply of energy and energy services, taking into account the principles of sustainable development.

49. In order to reach the aforementioned purpose, the EA-1 sets some principal objectives (Article 5 EA-1), which comprise:

- reliable energy supply;
- establishment of effective competition in the energy market;
- competitiveness in performing non-market activities;
- efficient energy transformation;
- reduced use of energy;
- energy efficiency;
- increased production and use of RES;
- transition to a low-carbon society with the application of low-carbon energy technologies;

- provision of energy services;
- assurance of social cohesions;
- protection of consumers as final customers of energy;
- provision of effective control over the implementation of the act provisions.

I. Energy Law and Policy in Slovenia

50. In the past twenty years, the energy law and policy in Slovenia have been influenced by the EU energy law and policy as best demonstrated by the chronology and contents of the amendments to the original EA and the EA-1 and their amendments and relating general and individual legal acts.[56] Article 22 of the new EA-1 expressly underlines that the obligations under international treaties and agreements, in particular those concerning the energy market, investments, the transmission of energy and energy sources, and integration into international energy networks, form an integral part of energy policy and planning of the development of energy sector activities.

51. In Article 20 EA-1, energy policy in Slovenia is defined as the implementation of measures in accordance with the principles of EA-1, which are used to achieve a reliable, sustainable, and competitive national supply of energy by means of promoting the objectives, most of which are in line with the objectives of energy law (*see* and compare with earlier references within this section). Article 20(1) EA-1 provides a list of the respective objectives, which includes security and quality of energy supply, balanced long-term development of energy economy based on trends in energy consumption, planned diversification of various primary energy sources, taking into account their economics, competitive energy supply, use of renewable and low-carbon energy sources, ensuring the priority of efficient energy use (EEU) over energy supply, environmentally acceptable production, generation, transmission and consumption of all types of energy, competition in the energy market, flexible energy users, and consumer protection.

52. Energy policy pursues the objectives of energy law by means of concretizing the measures in line with the principles set out in the energy legislation.

53. Let us mention that concretizing the energy policy measures is at the first stage a dynamic process of defining and classifying objectives. But above all, concretization must involve deliberate decisions on the use of means and methods that seem adequate, in view of the circumstances, for reaching the set objectives.

54. In line with Article 20(2) EA-1, the energy policy measures must be determined in long-term planning documents, namely, in the energy concept of Slovenia,

56. Earlier, the development of Slovenia's energy policy was influenced by the socio-economic model of the former SFRY (read more on that in Chapter 3).

in the comprehensive national energy and climate plan, and in operational and action plans for individual fields of energy supply and management.[57]

55. Ensuring efficient energy policy is necessarily associated with proper legislation, while at the same time it is the energy policy that directs the legislation.[58]

56. Energy law (a system of legal principles and rules concerning energy issues) and energy policy (selection of goals and their ranking, and implementation of appropriate measures) intertwine in a number of viewpoints. This is pretty obvious in the Energy Law and Policy Triangle or Energy Trilemma (energy security, equity, sustainability).[59] Nowadays, however, the situation seems to be even more complex since additional goals and objectives form energy law and policy, e.g. energy efficiency, economic efficiency and competition, etc. Each of the above-mentioned aspects tries to 'pull' energy policy and in turn energy law in its own direction. However, the effectiveness of energy law depends on the balance that is being established among the selected aspects. The principles of the Slovenian energy law, which are set out in section II EA-1 and introduced later in this chapter take into consideration all the above-mentioned aspects.

57. At the moment, a fundamental development document in Slovenia is national energy and climate plan as demanded by the EU legislation on Energy Union and Climate Action (governance mechanism), which tries to ensure, *inter alia*, the achievement of the 2030 and long-term objectives and targets of the EU in line with the so-called Paris Agreement (2015) through complementary, coherent and ambitious efforts by the EU and its Member States, while limiting administrative complexity. Slovenia adopted and published its final National Energy and Climate Plan in February 2020. This plan can be considered as a strategic document which defines public policies, i.e. aims and measures which will be carried out in all fields of the Energy Union until 2030 (with appropriate consideration of the desired development until 2040). With due consideration of the discussed document Slovenia plans to adopt a new national energy concept, which will represent a national energy programme and will be adopted via a resolution by the National Assembly at the proposal of the Government on the basis of projections of Slovenia's economic, environmental and social development, and on the basis of its international commitments to set targets for reliable, sustainable and competitive energy supply for the next twenty years and rough targets for the next forty years (albeit with interim controls, which should indicate whether the concept is still appropriate). A projection of the energy balance and the manner of energy supply and management are to be determined in this connection, on the basis of a twenty-year development projection for the country, taking account of technological, environmental and geopolitical trends of development; the national targets in energy supply and management; the requisite measures to meet the aforementioned targets; the commitments with regard to renewables; and indicators of corresponding energy policy targets in the state budget programme. At this point it is also worthy to point out the National Strategy for Decreased Use of Coal and for Restructuring of Coal Regions in Accordance with Principles of Fair Development. The preparation of the draft strategy is scheduled for September 2020, while the deadline for final version is still uncertain but it is reasonable to expect it in 2021. *See* more about the Slovenian energy policy in the chapters which deal with electricity and natural gas.
58. Cf. R.J. Heffron, *Energy Law: An Introduction*. SpringerBriefs in Law, 67.
59. Energy security: 'The effective management of primary energy supply from domestic and external sources, the reliability of energy infrastructure, and the ability of energy providers to meet current and future demand.' Energy equity: 'The accessibility and affordability of energy supply across the population'. Environmental sustainability: 'The achievement of supply and demand-side energy efficiencies and the development of energy supply from renewable and other low-carbon sources.' (sourced from World Energy Trilemma – Time to get real – the case for sustainable energy investment, World Energy Council, 2013, 8).

II. Basic Principles of Slovenian Energy Law

57. Simultaneous provision of all the objectives of EA-1 is hardly a simple thing but rather opposite. The section II EA-1 therefore defines the basic principles which need to be considered and which help persons – whom the norms are targeted at – to properly understand, interpret and apply the rules forming energy law. This concerns the principles that need to be considered in achieving all of the energy relating objectives and in implementing the energy policy measures.

58. As regards the objectives, a question may arise, at a certain point, as to what measures to use when there are several to choose from. The principle of priority in Article 7 of EA-1 defines the priority of measures or projects in case of comparable overall cost of alternative options. Hence, with regard to comparable costs considered in the life of a facility, energy efficiency measures have priority over the measures for the provision of new energy supply capacities. Yet, in cases where new capacities are unavoidable, the priority is given to the capacities that use RES. It is vital, however, to take into consideration the total cost in the lifetime of a project, which comprises energy expenditures in addition to the investment cost. All in all, this principle is fully reasonable and easy to understand since in reality, at least at current level of technical and technological development, there is no energy production with no harmful effects on nature and environment. We can just rank energy production modes according to high, moderate and low negative impact, and we can principally choose those with low negative impact, but unfortunately there is no neutral energy production mode on the menu. Since energy efficiency enables less energy production, it simply must be among the top priorities when looking from the environmental perspective.[60] In fact, where the latter is at stake there are three main pillars of combating climate change, i.e. increase of energy efficiency, decrease of fossil fuels until its total abandon and increase of renewables.

59. Also, cost-efficiency[61] is considered to be one of the basic principles, as it binds all national as well as local authorities to act rationally with regard to any measures (policy adoption, strategies, plans, and implementation), which implies keeping the external costs as low as possible in view of the results achieved, taking into consideration the principle of cost in the entire life. Since in the capitalism, *nomen est omen*, it is the capital that rules it is fully reasonable to anticipate principle according to which the capital is properly managed in order to achieve economic efficiency or better to say, one of its components (efficient production, allocation and innovation).

60. Article 9 EA-1 stipulates that energy supply shall enable suitable living conditions for poorer population groups or households. In other words, the social cohesion, which is among the constitutional aims of the EU,[62] must be properly

60. Moreover, in case of lower energy needs also energy security and equity are easier to achieve.
61. Article 8 EA-1.
62. *See* Art. 3(3) TEU.

incorporated in the energy policy. Moreover, the discussed principle is a clear manifestation of the concept of social or welfare state which is explicitly stipulated by the Slovenian Constitution.[63]

61. The state and/or local communities must ensure equal treatment for all participants in the procedures related to the construction of energy supply capacities as well as to energy supply and use,[64] and similar can be said for transparency.[65] Equal treatment is a universal constitutional principle, and it would be necessary to apply it even in case there would be no explicit provision in the EA-1. Equal treatment demands, to put it simply, equal treatment of persons or situations with the same essential characteristics (which must be legitimate according to the Constitution), and appropriate (proportionate) different treatment of persons or situations with different essential characteristics. On the other hand, the transparency is mainly ensured through mandatory public access to energy data (quantitative data on energy supply by types of consumer groups and by final consumer groups), public discussions of energy documents (strategies, policies, plans) and general legal acts.[66] Also, it explicitly defines transparency in favour of the consumers of energy supplied from the networks, who shall enjoy the right to energy supply performed in a transparent and non-discriminatory manner.[67]

62. In energy supply, one needs to bear in mind the protection of consumers as final customers of energy. This principle needs to be observed in terms of financial as well as physical accessibility to energy sources. As regards energy supply, the consumers are to some extent protected via consumer protection legislation, within which any contracts on the supply of goods (electricity and natural gas included) are under special protection in the light of the possibility to breach or establish a relationship (contractual obligation). In addition to these general rules on consumer protection, the EA-1 contains the principle (i.e., Article 13) as well as several specific rules (e.g., Articles 39–42).

63. The principle of integrity set out in Article 14 EA-1 provides that the state and local communities shall take into account their impact on energy efficiency and renewable energy use in all their activities. This is important since only this way we can achieve an acceptable balance in the discussed field.

64. The principle of incentives set out in Article 15 EA-1, which provides that the activities to increase energy efficiency and the share of renewable or other low-carbon energy sources shall be promoted, derives from Article 176 A of The Treaty of Lisbon, which provides that the promotion of energy efficiency and energy saving shall be one of the objectives of the Union's energy policy. Since there have been several incentives promoting other technologies, including the energy sector,

63. *See* Art. 2 of the Slovenian Constitution.
64. *See* Art. 10 EA-1.
65. *See* Art. 11 EA-1.
66. Articles 11 and 12 EA-1.
67. Article 16 EA-1.

it has been further provided that the installations, technologies, equipment, products, and services that are more environmentally friendly shall receive more favourable treatment compared to those that are less environmentally friendly. Moreover, the state, regional and local authorities shall take appropriate actions in order to raise awareness and knowledge about energy efficiency and RES.[68]

65. The principle of competitiveness defined in Article 17 EA-1 is of particular importance for the state of Slovenia, given state's participation and role in its public undertakings which are an important part of the Slovenian energy industry. This principle provides that the state shall be obliged to implement market rules and promote competition in the energy supply, treating individual producers or suppliers in a non-discriminatory manner all the way. This principle is further concretized by several legal acts, namely, not only by the EA-1 but also with ZPOmK-1 which defines general rules on competition as well as with the Treaty on the Functioning of the European Union's (TFEU's) provisions on internal market (free movement and competition rules).

66. In line with the 'polluter-pays' principle, energy producers shall bear the burdens and the risks of environmental pollution caused by their production (Article 18 EA-1). The state authorities and the authorities of local communities, however, shall act in line with the principle of sustainability, doing their best to minimize the negative environmental impacts and reduce the environmental burden of future generations when adopting policies, strategies, programmes, plans, general and concrete legal acts, and implementing measures (Article 19 EA-1).

68. Even though there is no explicit legislative provision for the public authorities to do so, we believe they would not act illegally in case they would point out indisputable negative effects of the use of fossil fuels when informing people about the energy efficiency and renewables.

Chapter 3. Historical Background and Development of Energy Law

67. The purpose of this section is to introduce some basic features of the development of the energy sector and energy legislation in Slovenia, which actually started on the territory of Slovenia before the country declared its independence. The development was marked by long-lasting processes of global historical importance (including, *inter alia*, material and spiritual cultures of the feudalism of Western Europe, capitalism under the rule of the Hapsburg or the Austro-Hungarian Monarchies, and later the attempt at the application of the Marxist theory when the Republic of Slovenia was an integral part of SFRY)[69] as well as by several historical milestones (WWI, WWII, and breakup of SFRY) as briefly discussed in the following sections of this chapter.

§1. Onset of Energy Development on Slovenian Territory

68. The history of energy development in Slovenia, just as elsewhere, began with the first use of fire.[70] Wood and charcoal were the most important energy sources until the second half of the nineteenth century (while as of the eleventh century in some places also running water (river, streams, etc.)[71] and sun were exploited) in spite of the fact that the public authorities already in the eighteenth century started a kind of a promotion of coal and peal.[72] Coal became the most important source of energy at the end of the nineteenth century and it retained the leading position for almost hundred years.[73]

69. The energy was used for all kinds of activities.[74] Traditionally, agriculture was the first and most widely conducted activity. Subsequently also other activities were conducted. For example, already in the ninth century a salt production was

69. Socialist Federal Republic of Yugoslavia, abbreviated to SFRY or shortened to Yugoslavia, was a state on the Balkan peninsula, which existed from 1963 to 1991. It appeared as Democratic Federal Yugoslavia soon after WWII on the land of the pre-war Kingdom of Yugoslavia (the delegates at the Third Session of the AVNOJ declared a new country on 10 Aug. 1945), while on 29 November the Constituent Assembly of Yugoslavia formally declared the state a republic, changing the name first to Federal People's Republic of Yugoslavia and in 1963 finally to SFRY.
70. Mechanical energy exploited by controlled or directed movement of animals, e.g. cows, donkeys and horses, is consciously ignored, but it is needless to say that this kind of energy was used as well, in particular in agriculture.
71. Cf. M. Seručnik, 'Izraba vode kot energijskega vira na slovenskem', in Ž. Lazarević & A. Lorenčič (eds), *Strategije in prakse energetske oskrbe v Sloveniji*. Založba INZ, 2015, 48.
72. Cf. M. Seručnik, 'Izraba trdih goriv na slovenskem do začetka dvajsetega stoletja', in Ž. Lazarević & A. Lorenčič (eds), *Strategije in prakse energetske oskrbe v Sloveniji*. Založba INZ, 2015, 90.
73. As discussed in the next section, after WWII hydro power and nuclear power gradually took the lead.
74. Cf. M. Seručnik, *supra* note 71.

conducted, mills in the eleventh century,[75] sawmills in the fifteenth century,[76] glass-making in the sixteenth century,[77] mining in the eighteenth century,[78] ironworks in the nineteenth century, etc.[79]

70. Towards the end of the nineteenth century, mill and sawmill owners, miners, and residents of some larger settlements and towns were the pioneers of lamp development in Slovenia. Thus, the first electrification on the Slovenian territory began over 130 years ago, in 1883, to be more precise, when the first light was lit in Maribor only four years after Edison had invented the light bulb. It was a mill owner, Karl Scherbaum, who set up the first power plant in Slovenia and the first light installation including thirty-six light bulbs. Slovenia's first public power plant was launched in 1884 in Škofja Loka, while the first thermal power plant started to operate in 1888 in Ljubljana.

71. After 1898, the development and the use of automobiles led to the use of oil products in Slovenia as well.

The early stages in the development of the power industry were hardly systematic or regulated, so the progress was slow in the beginning. The first attempt at systemization and regulation of electrification was initiated by the Carniolan Provincial Assembly back in 1898, but the regional authority in Vienna revoked the adopted decisions. As a result, the development of electrification was brought to a standstill until a resolution was adopted in 1909 with which all water sources became property of the province with the possibility of using them before private owners and the state. Between WWI and WWII, the electrification was taken over by the power companies of the occupying forces, while several power plants were developed by private owners.

72. In the discussed time period, there was not genuine energy law as was developed after WWII.

§2. From the End of WWII to Slovenia's Independence

73. After WWII all above-mentioned energy sources were used in Slovenia and the same can be said for the conducted activities. In fact, the list of used energy

75. Cf. M. Seručnik, *supra* note 71, 48.
76. Cf. M. Seručnik, *supra* note 71, 50.
77. Cf. M. Seručnik, 'Izraba trdih goriv na slovenskem do začetka dvajsetega stoletja', *supra* note 72, 69.
78. Cf. K Keber, 'Začetki uporabe "črnega zlata" in doba premoga', in Ž. Lazarević & A. Lorenčič (eds), *Strategije in prakse energetske oskrbe v Sloveniji*. Založba INZ, 2015, 184-185.
79. Cf. P. Vodopivec, 'Od vodnih koles k parnim strojem, od lesnega oglja k premogu', in Ž. Lazarević & A. Lorenčič (eds.), Strategije in prakse energetske oskrbe v Sloveniji. Založba INZ, 2015, 166.

sources and conducted activities was considerably expanded[80] due to the technical and economic development which, *inter alia*, effected the priorities.

74. Electrification of Slovenia was one of the key objectives of the country's after-war development.[81] Moreover, within the state-planned economy (command economy or administrative economy), the electricity industry was favourited over all other energy industries.[82] Having in mind that during WWII all energy infrastructure and companies were took over by the aggressors,[83] one of the first tasks in this regard was to settle the proprietary issues. Not surprisingly, since the country was organized as a socialist country with state-planned economy, also in the energy sector public property was predominant. Based on the federal (Yugoslav) act on nationalization from 1946, all power facilities were made socialized undertakings and declared, in November 1947, undertakings of national importance for the state and the Republics.[84] Yet in 1950, a new federal law (Basic Law on Management of State Economic Enterprises and Higher Economic Associations by the Workers' Collective) brought several social and economic changes. Centralist state relations were replaced by self-governing model of corporate governance, which the workers implemented through workers' councils and management boards. The first sectoral law at the national (republic) level which was adopted by the then Socialist Republic of Slovenia in 1965 (Basic Law on Power Industry) was aimed at ensuring a more rational and harmonized operation, maintenance, production planning, and transmission of electricity across Slovenia's regions. Based on the new federal constitution in 1974 and the Law on Formation of Organizations of Associated Labour in 1976, all of the existing companies were transformed into organizations of associated labour, which in turn affected the way power industry had been organized. Basic organizations of associated labour (BOAL) were formed, covering the narrowest work process segments. They were further organized into labour organizations, which sometimes associated with composite organizations of associated labour. BOAL introduced mutual solidaritous responsibility, made commitments to cover losses for one another, and merged part of resources for tasks of common interest, which were performed by a working community for corporate services.

75. In this context the assembly of the then Socialist Republic of Slovenia in 1981 adopted the Act on Energy Economy (AEE).[85] The AEE has eight chapters,

---

80. Oil and natural gas and later even a nuclear energy become more and more important. The energy was crucial since the Slovenian after-war economy combined almost all business activities known at that time, including heavy industry.
81. Cf. J. Prinčič, 'Pospešena elektrifikacija temelj energetske strategije Slovenije v času obnove in centralnoplanske ureditve', in Ž. Lazarević & A. Lorenčič (eds), *Strategije in prakse energetske oskrbe v Sloveniji*. Založba INZ, 2015, 291–293.
82. *Ibid.*
83. Cf. J. Prinčič, *supra* note 81, 293.
84. Of course, some of the energy companies were established later by the country itself and the same is true for the power plants and other energy infrastructures. The country was heavily oriented towards coal, but at the same time it is worthy to point out that already in 1966, the first pilot nuclear reactor was launched in Podgorica near Črnuče, later followed by the nuclear power plant in Krško which has been online since 1981.
85. Official Gazette of the Socialist Republic of Slovenia, No. 33/82.

i.e. energy activities (Articles 2–13), ways of achieving the special interest with energy activities (Articles 14–59), rational use of energy (Articles 60–64), energy consents or permits (Articles 65–71), supply of energy sources from energy networks (Articles 72–76), inspection control (Articles 77–83), penalties (Articles 84–88), and transitional and final provisions (Articles 89–95). A starting point was the finding that the energy is of essential importance for the development of the society as well as for each individual; therefore, it has to be accessible for all people.[86] The AEE was designed with respect to the three core principles. First, energy activities shall be treated as activities of special importance for the society, which means special public law obligations are attached to those activities. Second, users and energy producers (or better to say vertically integrated energy companies) must cooperate in a self-governing interest community, which binds both sides to negotiations and to a consensual way of resolving problems. And third, a common energy policy shall be established.

76. Late in the 1980s and early in the 1990s the sociopolitical system on the territory of Yugoslavia underwent some drastic changes, which in turn reflected itself in the economy as well. The socialist system the economy had been based upon started to change. The federal law on companies which was adopted in 1988 enacted socially owned, mixed, contractual, and private companies. Slovenian power industry began its transition from self-governing systems to organizations that were closer to the ones found in Western Europe.

§3. The Period after Slovenia's Independence

77. With the declaration of Slovenia's independence in 1991, the Slovenian energy industry separated from the once common Yugoslav energy system. The country's transformation into capitalist country with social market economy affected also the energy sector. Its development was largely influenced by the country's endeavour to join the EU and even more after 2004 when this aim was achieved. Namely, already the first energy legislative package which was adopted by the EU in the second half of the nineties was more or less transposed in the Slovenian legal system due to the aforementioned country's endeavour to join the EU. It is needless to explain in detail that this is evermore true for the second and third energy (and now even the fourth) legislative packages and more generally for the whole acquis communautaire associated with the energy sector as discussed in this monograph. In fact, after 1991, the transformation of the Slovenian energy sector due to the liberalization process as facilitated by the EU and more generally due to the overall effect of the supranational rules on the Slovenian legal system was very similar to the development of energy sectors in the 'old' Member States.[87]

86. *See* the draft of the AEE, Poročevalec Skupščine SR Slovenije in Skupščine SFR Jugoslavije za delegacije in delegate, No. 19/79.

87. Namely, even in the 'old' Member States the energy sector was not subject to genuine market principles while public monopolies controlled the market and only as late as in the nineties this started to change. Although the field of energy was from the very beginning covered by the Treaties (two

I. The First Energy Act of 1999 (EA)

78. The first legislative act explicitly dealing with energy in independent Slovenia, which was adopted in 1999 (EA), brought considerable changes to the energy industry and energy policy. This is not to say that until the adoption of EA the Slovenian energy sector was organized in the same way as in the times of SFRY, yet, the truth is that energy sector remained more or less in public hands and with no significant competition until the EA. Among the most important reasons for its adoption was to modernize energy sector according to the 'West European model'. Moreover, according to the Association Agreement which Slovenia concluded with the European Community and its Member States, it was necessary to follow the supranational rules.

79. Thus, the EA was an important step towards aligning the national energy legislation with the EU energy legislation although it had been adopted prior to Slovenia's accession to the EU. The documentation supplementing the EA draft explicitly pointed out that its provisions follow Directive 96/92/EC of the European Parliament and of the Council of 19 December 1996 concerning common rules for the internal market in electricity,[88] Directive 98/30/EC of the European Parliament and of the Council of 22 June 1998 concerning common rules for the internal market in natural gas,[89] Council Directive 90/547/EEC of 29 October 1990 on the transit of electricity through transmission grids,[90] Council Directive 91/296/EEC of 31 May 1991 on the transit of natural gas through grids,[91] and Council Directive 90/377/EEC of 29 June 1990 concerning a Community procedure to improve the transparency of gas and electricity prices charged to industrial end users.[92] Indeed, the EA did introduce more or less the same principles and rules as set out in two of the then directives on natural gas and electricity market liberalization and the Directive on the indication of energy consumption by labelling as well as transit through grids. Thus, the EA can be considered as a trigger of a real transformation of the Slovenian energy sector.

80. The adoption of the EA initiated the process of the liberalization and deregulation of the energy sector, which in turn laid the foundations for the new Slovenian energy market. With the implementation of the EA, EU directives were gradually incorporated into the Slovenian electricity market, as Slovenia started to move towards EU membership soon after it declared its independence. Slovenia's internal electricity market formally opened in 2001 after the expiry of the transitional period set out in the EA, which was a significant milestone in Slovenia's energy industry.

---

of the original Treaties even explicitly covered the field of energy), the primary law was rarely used or in rather limited extent almost until the new millennium. In other words, for a long time, the energy sector and national energy monopolies were protected from the effects of European Union law; cf. Kim Talus, *Introduction to EU Energy Law,* Oxford University Press, 2016, 3.

88. Official Journal of the European Union, L 27, 30.1.1997, 20–29.
89. Official Journal of the European Union, L 204, 21.7.1998, 1–12.
90. Official Journal of the European Union, L 313, 13.11.1990, 30–33.
91. Official Journal of the European Union, L 147, 12.6.1991, 37–40.
92. Official Journal of the European Union, L 185, 17.7.1990, 16–24.

In the same year, newly established entities, such as electricity market operator Borzen, d.o.o. (company, 100-owned by the Republic of Slovenia) and the Energy Agency, were launched. Furthermore, power companies made the necessary adjustments so as to align their operation with the EA. As of 1 January 2003, the electricity market opened internationally as well.

81. Natural gas market began to open only in 2003.

82. The EA is an organic law on the functioning of the energy industry system, which has been changed five times (amendments EA-A to EA-D). The objective of all of the amendments apart from EA-D was to align the national legislation to the European acquis, lay down the conditions for the functioning of the electricity market and regulator, to regulate the performance of commercial public services in the electricity and gas sectors, and to ensure efficient use of energy and RES.

83. With the Act Amending the EA – EA-A (Official Gazette of the Republic of Slovenia, No. 51/04) the provisions set out in Directive 2003/54/EC of the European Parliament and of the Council concerning common rules for the internal market in electricity and repealing Directive 96/92/EC and those of Directive 2003/55/EC of the European Parliament and of the Council concerning common rules for the internal market in natural gas and repealing Directive 98/30/EC were fully transposed into Slovenia's legislation.

84. The Act Amending the EA – EA-B (Official Gazette of the Republic of Slovenia, No. 118/06) fully transposed into our national legislation the provisions of the Council Directive 2004/67/EC concerning measures to safeguard security of natural gas supply. The provisions of Directive 2002/91/EC of the European Parliament and of the Council on the energy performance of buildings were partly transposed. The provisions of Directive 2002/91/EC concerning the methodology of calculation of energy performance and requirements for energy efficiency of buildings have been transposed through the Construction Act, while the provisions dealing with the inspection of boilers through the act on environmental protection.

85. The Act Amending the EA – EA-C (Official Gazette of the Republic of Slovenia, No. 70/08) introduced a new support scheme for electricity from renewable sources and from combined heat and power (CHP) systems. This act and the implementing regulations based on it have fully transposed the provisions from the following directives:

- Directive 2001/77/EC of the European Parliament and of the Council on the promotion of electricity produced from RES in the internal electricity market.
- Directive 2004/8/EC of the European Parliament and of the Council on the promotion of cogeneration based on a useful heat demand in the internal energy market and amending Directive 92/42/EEC.

- Directive 2005/32/EC of the European Parliament and of the Council establishing a framework for the setting of eco-design requirements for energy-using products and amending Council Directive 92/42/EEC and Directives 96/57/EC and 2000/55/EC of the European Parliament and of the Council.
- Directive 2006/32/EC of the European Parliament and of the Council of 5 April 2006 on energy end-use efficiency and energy services and repealing Council Directive 93/76/EEC.
- Directive 2005/89/EC of the European Parliament and of the Council concerning measures to safeguard security of electricity supply and infrastructure investment.

86. The Act Amending the EA – EA-D (Official Gazette of the Republic of Slovenia, No. 22/10) did not transpose any new directives into Slovenia's legislation, though it did eliminate some weaknesses of the existing regulation concerning energy infrastructure development, issuing of energy permits, efficient use of energy, use of renewables, and safeguarding security of energy supply. It also eliminated some drawbacks related to the functioning of the electricity and natural gas markets and the operation of the regulatory authority.

87. The Act Amending the EA – EA-E (Official Gazette of the Republic of Slovenia No. 10/12) has fully transposed into the national legislation the provisions of Directive 2009/28/EC of the European Parliament and of the Council on the promotion of the use of energy from renewable sources and amending and subsequently repealing Directives 2001/77/EC and 2003/30/EC, Directive 2009/125/EC of the European Parliament and of the Council establishing a framework for the setting of eco-design requirements for energy-related products (renewed), and Directive 2010/30/EU of the European Parliament and of the Council on the indication by labelling and standard product information of the consumption of energy and other resources by energy-related products. In addition, it transposed some of the provisions of Directive 2009/31/EC of the European Parliament and of the Council on the geological storage of carbon dioxide (CO_2) and amending Council Directive 85/337/EEC, European Parliament and Council Directives 2000/60/EC, 2001/80/EC, 2004/35/EC, 2006/12/EC, 2008/1/EC and Regulation (EC) No. 1013/2006, and Directive 2009/73/EC of the European Parliament and of the Council concerning common rules for the internal market in natural gas and repealing Directive 2003/55/EC.[93]

II. The Second Energy Act of 2014 (EA-1)

88. The EA has been amended five times, which not only made it non-transparent but also outdated and useless. Having in mind additional directives

93. On the other hand, the EA-E did not transpose Directive 2009/72/EC. This was left for the EA-1 as follows.

which the Slovenian legislator was obliged to transpose in the Slovenian legal system, the situation would only get worst. In fact, the adoption of the new EA-1 (EZ-1) in March 2014 was an urgent step, as Slovenia was already lagging behind with the transposition of several European directives governing the natural gas and electricity markets, energy efficiency, and RES (altogether ten EU directives),[94] which earned Slovenia several formal reminders by the European Commission which finally filed two lawsuits against Slovenia before the EU Court of Justice.[95]

89. The adoption of the EA-1 means that the Slovenian energy legislation is principally in line with the EU's Third Energy Package. This is not to say, however, its content is fully in line with the acquis communautaire. As will be discussed later in the text, here and there it was possible to find provisions which did not fully correspond to the EU energy law.[96] The impact of the EU legislation onto the development of the legislation in Slovenia and the EA-1 are dealt with in Chapter 5 and in some sections of Parts I–IV.

90. The EA-1 has not only transposed the European legislation into the national legal order but also tackled issues, such as energy infrastructure, heat supply, and other areas of energy policy, thus making the legislative regulation concerning the energy sector much more transparent. That, in turn, has improved the legal security of citizens, by giving greater power and influence to final customers as consumers. It has also redressed the infringements identified by the Constitutional Court of the Republic of Slovenia in their decision U-I-257/009-22 of 14 April 2011 (Official Gazette of the Republic of Slovenia, No. 37/11). Hence, the decision of the Constitutional Court of the Republic of Slovenia showed that the entire section of the EA on network charges and fees was rather poorly formulated and unclear. Since this regards public levies, it is imperative to have a precise legal basis that specifies each item of the network charge, its purpose and the way it is calculated. Also, it needed to be made clear that the network charge is set by the Agency, while additional charges on electricity bills are set by the Government. Hence, everything that concerns network charges has now been regulated with the EA-1 anew, in line with the principles of clarity and transparency. On the other hand, however, Case U-I-133/13-24 (and U-I-134/13-22)[97] revealed the constitutional shortcomings of the EA-1 which are now already remedied. Moreover, eventually, several other shortcomings became obvious and, together with the development of the EU energy law

94. In addition, it was also necessary to ensure a compatibility of the national legislation with EU regulations.
95. Infringement procedure No. 2011/1125 and Case C-8/13 and infringement procedure No. 2011/1126 and Case C-9/13.
96. For example, the EA-1 was not fully in line with Art. 13(2) of Directive 2010/31/EU of the European Parliament and of the Council of 19 May 2010 on the energy performance of buildings (Official Journal of the European Union, L 153, 18.6.2018, 13), and with Art. 2 of Directive 2012/27/EU of the European Parliament and of the Council of 25 Oct. 2012 on energy efficiency, amending Directives 2009/125/EC and 2010/30/EU and repealing Directives 2004/8/EC and 2006/32/EC (Official Journal of the European Union, L 315, 14.11.2012, 1).
97. ECLI:SI:USRS:2016:U.I.133.13.

and with the endeavour to ensure compatibility of the EA-1 with the acquis communautaire, therefore, also the EA-1 was amended three times so far.

91. The Act Amending the EA-1 – EA-1A (Official Gazette of the Republic of Slovenia, No. 81/15) modified provisions on out-of-court dispute settlement between undertakings and consumers. More precisely, the legislative act in question aimed at the full alignment of the EA-1 with Directive 2013/11/EU of the European Parliament and of the Council of 21 May 2013 on alternative dispute resolution for consumer disputes and amending Regulation (EC) No 2006/2004 and Directive 2009/22/EC.[98] The following provisions of the EA-1 were modified: Article 50, Article 175, Article 490, and Article 491.

92. The Act Amending the EA-1 – EA-1B (Official Gazette of the Republic of Slovenia, No. 43/19) was adopted to achieve three main aims. First, the amendment shall ensure the compatibility with the acquis communautaire. In this regard, it specifically aimed at compatibility with Article 13(2) of Directive 2010/31/EU of the European Parliament and of the Council of 19 May 2010 on the energy performance of buildings (Official Journal of the European Union, L 153, 18. 6. 2018, 13), and with Article 2 of Directive 2012/27/EU of the European Parliament and of the Council of 25 October 2012 on energy efficiency, amending Directives 2009/125/EC and 2010/30/EU and repealing Directives 2004/8/EC and 2006/32/EC (Official Journal of the European Union, L 315, 14. 11. 2012, 1). Moreover, the EA-1A aims at compliance with the Communication from the Commission – Guidelines on state aid for environmental protection and energy 2014–2020.[99] Second, the amendment shall ensure full execution of the judgment of the Constitutional Court issued in Case U-I-133/13–24 (and U-I-134/13–22),[100] which deals with a right to build and related land easement. Third, the amendment shall overcome the shortcomings which became clear after the application of the EA-1 a daily practice, e.g. personal data protection, reliability of suppliers who appoint agents, disconnection of electricity. Due to the above-mentioned amendments the following provisions of the EA-1 were modified: Article 2, Article 4, Article 6(2), Article 20(2), Article 23(5), Article 24, Article 30(1), Article 36, Article 46(2), Article 48(2), Article 51, Article 74, Article 114(4), Article 119(5), Article 151(1), Article 159, Article 166(1), Article 167, Article 168, Article 169, Article 171(5), Article 200(1), Article 249(1), Article 274(1), Article 275, Article 313(1), Article 316, Article 322(1), Article 328, Article 336, Article 354(3), Article 358(1), Article 365(1), Article 368(2), Article 372(6), Article 373, Article 413(1), Article 432, Article 434, Article 451(2), Article 460(1), Article 464(1), Article 472, Article 473(4) and (5), Article 474, Article 490(3), Article 491(3), Article 491(1), Article 494(6), Article 495(1), Article 500, and Article 501. In addition, the following new provisions were included: Article 157 a–157 č, Article 314(3) and (4), Article 367(3), Article 382 a, Article 485 a, Article 493 a, Article 512(2), and Article 554(7).

98. Official Journal of the European Union, L 165, 18.6.2013, 63.
99. Official Journal of the European Union, C 200, 28.6.2016, 1.
100. ECLI:SI:USRS:2016:U.I.133.13.

93. The Act Amending the EA-1 – EA-1C (Official Gazette of the Republic of Slovenia No. 65/20) was adopted mainly because of the transposition of Directive (EU) 2019/692 of the European Parliament and of the Council of 17 April 2019 amending Directive 2009/73/EC concerning common rules for the internal market in natural gas[101] into the Slovenian legal system. The following provisions of the EA-1 were modified: Article 2, Article 159, Article 246(2), Article 261(2), Article 262(2), and Article 265(1). In addition, the following new provisions were included: Article 177(6), Article 281 a, and Article 386(8).

101. Official Journal of the European Union, L 117, 3.5.2019, 1.

Chapter 4. Role of Key Government Institutions

94. This chapter presents the main players in Slovenian energy law and policy, with a particular focus on the Government or let us say on some bodies of executive branch, i.e., on the ministries and bodies under the aegis of the ministries, and on public agencies that have a direct or indirect influence on the Slovenian energy sector. The most notable are, inside the Ministry of Infrastructure, the Energy Directorate[102] and the Infrastructure Inspectorate of the Republic of Slovenia (and its inspection departments),[103] and inside the Ministry of the Environment and Spatial Planning, the Slovenian Nuclear Safety Administration[104] and the Environment Agency at the very least.[105] Furthermore, the Energy Agency[106] and the Slovenian Competition Protection Agency should be noted as extra-governmental institutions.[107] Before a brief presentation of the aforementioned institutions, it should be noted that they have not been ordered in terms of their importance or impact on the Slovenian energy sector.

95. The Energy Directorate is a specialist administrative body that within the legal and political framework set out by the applicable regulations and strategic documents on national energy policy performs administrative tasks and exercises measures aimed at ensuring a reliable, sustainable and competitive energy supply, increasing energy efficiency, and expanding the supply of renewable energy. To this end the directorate primarily supervises the functioning of the utilities; participates in the preparation of regulations, documents and measures for planning energy supply, energy consumption in Slovenia and the sustainable development of energy systems; draws up (drafts) national programmes and regulations in the area of energy efficiency and renewables policy, and implements, coordinates and participates in promotional programmes for these policies; rules in certain administrative proceedings in the first and second instances; participates in the preparation of material for the State Prosecutor's Office in judicial proceedings; monitors EU regulations, harmonizes national legislation, and participates in the drafting of proposed EU regulations and other acts; formulates Slovenia's position for EU organs and working bodies; and participates in international energy links. The directorate is also responsible for the mining sector.[108]

96. The Infrastructure Inspectorate is a specialist administrative body that conducts inspection supervision of, *inter alia*, the implementation of regulations in the areas of the energy industry, the electricity industry and mining.[109]

102. http://www.mzi.gov.si/en/areas_of_work/energy/.
103. http://www.ii.gov.si/.
104. http://www.ursjv.gov.si/en/.
105. http://www.arso.gov.si/en/.
106. http://www.agen-rs.si/.
107. http://www.varstvo-konkurence.si/en/.
108. *See* the website of the Energy Directorate as cited in Footnote 102.
109. *See* the website of the Infrastructure Inspectorate as cited in Footnote 103.

97. The Slovenian Nuclear Safety Administration is a specialist administrative body responsible for performing special expert and developmental administrative tasks, and for conducting inspection supervision of the implementation of regulations in the area of nuclear energy.[110]

98. The Environment Agency is an administrative body that is primarily active in the area of the environment (weather, water, environmental protection, nature, climate change, earthquakes and noise), and not energy, although given the close link between environment and energy it is of at least indirect significance to the latter, particularly in the sense of credible measurements and databases of environmental indicators in Slovenia, including those revealing the environmental load entailed by the energy sector.[111]

99. The Energy Agency is a legal person under public law that does not fall under the aegis of the Government or a ministry. On the basis of a public authorization it functions as the national regulatory authority in the area of the energy market. It autonomously[112] and independently[113] pursues the objectives stipulated by law,[114] and in this connection, it primarily monitors, guides and supervises[115] energy

---

110. *See* the website of the Slovenian Nuclear Safety Administration as cited in Footnote 105.
111. *See* the website of the Environment Agency as cited in Footnote 106.
112. It must nevertheless enforce legally binding decisions by the European Commission and by the ACER, and must cooperate with ACER and with other national regulators in the area of energy that are responsible for protection of competition and securities market regulation.
113. Its functional, legal institutional and financial independence is guaranteed; *see infra.*
114. Article 385 EA-1 sets out the following fundamental objectives for the Agency:

   - encouraging a competitive, reliable and environmentally sustainable market in electricity and natural gas, and effectively opening the market to all consumers and suppliers;
   - developing competitive and properly functioning regional markets in electricity and natural gas;
   - removing barriers to trading in electricity and natural gas;
   - cost-effectively encouraging the development of safe, reliable and efficient non-discriminatory consumer-focused systems that encourage sufficient capacity in the system and, in accordance with the general objectives of energy policy, energy efficiency and the inclusion of electricity and gas production from renewable energy resources and the distribution of production in transmission and distribution networks;
   - facilitating easier inclusion in the network of new production capacity, particularly by removing barriers that could prevent new participants from entering the market for electricity and gas from renewables;
   - providing appropriate incentives for operators and for users of systems to increase network efficiency and to encourage market integration in the short-term and long-term;
   - providing benefits to consumers of electricity and natural gas via the efficient functioning of the market, the encouragement of effective competition, and aid in ensuring consumer protection;
   - helping to meet high standards of service for consumers of electricity and natural gas, and helping to protect vulnerable consumers and to ensure compliance in the requisite data exchange procedures for all consumers.

115. The Agency supervises the implementation of the EA-1 in the area of the market in electricity and natural gas, and regulations and general acts issued on its basis, except in cases falling under the jurisdiction of individual inspection bodies (primarily the Infrastructure Inspectorate). It should

providers in the electricity and natural gas sectors, and performs tasks of regulating energy providers in the area of heat and other energy gases. These are very sensitive tasks which should be tackled by highly qualified persons pursuant to the law and according to professional guidelines, without any undue and unlawful pressure from outside. Therefore, in performing their tasks, the Agency's director, the Agency's staff and the members of the Agency's Council shall not be subject to any decisions, positions, instructions or guidance from government, local community or other authorities, legal persons or individuals, and shall not seek them. The Agency shall lay down its internal organization and job classification in an autonomous manner, and in the same manner it shall also decide on the required number of staff and on the financial sources needed to efficiently perform its tasks and competences, and shall define them in the work programme and financial plan. In this context, one shall also consider that the Agency shall be financed exclusively from the compensations from gas and electricity transmission system operators (TSOs) for the Agency's regulatory tasks, and from other revenue generated by the Agency through its operations.[116] Any revenue in excess of the expenditure of the Agency related to the performance of its tasks shall be saved in the Agency's reserves. The Council of the Agency shall determine the minimum amount of reserves that the Agency must hold permanently, except in the case of temporarily covering of deficit. If, in a particular calendar year, the amount of reserves exceeds the minimum amount of permanent reserves, the surplus shall be used to finance the Agency in the following year. If, in a particular calendar year, the Agency does not cover all its expenditure from the revenue, including the reserve surplus, the deficit shall be temporarily covered from the Agency's minimum reserves. All the abovementioned shall ensure financial autonomy of the Agency. For this reason a supervision of the lawfulness, designated use, and efficient and effective use of the Agency's resources shall be carried out (only)[117] by the Court of Audit of the Republic of Slovenia. All the said measures shall ensure professional work of the Agency. Within the framework of the performance of the administrative and other tasks imposed on the Agency by the law, EU acts and its own general acts issued on the basis of its explicit legal powers, it issues general acts, e.g. on the network charge and tariff for the use of the system, and individual acts[118] (as part of its functioning it also undertakes real acts and commercial acts). The Agency's rulings and

additionally be noted that the Agency also supervises the implementation of the EU regulations in the area of the single market in electricity and natural gas. It conducts the proceedings in this connection and imposes measures ex officio (solely).

116. In relation to its tasks, the Agency shall not accept donations or payments other than those defined by the EA-1.

117. The Agency shall, at least once a year by 30 June for the preceding year, submit a report on the state of the energy sector to the Government and the National Assembly of the Republic of Slovenia, however, this report only generally describes the situation within the energy market, and it does not include any information of the Agency's financial situation.

118. The Agency mainly issues administrative decisions within an special administrative procedure. Yet, the Agency is *inter alia* responsible for ruling under certain conditions on disputes between, on the one hand, (potential) users of electricity or natural gas system or suppliers, and, on the other, the operator(s) with regard to access to the system; charging for use of the system; breaches of system operating instructions; the identification of anomalies and the coverage of costs for rectifying

resolutions cannot be appealed, and its rulings cannot be cancelled or overturned under the supervisory right: a ruling can only be annulled by the Agency (all of this is to a great extent the result of the drive for specialization and the elimination of political pressures). An administrative dispute is nevertheless allowed against individual acts of the Agency.[119]

100. The Slovenian Competition Protection Agency is a legal person under public law that is responsible for supervising the implementation of competition law and rules, including Articles 101 and 102 of the TFEU. To this end it monitors and analyses the situation on the market where this is significant to the development of effective competition, it conducts special administrative proceedings (and misdemeanours proceedings) and issue rulings[120] in accordance with the law, and provides opinions on general issues within its competence to the National Assembly and to the Government. It can lodge a suit before the competent court to establish the nullity of a restrictive agreement or preventive acts in connection with a particular market concentration. The Agency is autonomous and independent in exercising its tasks and powers. As is evident from the above, the Agency is not a sector-specific body, but it nevertheless has great significance or at least potential significance in the energy sector, particularly if it is borne in mind that in recent years the European Commission has primarily realized its liberalization targets in the energy sector by means of general rules of competition law (*see infra*, Part VI).

101. In light of all of the above, what is self-evident should be reiterated, namely that the legislative and judicial branches of power are also of great significance to the energy sector (*see supra*; Introduction, Chapter 1 §3). The legislator determines the boundaries of the functioning of the executive branch, which in principle can only function in cases when it has lawful power and only within the boundaries of this power. However, the competent courts exercise control of legality of the work

---

anomalies and breaches of general acts governing anomalies and their rectification; and other matters so stipulated by the law (*see* Art. 413(1) EA-1).

In this connection it is the authors' opinion that although the Agency is a holder of a public authorization to perform delegated administrative tasks, it can be deemed a court in the sense of Art. 267 of the TFEU when settling the above-mentioned disputes, and consequently it is allowed to refer a matter to the EU Court of Justice for a preliminary ruling. In this case, where the dispute is not settled in a classical administrative procedure, the Agency also meets a condition that is usually missing when ruling in administrative proceedings, namely that it rules in a dispute between two parties. In the case of the aforementioned dispute between (potential) users and operators, in contrast to administrative proceedings it is not a bilateral relationship, but instead a trilateral relationship typical of judicial proceedings. The other conditions for the recognition of 'court' status, i.e. permanent establishment by law, functioning on the basis of law, and independence of work, are more or less beyond dispute with regard to the Agency when dealing with above-mentioned disputes. The situation is, however, different when the Agency deals with other issues in administrative procedures. In short, in principle the Agency cannot be considered as a 'court' in the sense of Art. 267 TFEU except when it settles aforementioned disputes.

119. Given the Agency's very significant role with regard to energy and the energy sector, here we refer to Arts 383–450 EA-1, which relate to the Agency.

120. The Agency's rulings and resolutions cannot be appealed, but extraordinary legal remedies in administrative proceedings and administrative disputes are allowed.

of the executive, including the state administration, and in general provide the constitutionally envisaged judicial controls of the work of bodies in the system of the executive branch.

Chapter 5. Sources of Slovenian Energy Law

102. This chapter presents some of the key sources that make up the present[121] general part of Slovenian energy law, which means that in principle, unless stipulated otherwise for the particular case, they apply to all areas within the energy sector, while the specific part of Slovenian energy law formed by sources relating to individual areas of the energy sector such as electricity, natural gas, oil and coal, is discussed later in this monograph (Parts I–III).

103. This chapter also presents some of the other sources that are of significance to the energy sector, despite not relating exclusively to it. These are, most notably but not exclusively, sources in the areas of environmental protection, spatial planning, protection of competition, consumer protection and tax law. Some of these sources are discussed in detail later in this monograph (Parts IV to VI).

§1. EU Law

104. Slovenian energy law is an integral part of Slovenian law. Its sources form, together with all other legal sources, the Slovenian legal system, which was presented in brief above (*see* Introduction, Chapter 1 §4) and to avoid repetition will not be addressed again here, although for practical reasons the primacy of EU law, which sets the external boundaries of Slovenian energy law, should be reiterated.[122] This primarily refers to the EU rules that make up primary and secondary law, and in general the acquis communautaire in the area of internal policy,[123] which also includes competition policy and general competition law, which over recent years has partly supplanted (de facto, not de jure) specific sectoral (*ex ante*) regulation.[124]

---

121. It is meant July 2020.
122. The term 'of domestic origin' is applied to the law of EU Member States because EU law is part of the law of the Member States. In light of the above, there is a distinction between (authentic) Slovenian law adopted directly by the Slovenian authorities, and (transposed) Slovenian law adopted by the EU institutions or generally at the EU level to which Slovenia has in this connection transferred the execution of certain of its sovereign rights.
123. *See*, e.g., Part Three of the TFEU:

 - internal market (title I);
 - common rules on competition, taxation and approximation of laws (title VII);
 - trans-European networks (title XVI);
 - economic, social and territorial cohesion (title XVIII); and
 - energy (title XXI).

124. At the EU level, this trend is particularly notable in European Commission practice since completing the sector enquiry in 2007.

§2. The Constitution

105. The Constitution is Slovenia's most authentic formal legal act, almost all the provisions of which have at least an indirect impact on the energy sector, particularly those governing human rights and freedoms, and their implementation, economic and social relations, the powers of individual government bodies and relations between these bodies, and the legal system. For the purpose of orientation, examples of constitutional provisions that have significance for Slovenian energy law are the following:

- Article 2 (rule of law and social state).
- Article 14 (equality before the law).
- Article 33 (right to private property and inheritance).
- Article 35 (right to privacy).
- Article 67 (restriction of property rights).
- Article 72 (healthy living environment).
- Article 74 (free enterprise, limits thereon and protection of competition).
- Article 147 (taxes).
- Article 153 (hierarchy of formal legal acts).

§3. International Treaties and Other Sources of Classical International Law

106. International treaties that have been validly concluded and by which Slovenia is bound are transposed into the Slovenian legal system by ratification and publication in the Official Gazette of the Republic of Slovenia. International treaties ratified via a law by the legislator, i.e. the National Assembly, rank below the Constitution and above the laws and other regulations in the hierarchy.[125] Examples of multilateral[126] international treaties that relate directly to the Slovenian energy sector include:

- the Energy Charter Treaty and Energy Charter Protocol on Energy Efficiency and Related Environmental Aspects;[127]
- the Statute of the International Renewable Energy Agency;[128]
- the Statute of the International Atomic Energy Agency;[129]

125. International treaties ratified via a decree by the government rank below laws and above other secondary legislation in the hierarchy.
126. Of course, Slovenia has concluded numerous bilateral international agreements which relate to Slovenian energy sector.
127. Official Gazette of the Republic of Slovenia (International Treaties), No. 12/97.
128. Official Gazette of the Republic of Slovenia (International Treaties), No. 1/10.
129. Official Gazette of the Republic of Slovenia (International Treaties), Nos 9/92, 9/93, 5/99, 9/08, 13/11, 9/13 and 5/17.

- the Agreement between the Government of the Republic of Slovenia and the Government of the Russian Federation on Cooperation in Construction and Operation of the Gas Pipeline on the Territory of the Republic of Slovenia.[130,131]

§4. LAWS

107. Laws or legislative acts of parliament only occupy the third rank (or even fourth rank when taking into account the EU law) of formal legal acts[132] in the Slovenian legal system,[133] but have a central role in the energy sector. They systematically and comprehensively regulate the energy sector and the major areas within it. The following laws that directly regulate the energy sector are particularly notable:[134]

- the EA-1;[135]
- the Act Regulating the Basic Safety of Transport Along Oil and Gas Pipelines;[136]
- the Conditions of the Concession for Exploitation of the Energy Potential of the Lower Sava River Act;[137]
- the Fund for Financing Decommissioning of the Krško Nuclear Power Plant Krško and Disposal of Radioactive Waste from the Krško Nuclear Power Plant Act;[138]
- the Mining Act (ZRud-1);[139] and
- the Act Regulating the Gradual Closure of the Trbovlje-Hrastnik Mine and the Economic Development Restructuring of the Region.[140]

108. In Slovenia, the EA-1 of 2014 is the core and systemic legislative act in the field of energy. It was adopted primarily to harmonize with the third energy package and with other EU energy legislation,[141] but also for the purpose of greater

130. Official Gazette of the Republic of Slovenia (International Treaties), Nos 4/10 and 14/12.
131. The EZ-1C provides for modification of the agreement in question according to Art. 281a EA-1.
132. As stated, the first rank consists of EU law and the Constitution of the Republic of Slovenia (considering the theory of constitutional pluralism), and the second rank of international treaties ratified by the legislator.
133. *See* Art. 157 of the Slovenian Constitution.
134. Not all such laws are cited below, as some relate to very narrow issues, such as the closure of a specific mine or the operation of the nuclear power plant.
135. Official Gazette of the Republic of Slovenia, Nos 17/14, 81/15, 43/19 and 65/20.
136. Official Gazette of the SFRY, No. 64/73.
137. Official Gazette of the Republic of Slovenia, Nos 87/11, 25/14 – ZSDH-1, 50/14, 90/15, 67/17 and 65/20.
138. Official Gazette of the Republic of Slovenia, Nos 75/94, 24/03, 47/03 and 68/08.
139. Official Gazette of the Republic of Slovenia, Nos 61/10, 62/10, 76/10, 57/12, 111/13 and 14/14.
140. Official Gazette of the Republic of Slovenia, Nos 61/00, 42/03, 55/03, 71/04, 26/05, 43/10, 49/10, 40/12, 25/14, 46/14, 82/15 and 84/18.
141. Under the EA-1, the following EU directives are transposed into Slovenian legislation:

   - Directive 2009/72/EC of the European Parliament and of the Council of 13 Jul. 2009 concerning common rules for the internal market in electricity and repealing Directive 2003/54/EC, Official Journal of the European Union, L 211, 14.8.2009, 55.

- Directive 2009/73/EC of the European Parliament and of the Council of 13 Jul. 2009 concerning common rules for the internal market in natural gas and repealing Directive 2003/55/EC, Official Journal of the European Union, L 211, 14.8.2009, 94.
- Directive 2005/89/EC of the European Parliament and of the Council concerning measures to safeguard security of electricity supply and infrastructure investment, Official Journal of the European Union, L 33, 18.1.2006, 22.
- Directive 2009/28/EC of the European Parliament and of the Council on the promotion of the use of energy generated from renewable sources and amending and subsequently repealing Directives 2001/77/EC and 2003/30/EC, Official Journal of the European Union, L 140, 5.6.2009, 16.
- Directive 2009/125/EC of the European Parliament and of the Council of 21 Oct. 2009 establishing a framework for the setting of eco-design requirements for energy-related products, Official Journal of the European Union, L 285, 3.10.2009, 10.
- Directive 2010/30/EU of the European Parliament and of the Council of 19 May 2010 on the indication by labelling and standard product information of the consumption of energy and other resources by energy-related products, Official Journal of the European Union, L 153, 18.6.2010, 1.
- Directive 2010/31/EU of the European Parliament and of the Council of 19 May 2010 on the energy performance of buildings, Official Journal of the European Union, L 153, 18.6.2010, 13.
- Directive 2012/27/EC of the European Parliament and of the Council of 25 Oct. 2012 on energy efficiency, amending Directives 2009/125/EU and 2010/30/EU and repealing Directives 2004/8/EC and 2006/32/EC, Official Journal of the European Union, L 315, 14.11.2012, 1.
- Directive 2004/8/EC of the European Parliament and of the Council of 11 Feb. 2004 on the promotion of cogeneration based on a useful heat demand in the internal energy market and amending Directive 92/42/EEC, Official Journal of the European Union, L 52, 21.4.2004, 50.
- Directive 2009/31/EC of the European Parliament and of the Council on the geological storage of carbon dioxide and amending Council Directive 85/337/EEC, European Parliament and Council Directives 2000/60/EC, 2001/80/EC, 2004/35/EC, 2006/12/EC, 2008/1/EC and Regulation (EC) No. 1013/2006, Official Journal of the European Union, L 140, 5.6.2009, 114.
- Directive (EU) 2019/692 of the European Parliament and of the Council of 17 April 2019 amending Directive 2009/73/EC concerning common rules for the internal market in natural gas, Official Journal of the European Union, L 117, 3.5.2019, 1.

Furthermore, the EA-1 also defines the competent authorities for implementation, and sanctions for breaches of the following EU regulations:

- Regulation (EC) No. 714/2009 of the European Parliament and of the Council of 13 Jul. 2009 on conditions for access to the network for cross-border exchanges in electricity and repealing Regulation (EC) No. 1228/2003, Official Journal of the European Union, L 211, 14.8.2009, 15.
- Regulation (EC) No. 715/2009 of the European Parliament and of the Council of 13 Jul. 2009 on conditions for access to the natural gas transmission networks and repealing Regulation (EC) No. 1775/2005, Official Journal of the European Union, L 211, 14.8.2009, 36.
- Regulation (EU) No. 994/2010 of the European Parliament and of the Council of 20 Oct. 2010 concerning measures to safeguard security of gas supply and repealing Council Directive 2004/67/EC, Official Journal of the European Union, L 295, 12.11.2010, 1.
- Regulation (EC) No. 713/2009 of the European Parliament and of the Council of 13 Jul. 2009 establishing an Agency for the Cooperation of Energy Regulators, Official Journal of the European Union, L 211, 14.8.2009, 1.
- Regulation (EU) No. 1227/2011 of the European Parliament and of the Council of 25 Oct. 2011 on wholesale energy market integrity and transparency, Official Journal of the European Union, L 326, 8.12.2011, 1.

transparency.[142] It is the umbrella law in the energy sector, which lays down the principles of energy policy, energy market operation rules, manners and forms of providing public services in the energy sector, principles and measures for achieving a secure energy supply, for increasing energy efficiency and energy saving and for increasing the use of energy generated from RES, and lays down the conditions for the operation of energy installations, regulates the responsibilities, organization and tasks of the Energy Agency and the competences of other authorities operating in the field of energy.[143] The principal objectives in the field of energy supply and use are as follows:

- reliable energy supply;
- to establish effective competition in the energy market;
- competitiveness in performing non-market activities;
- efficient energy transformation;
- reduced use of energy; efficient use of energy;
- energy efficiency;
- increased production and use of RES;
- transition to a low-carbon society with the application of low-carbon energy technologies;
- provision of energy services;
- ensuring social cohesiveness;

- Regulation (EU) 2018/1999 of the European Parliament and of the Council of 11 December 2018 on the Governance of the Energy Union and Climate Action, amending Regulations (EC) No 663/2009 and (EC) No 715/2009 of the European Parliament and of the Council, Directives 94/22/EC, 98/70/EC, 2009/31/EC, 2009/73/EC, 2010/31/EU, 2012/27/EU and 2013/30/EU of the European Parliament and of the Council, Council Directives 2009/119/EC and (EU) 2015/652 and repealing Regulation (EU) No 525/2013 of the European Parliament and of the Council, Official Journal of the European Union, L 328, 21.12.2018, 1.
- Regulation (EU) 2017/1369 of the European Parliament and of the Council of 4 July 2017 setting a framework for energy labelling and repealing Directive 2010/30/EU, Official Journal of the European Union, L 198, 28.7.2017, 1.

142. The predecessor to the current EA-1, i.e. EA, was adopted before Slovenia joined the EU (namely in 1999), and was then updated several times, primarily for reason of convergence with EU law, as a result of which it became relatively lacking in transparency, and any further amendments for convergence with EU law would have merely resulted in further deterioration. For more, *see* above in Chapter 3.
143. The Energy Act (EA-1) has the following structure:

   - Part 1: General provisions, Articles 1–33
   - Part 2: Electricity, Articles 34–157
   - Part 3: Natural gas, Articles 158–281
   - Part 4: Heat and other energy gases from isolated distribution systems, Articles 282–311
   - Part 5: Energy efficiency and renewable energy sources, Articles 312–382
   - Part 6: Energy agency, Articles 383–450
   - Part 7: Inspection, Articles 451–461
   - Part 8: Energy infrastructure, Articles 462–477
   - Part 9: Other common provisions, Articles 478–485
   - Part 10: Carbon dioxide transport, Articles 486–488
   - Part 11: Penal provisions, Articles 489–502
   - Part 12: Transitional and final provisions, Articles 503–557.

– protecting consumers as final customers of energy;
– ensuring effective control of the implementation of the provisions of this act.

109. The Act Regulating the Basic Safety of Transport along Oil and Gas Pipelines regulates the transport of liquid and gaseous hydrocarbons, i.e. crude oil, natural gas and their derivatives, and other materials along oil and gas pipelines. These include underground and undersea oil and gas pipelines, buried oil and gas pipelines with fittings, underground crossings for oil and gas pipelines below watercourses, paths and roads, tunnels built exclusively for oil and gas pipelines, overground sections of oil and gas pipelines, and bridges for oil and gas pipelines not intended for public transport.

110. The Conditions of the Concession for Exploitation of the Energy Potential of the Lower Sava River Act regulate, as already indicated by the Act's name, the conditions of the concession for exploitation of the river Sava's energy potential and conditions which must be fulfilled by the concessionaire when planning and building the infrastructure needed for the implementation of the concession.

111. The Fund for Financing Decommissioning of the Krško Nuclear Power Plant Krško and Disposal of Radioactive Waste from the Krško Nuclear Power Plant Act regulates the establishment and operation of the Fund for Financing Decommissioning of the Nuclear Power Plant Krško and disposal of radioactive waste from the Nuclear Power Plant Krško.

112. The ZRud-1[144] sets out the conditions for prospecting, exploring and exploiting mineral commodities, irrespective of whether they are in the ground, on the surface or in water, the conditions for decommissioning their exploitation, and the conditions for ensuring occupational health and safety during the exploration, exploitation and decommissioning of the exploitation of mineral commodities, and regulates inspection supervision.[145]

113. The Act Regulating the Gradual Closure of the Trbovlje-Hrastnik Mine and the Economic Development Restructuring of the Region regulates, first, foundations for definition of a plan of gradual closure of the mine Trbovlje-Hrastnik as

144. Official Gazette of the Republic of Slovenia, No. 14/14 – official consolidated version, and 61/17-GZ.
145. The Mining Act *inter alia* implements the following:

- Directive 94/22/EC of the European Parliament and of the Council of 30 May 1994 on the conditions for granting and using authorizations for the prospection, exploration and production of hydrocarbons, Official Journal of the European Union, L 164, 30.6.1994, 3.
- Directive 2006/123/EC of the European Parliament and of the Council of 12 Dec. 2006 on services in the internal market, Official Journal of the European Union, L 376, 27.12.2006, 36.
- Directive 2013/30/EU of the European Parliament and of the Council of 12 Jun. 2013 on safety of offshore oil and gas operations and amending Directive 2004/35/EC, Official Journal of the European Union, L No. 178, 28.7.2013, 66.

well as the financial resources for this activity, second, financial resources for payment of a direct damage caused by the operation of the mine, and, third, foundations for the definition of a plan for the region restructuring.

114. As stated, numerous other legislative acts are of significance to the energy sector; although they do not relate exclusively to it, they intervene in the energy sector directly, such as:

- the Spatial Management Act;[146]
- the Building Act;[147]
- the Environmental Protection Act;[148]
- the Public Procurement Act;[149]
- the Public-Private Partnership Act.[150]

§5. Secondary Acts

115. The aforementioned laws are further concretized by numerous (horizontal) secondary acts, such as on the energy infrastructure and its spatial implementation, on local energy systems, on energy efficiency, on the sectoral regulator, etc.[151] In addition, there are also numerous (sectoral) secondary acts, which regulate electricity, natural gas, oil or coal, that for practical reasons cannot be cited here, but are cited in individual parts of this monograph that discuss electricity, natural gas, oil and coal. However, for an illustration, let us point out that there are almost two-hundred general secondary acts issued by the Slovenian government, competent ministries, the Energy Agency, and the operators of the transmission and distribution systems of electricity, natural gas and heat. This clearly confirms the thesis that the adoption of the legislative act (such as EA-1) or acts does not necessarily mean the end of the transposition of EU directives and more generally of implementation of the acquis communautaire in the field of energy or energy sector.

§6. Case Law

116. Since the new EA-1 was adopted, the competent courts in Slovenia, in particular the Administrative Court of the Republic of Slovenia and the Supreme Court of the Republic of Slovenia, issued numerous judgments and decisions. It seems that

146. Official Gazette of the Republic of Slovenia, No. 61/17.
147. Official Gazette of the Republic of Slovenia, Nos 61/17, 72/17 and 65/20.
148. Official Gazette of the Republic of Slovenia, Nos 96/04,– official consolidated version, 61/06, 8/10, 46/14, 21/18, 31/18 and 82/20.
149. Official Gazette of the Republic of Slovenia, Nos 91/15 and 14/18.
150. Official Gazette of the Republic of Slovenia, No. 127/06.
151. There are numerous secondary acts. Some of them are listed or even discussed within the individual chapters on electricity, natural gas, etc.

the main areas of case law are subvention and other forms of state aid,[152] regulatory framework and financing of public services obligations,[153] access to the network,[154] permits,[155] easements and other limitations of property right,[156] treatments of vulnerable consumers,[157] change of supplier,[158] etc. Moreover, there are few judgments and decisions of the Constitutional Court of the Republic of Slovenia. In most cases, the Constitutional Court dismissed the claim or proposal, but this is not to say there were no provisions in the EA-1 which are not in line with the Slovenian Constitution as discussed in this monograph.[159]

---

152. For example, ECLI:SI:VSRS:2017:X.IPS.194.2015; ECLI:SI:VSRS:2017:X.IPS.239.2015; ECLI:SI:VSRS:2017:X.IPS.243.2015; ECLI:SI:UPRS:2015:I.U.1255.2014; ECLI:SI:UPRS:2019 :I.U.2293.2018.11; ECLI:SI:VSLJ:2017:I.CPG.1343.2016; ECLI:SI:VSCE:2019:CPG.68.2019.
153. For example, ECLI:SI:VSLJ:2018:I.CPG.701.2018; ECLI:SI:VSLJ:2017:I.CPG.627.2016; ECLI:SI:VSRS:2020:I.UP.7.2020; ECLI:SI:VSLJ:2018:I.CPG.701.2018; ECLI:SI:UPRS:2016 :II.U.17.2016; ECLI:SI:UPRS:2016:II.U.17.2016. ECLI:SI:UPRS:2016:II.U.467.2015; ECLI:SI :UPRS:2016:II.U.467.2015; ECLI:SI:UPRS:2019:I.U.135.2019.14.
154. For example, ECLI:SI:VSLJ:2018:I.CP.2918.2017; ECLI:SI:VSMB:2018:I.CP.995.2018; ECLI:SI:UPRS:2018:IV.U.97.2016.9; ECLI:SI:UPRS:2019:I.U.1313.2018.16; ECLI:SI:UPRS :2017:II.U.304.2016.32; ECLI:SI:VSLJ:2018:II.CPG.9.2018.
155. For example, ECLI:SI:VSRS:2018:X.IPS.254.2017.
156. For example, ECLI:SI:VSRS:2018:X.IPS.254.2017; ECLI:SI:VSCE:2018:CP.160.2018; ECLI:SI:VSLJ:2016:I.CP.2553.2015; ECLI:SI:UPRS:2017:I.U.747.2016; ECLI:SI:VSRS:2017:I. UP.199.2017.
157. For example, ECLI:SI:VSLJ:2018:I.CP.2918.2017, ECLI:SI:VSMB:2018:I.CP.995.2018.
158. For example, ECLI:SI:VSLJ:2019:II.CPG.579.2019.
159. *See*, e.g., Case U-I-133/13-24 (and U-I-134/13-22), ECLI:SI:USRS:2016:U.I.133.13.

Part I. Regulatory Framework Concerning Electricity

117. The first part of the contents deals with the regulatory framework concerning electricity. This is comprised of the following five chapters.

118. Chapter 1 (General Introduction), which serves as an introduction to the regulatory framework concerning electricity, presents the main properties and characteristics of the Electricity Sector in the Republic of Slovenia and provides an overview of Slovenian energy policy. This is followed by a presentation of the general legal framework applicable to electricity infrastructure and a discussion of certain special characteristics in the operations of electricity undertakings. In the end, some key acts and other regulations governing the sector and which constitute the main Slovenian legal acts in the field of electricity, are presented.

119. Chapter 2 (Production) mainly discusses the conditions that need to be fulfilled for the production of electricity. This chapter focuses on obtaining various approvals or consents and permits needed to construct and operate an electricity plant or a unit generating electricity. In addition, the chapter also discusses the technical conditions for constructing above-terrain high-voltage electricity pylons as well as the manner of ensuring the lacking new capacities for electricity production.

120. Chapter 3 (Transport) discusses the transport of electricity through the transmission network or system. First, the term transmission system is defined; this is followed by an overview of the fundamental characteristics of specific public law obligations relating to conducting activities as a TSO which is deemed a public utility. The chapter then discusses the unbundling (separation) of the activity of the TSO from other activities in the electricity sector, and discusses the provision of system services, data confidentiality and select questions relating to the access to the system of third persons.

121. Chapter 4 (Distribution) discusses the transport of electricity through the distribution network or system. First, the term distribution system is defined; this is followed by an overview of the fundamental characteristics of specific public law obligations relating to conducting activities as a distribution system operator (DSO) which is deemed a public utility. The chapter then discusses the unbundling (separation) of the activity of the DSO from other activities in the electricity sector, and discusses the closed distribution system, select questions relating to the access to the system of third persons and leasing a significant part of the distribution network.

122. Chapter 5 (Consumption) discusses the consumption of electricity. This chapter mainly focuses on the protection of final electricity consumers and especially on the protection of (vulnerable) household electricity consumers and emergency electricity supply.

Chapter 1. General Introduction

123. This chapter is designed as an introduction to a more detailed discussion of the regulatory framework concerning electricity. It first presents the main properties and characteristics of the Electricity Sector in the Republic of Slovenia and provides an overview of Slovenian energy policy. This is followed by a presentation of the general legal framework applicable to electricity infrastructure and a discussion of certain special characteristics in the operations of electricity undertakings. In the end, some key acts and other regulations governing the sector and which constitute the main Slovenian legal acts in the field of electricity are presented.

§1. Electricity Sector in Slovenia

124. Using selected figures such as those for domestic production imports and consumption of electricity, data on the transmission and distribution systems, and data on market structure, the electricity sector in Slovenia was presented in the introduction to this monograph, in Chapter 1 §2 General Information about the Slovenian Energy Sector, but for practical reasons certain additional useful information and explanations relating to individual sectors and markets within the Slovenian electricity sector are given here.

125. In the technical sense, the Slovenian electricity sector is by its very nature comparable to the electricity sectors of other EU Member States, and can be similarly divided into several mutually reliant economic activities or branches that together form a complementary whole. These are production, organization and support of the electricity market, trading, transport along transmission and distribution networks, and supply to electricity consumers.[160] Of the aforementioned branches, production, trading and supply to consumers are pursued freely on the market,[161] in a similar fashion to other competitive markets (of course, considering the specific

160. Undertakings performing at least one of these activities shall be considered as electricity undertakings. All electricity undertakings shall, in the public interest, perform tasks that refer to the reliability, regularity, quality and price of supply and to environment protection, including the efficient use of energy, energy generated from renewable sources and climate protection. In addition to these general obligations, electricity undertakings entrusted with the operation of services of general economic interest in the sense of the Art. 106(2) TFEU shall perform special tasks (*see infra*).

161. More precisely, the functions of the production and supply of electricity shall be carried out freely in the market, in which participants shall freely agree on the price and quantity of electricity to be supplied, final customers shall have the right to choose and switch the supplier from which they purchase electricity, and producers shall have the right to choose and switch the supplier to which they sell electricity. Traders shall conclude contracts among themselves, save for the congestion of the system, when the right to conclude contracts shall be granted in accordance with the EA-1. Suppliers to users shall conclude open contracts on the supply to final customers and purchasing from producers regardless of the connection point. Suppliers shall have an offset balance; any imbalances shall be calculated in accordance with the rules adopted by the market operator on the basis of the EA-1.

characteristics of electricity and the electricity sector), while the transport of electricity along transmission and distribution networks and the organization and support of the electricity market are pursued in conditions of restricted market competition, under a special regime of public law that includes the obligations of the utilities or public services obligations.[162] The electricity undertakings providing the services of general economic interest in the sense of Article 106(2) TFEU shall ensure: permanent and uninterrupted system operation within the limitations set by the technical condition of equipment and quality supply standards; safe and reliable operation and maintenance of the system; system development; connection of system users in accordance with general and non-discriminatory conditions; a system that enables customers to freely choose their supplier and enables producers and suppliers to freely sell and purchase electricity; billing the use of the system; long-term planning of system development; provision of emergency supply to vulnerable users; provision of sustaining supply; other obligations specified in a specific act or regulation.[163] Of course, in addition to these general obligations such undertakings are also bound to fulfil specific public services obligations.

126. The Government shall provide each of the aforementioned public service providers with exclusive rights[164] to provide mandatory public services in the electricity industry.[165]

127. Immediately below there follows a brief explanation of certain basic attributes of the aforementioned branches of the electricity sector, which first examines the market-based branches, followed by the transport of electricity along the transmission and distribution networks and the organization of the electricity market, whose operation is provided as a mandatory state public utility.

128. Electricity production is inseparable from the corresponding infrastructure (power stations), which in terms of technical matters, safety, environmental protection and planning are such demanding facilities that they require a special system of permits to ensure that the principal risks are managed. It can nevertheless be concluded that there are a relatively large number of power stations in Slovenia, particularly (small) hydro stations. The largest electricity producers include Jedrska elektrarna Krško (Nuclear Power Plant Krško), Termoelektrarna Šoštanj (Thermal Power Plant Šoštanj), Termoelektrarna Trbovlje (Thermal Power Plant Trbovlje), Dravske elektrarne Maribor (Drava Hydro Power Plants Maribor) and Hidroelektrarne na spodnji Savi (hydro power plants on Lower Sava). Electricity production in Slovenia is diverse, and it could be said that electricity is produced from almost

162. For more about public service obligations, universal services and services of general economic interest *see* A. Ferčič, *Public Services and Related Concepts in the European Union: Understanding European Union's Legal Framework for Services of General Economic Interest,* Nova Science Publishers, 2020, 53–66.
163. Article 37(2) EA-1.
164. The EA-1 does not contain the definition of the exclusive right, however, considering the whole context one can come to the conclusion that it is meant the exclusive right in the sense of Art. 106(1) TFEU.
165. Article 38 EA-1.

all sources known at present, both renewable and non-renewable, but in terms of the proportion of total domestic electricity production that they account for, the most notable are nuclear, hydro and thermal (lignite).[166]

129. In principle, trading in electricity takes place on the wholesale and retail markets. Trading in electricity on the wholesale market is conducted solely between members of the balancing scheme,[167] i.e., between traders[168] and suppliers[169] within the balancing scheme, who conclude closed agreements between each other.[170] Trading may be undertaken via direct agreements, or may be organized within the framework of a special exchange.[171] The wholesale market also allows for cross-border trading,[172] in which it is necessary to take into account that the capacities of the transmission lines that connect the grids of two or more countries are limited. It is therefore necessary to provide cross-border transmission capacity through explicit auctions where participants bid solely for transmission capacity expressed in MW, while the energy has to be provided separately, in implicit auctions, where market participants bid for electricity in addition to transmission capacity. By contrast, electricity trading on the retail market is undertaken between suppliers[173] and consumers, who conclude open agreements in which the quantities of energy supplied and the timing of supply are not determined in advance; consumers pay for the supplied electricity on the basis of the actual consumption of electricity units, which is measured using special metres.

---

166. The sources are given in the order of their contribution to total domestic electricity production in recent years.
167. The balancing scheme is a hierarchical arrangement for the Slovenian electricity market. The balancing scheme is operated by Slovenia's market operator, Borzen d.o.o., a public company.
168. A trader is a legal or natural person who buys electricity for onward sale inside or outside the system where the trader is based.
169. A supplier is a legal or natural person who pursues supply activities, i.e., sells electricity to consumers (including onward sale), and does not mean a producer, unless the producer joins the balancing scheme and is given membership of the balancing scheme.
170. A closed electricity supply agreement is a legal transaction between members of the electricity market balancing scheme, in which the quantity of electricity supplied during the relevant period is defined for each accounting interval, which means that the agreement is independent of the actual quantity of electricity supplied; any difference between the contractually agreed quantity and the quantity actually supplied is the subject of the balancing calculation (Art. 36(47) EA-1).
171. After the close of day-ahead exchange trading, trading on the intraday market begins. In contrast to day-ahead trading, which operates according to the principle of auction trading (all purchase and sale bids are combined after the close of trading in a supply/demand curve, and their intersection determines the market price), intraday trading operates on the principle of current trading, which means that an individual transaction is concluded as soon as an individual supply and an individual demand meet. It should be further noted that in the final hour before supply begins the intraday market transforms into the balancing market, in which the system operator acts as the sole buyer of balancing energy (positive or negative).
172. It is of interest to Slovenian firms partly because of the access to forms of trading and transactions in electricity that do not exist on the Slovenian market, such as transactions in derivatives (futures and options).
173. A firm that wishes to act as a supplier in the Slovenian retail market must be registered for this business activity in an EU Member State. Before pursuing this activity, it has to become a member of the balancing scheme and to meet other requirements set out by applicable energy regulations, such as the obligation to separate supply from distribution at affiliates.

130. The organization of and support for the electricity market, which in Slovenia is provided as a mandatory state economic public utility, is (at the moment) provided exclusively[174] by the market operator Borzen, organizator trga z električno energijo, d.o.o., which performs the following tasks and activities:

- operation of the electricity market's balancing scheme;[175]
- recording of agreements on membership of the balancing scheme, open agreements and closed agreements;[176]
- implementation of the balancing market in electricity;
- execution of the balancing calculation;
- pursuit of the activities of the Support Centre;[177]
- collection and publication of data to ensure transparency in the operation of the electricity market; and
- execution of accounting and financial settlement of transactions related to the aforementioned tasks.[178]

131. With respect to pursuing such tasks and activities, the operator shall, pursuant to public authorization, issue regulations on the functioning of the market and on organizing the balancing market, as well as regulations governing the functioning of the Support Centre. However, the latter shall be subject to the Government's approval (consent), while both the former shall be subject to the Energy Agency's approval (consent). A market operator shall ensure the transparency, non-discrimination and fairness of its operations, observing the fundamental principles of a state governed by the rule of law.[179]

132. The transport of electricity is undertaken along the transmission and distribution networks. As illustrated below, the fundamental difference between the two

174. As concession grantor, the Republic of Slovenia shall grant the (non-payable) concession for providing the electricity market operator service of general economic interest to one market operator and for the entire territory of the Republic of Slovenia (Art. 99 EA-1).

175. The electricity market shall be hierarchically structured in a balance scheme in which the relations between the balance scheme members and their respective inflow and outflow balance keeping are specified in a uniform manner by the balance scheme membership agreements. The membership and structure of the balance scheme shall be established in the balancing contracts and compensation agreement. An individual natural or legal person may join the balance scheme as a member only through a single balancing contract or a single compensation agreement, with the exception of the providers of services of general economic interest, which may, in order to carry out individual tasks of the services of general economic interest in a transparent and economically effective manner, in addition to the mandatory establishment of their own balancing group also establish separate balancing groups or subgroups. The rules for electricity market operation may envisage special statuses for balance scheme members providing services of general economic interest under this Act. *See* Art. 102 EA-1.

176. Closed agreements are used for electricity traders.

177. The Centre for Support shall draw up and implement programmes to provide information, training and awareness-raising of various target groups with regard to the benefits and practical aspects of the development and use of energy efficiency and renewable energy technologies. *See* Art. 351 EA-1.

178. Article 97 EA-1.

179. *Ibid.*

networks is the voltage levels that they operate at, but both networks are organized as a public utility. There are two public companies primarily responsible for the transport of electricity in Slovenia, namely ELES, sistemski operater prenosnega elektroenergetskega omrežja, d.o.o., which holds the exclusive right to provide the public utility of acting as the system operator for the transmission network in Slovenia (for voltages of 400, 220 and 110 kV) and is under 100% public ownership, and SODO, sistemski operater distribucijskega omrežja z električno energijo, d.o.o., which provides the public utility of acting as the system operator for the distribution network in Slovenia (for voltages of 0.4, 10, 20 and 35 kV, and exceptionally 110 kV),[180] whereby it should be noted that on the basis of a separate agreement on behalf of SODO d.o.o. several other companies provide services in the distribution network, namely Elektro Celje d.d., Elektro Gorenjska d.d., Elektro Ljubljana d.d., Elektro Maribor d.d. and Elektro Primorska d.d. As illustrated later in this monograph (*see* Part VI), Slovenia's competition ombudsman has already fined these companies for cartel behaviour.

§2. Slovenia's Electricity Sector Policy

133. Slovenia's policy with regard to the electricity sector can be inferred from the EA-1, which is the fundamental and systemic regulation for the energy sector, and can also be inferred from the various strategic documents and decisions in individual cases made by national bodies and authorities responsible for the electricity sector. An awareness of public policy in this area is the key to understanding and correctly interpreting the relevant laws, regulations and other rules, as only in this way are the public objectives and measures revealed, in short, the national vision and related strategy for the electricity sector in a specific period.

---

180. Article 512 of the original EA-1 provided for transfer of 110 kV network sections, namely, companies owning such network sections shall transfer it for a fee in three years after the EA-1 came in force, i.e. until March 2017. However, this obligation was not fulfilled in due time but nothing really happened since the discussed provision did not define any sanction in case of the delay of the network transfer (*lex imperfecta*). The owners of the network, which can be considered as public undertakings in the sense of Directive 2006/111/ES, demanded a relatively high price but the TSO was not willing to paid it. On the one hand, the owners tried to sell the discussed network for appropriate price according to market economy vendor principle to avoid a state aid in the sense of Art. 107 (1) TFEU, but, on the other hand, the TSO tried to follow the logic of market economic purchaser principle. At the abstract level, the endeavour of both sides is reasonable, yet, when it comes to the real case, this status quo position can be only solved in the intersection of both principles, i.e. that of market economy vendor and market economy purchaser. In this vein, the EZ-1B included an additional paragraph according to which the discussed transfer shall be carried out at the value assessed by a certified appraiser of real estate and equipment, selected jointly by the TSO and the network owner(s). The assessment must take into account the Agency's methodology for the determination of the regulatory framework and in particular the method of determining the value of assets used by the Agency to determine the recognized depreciation and return. The procedure and way of determining the value assessment shall also be applied to funds or assets which were not taken into account in the network charge until the entry into force of the EA-1B.

134. The supreme objectives of current energy policy, which could of course also be mapped to the electricity sector, are the reliable, sustainable and competitive supply of energy to the country, via the promotion of:

- a reliable and high-quality energy supply;
- long-term balance in the development of the energy economy with regard to developments in energy consumption;
- planned diversification of various primary energy sources, taking their economics into account;
- a competitive energy supply;
- the use of renewables and low-carbon energy sources;
- the prioritization of energy efficiency over energy supply;
- a low environmental impact in the acquisition, production, transport and use of all types of energy;
- competition on the energy market;
- flexible energy consumers;
- consumer protection.[181]

135. The measures to achieve the aforementioned are set out in detail in special long-term planning documents, such as fundamental development plan in the field of energy sector (national energy and climate plan), energy concept or plan, and operational and action plans for individual areas of energy supply and management. Of the aforementioned documents, the current fundamental development document in Slovenia is national energy and climate plan as demanded by the EU legislation on Energy Union[182] and Climate Action (governance mechanism),[183] which tries to ensure, *inter alia*, the achievement of the 2030 and long-term objectives and targets of the EU in line with the so-called Paris Agreement (2015) through complementary, coherent and ambitious efforts by the EU and its Member States, while limiting administrative complexity.[184]

136. Slovenia adopted and published its final National Energy and Climate Plan in February 2020.[185] This plan can be considered as a strategic document which

181. For example, an additional objective is efficiency and reduced consumption of electricity. *See* Arts 5 and 20 EA-1.

182. The Energy Union rests on five pillars, i.e. energy security; the internal energy market; energy efficiency; decarbonization; and research, innovation and competitiveness.

183. *See* Regulation (EU) 2018/1999 of the European Parliament and of the Council of 11 Dec. 2018 on the Governance of the Energy Union and Climate Action, amending Regulations (EC) No. 663/2009 and (EC) No. 715/2009 of the European Parliament and of the Council, Directives 94/22/EC, 98/70/EC, 2009/31/EC, 2009/73/EC, 2010/31/EU, 2012/27/EU and 2013/30/EU of the European Parliament and of the Council, Council Directives 2009/119/EC and (EU) 2015/652 and repealing Regulation (EU) No. 525/2013 of the European Parliament and of the Council, Official Journal of the European Union, L 328, 21.12.2018, 1.

184. *See* the first paragraph of the preamble to the aforementioned regulation.

185. The final document was prepared with due consideration of the European Commission's observations as pointed out in relation to the draft plan. Moreover, when drafting the discussed plan the Strategy for Slovenia's Development until 2030 was considered. The latter puts great emphasis on low-carbon circular economy and sustainable management of natural resources.

defines public policies, i.e. aims and measures which will be carried out in all fields[186] of the Energy Union until 2030[187] (with appropriate consideration of the desired development until 2040).[188] With due consideration of the discussed document, Slovenia plans to adopt a new[189] national energy concept, which will represent a national energy programme and will be adopted via a resolution by the National Assembly at the proposal of the Government on the basis of projections of Slovenia's economic, environmental and social development, and on the basis of its international commitments to set targets for reliable, sustainable and competitive energy supply for the next twenty years and rough targets for the next forty years (albeit with interim controls, which should indicate whether the concept is still appropriate). A projection of the energy balance and the manner of energy supply and management are to be determined in this connection, on the basis of a twenty-year development projection for the country, taking account of technological, environmental and geopolitical trends of development; the national targets in energy supply and management; the requisite measures to meet the aforementioned targets; the commitments with regard to renewables; and indicators of corresponding energy policy targets in the state budget programme. At this point, it is also worthy to point out the National Strategy for Decreased Use of Coal and for Restructuring of Coal Regions in Accordance with Principles of Fair Development. The preparation of the draft strategy is scheduled for September 2020 while the deadline for final version is still uncertain but it is reasonable to expect it in 2021.

§3. Electricity Infrastructure

137. The electricity infrastructure comprises facilities and production installations and the electricity network,[190] which reflects its decisive effect on the provision of electricity, which is an essential asset in modern society. In view of this, it is clear that the electricity infrastructure must be planned and constructed in such a

---

186. *See* Footnote 182.
187. For illustration, the selected targets for 2030 are as follows: decrease of total emissions of greenhouse gasses (–36%), decrease of non-ETS emissions of greenhouse gasses (at least–20%), appropriate share of renewable energy sources in the final energy consumption (at least 27%), appropriate share of efficient use of energy (at least 35%), share of research and innovation (3% of the GDP / 1% from public sources and 2% from private sources). Of course, all these targets are further elaborated and concretized in the National Energy and Climate Plan which is accessible, *inter alia*, at the European Commission web page. In fact, at the latter one can access draft plans, European Commission's observations and final plans of all Member States, *see* https://ec.europa.eu/energy/topics/energy-strategy/national-energy-climate-plans_en.
188. The plan provides for modifications or adjustments in 2023 and 2024, and in this regard also new EU legislation and other acts, which will be adopted in accordance to the European Green Deal, shall be properly considered.
189. In fact, the old national energy concept as was proposed with a substantial delay by the government in March 2018 was not adopted by the National Assembly.
190. Each element of the electricity infrastructure is important, but in practice the network constitutes the greatest regulatory challenge, taking into account the fact that it is characterized by a combination of a natural monopoly and the economic irreversibility of fixed costs, which is known as a monopolistic bottleneck.

way as to correspond to the current state of the art and be economically efficient, and must be maintained so as to ensure optimal technical operation and economic efficiency.[191]

138. In order to ensure the provision of public utility services in the energy sector, the Government defines by decree the types of maintenance work on the electricity network in the public interest and the method of carrying out that work, under the provisions of the act governing construction.[192]

139. The construction and acceptance of the facilities and land required for the production, transmission and distribution of electricity are in the public interest, which justifies expropriation, the establishing of a special right in favour of the operator which for a certain time period limits the use or owner's power to use the relevant land or the (public) easements, which can be temporary or permanent (in certain cases this occurs *ex lege*).[193] For all issues relating the expropriation or limitation of the property right which are not covered by the EA-1, the legislative act on expropriation and limitation of property right applies.[194]

140. For reasons of security, a buffer zone is provided for electricity systems, which can be described as a belt of land alongside electricity lines and facilities in which other facilities and installations may be constructed and work carried out that could affect the operation of the network only under certain conditions and at a certain distance from the lines and facilities of this network. The width of the buffer zone for an electricity network extends on each side from the axis of the electrical line or from the outermost fence of the substation or transformer station, and measures:

- 40 m for above-ground multisystem power lines and for substations with a nominal voltage of 400 kV and 220 kV;
- 10 m for underground cable systems with a nominal voltage of 400 kV and 220 kV;
- 15 m for above-ground multisystem power lines and for substations with a nominal voltage of 110 kV and 35 kV;
- 3 m for underground cable systems with a nominal voltage of 110 kV and 35 kV;
- 10 m for above-ground multisystem power lines with nominal voltages of between 1 kV and 20 kV;
- 1 m for underground cable systems with a nominal voltage of up to 20 kV;
- 1.5 m for above-ground lines with a nominal voltage of up to 1 kV;
- 2 m for medium-voltage substations and medium-voltage transformer stations.[195]

191. The owners of individual parts of the electricity infrastructure are obliged to make continuous investments in maintenance and provide an appropriate level of indemnity insurance.
192. *See* Art. 463 EA-1.
193. *See* Arts 472–474 EA-1.
194. *See* Art. 472 EA-1.
195. *See* Art. 468 EA-1.

§4. Selected Special Characteristics in the Operations of Electricity Undertakings

141. For reasons of general interest, that activities necessary to the desired provision of electricity can be carried out without disruption, the EA-1 restricts enforcement proceedings on the electricity infrastructure, as it stipulates that the facilities, installations and network of the electricity infrastructure which are required for the operation of a public utility service cannot be subject to enforcement proceedings.[196] However, this does not apply absolutely, since exemption from enforcement does not apply in cases where enforcement is conducted for the repayment of a claim arising from a loan whereby an item was purchased or a loan granted for the development of a public service activity, and in cases where enforcement is conducted for the repayment of a loan secured by a contractual lien on that item.[197]

142. In the spirit of providing uninterrupted operation of essential activities, the right of workers to strike, which is otherwise a general legally recognized right, is limited if it concerns workers employed by an operator of a public utility service or by system service providers. Total strikes are not permitted, since a minimum work process must be ensured despite the strike, so that the electricity system functions to an extent and in a manner that it is capable of carrying out its mission, i.e., that objectives in that area are not threatened.[198]

143. And finally, for the reasons stated above, bankruptcy proceedings may not be initiated against companies, wholly owned by the Republic of Slovenia or a local community, which have been awarded a concession to provide a public utility service, or against public companies wholly owned by the state or local communities which provide a public utility service under the Act (the founders of the aforementioned legal entities bear subsidiary liability).[199] Since it is possible for an aforementioned legal entity to gradually lose the special status which protects it from bankruptcy, the Act also governs this situation and in this connection stipulates that energy infrastructure and property rights that are required to be intact for the provision of a public utility service may only be sold as a (indivisible) business entity in bankruptcy proceedings. If the bankruptcy debtor is a legal entity or natural person that does not provide a public utility service, a public utility service provider has a pre-emptive right in the sale of assets as a business entity in bankruptcy proceedings and in the sale of energy infrastructure and property rights that comprise infrastructure in bankruptcy proceedings. The pre-emptive right of a public utility service provider also relates to land that forms part of the bankruptcy estate and on

196. This however does not apply to facilities for the production of electricity or natural gas owned by natural persons and legal entities and in which the Republic of Slovenia does not have a direct or indirect ownership stake. Such statutory regulation could raise the question of compliance with the principle of the prohibition of special treatment for public enterprises.
197. *See* Art. 478 EA-1.
198. *See* Arts 483–485 EA-1.
199. Here as well there is a possible concern about the principle of special or favoured treatment of public enterprises.

which the public utility service provider's facilities, installations and lines are located. Where the bankruptcy debtor is a public utility service provider under the Act on the basis of a work or service concession, the method of sale of the assets and the pre-emptive right do not affect the concession-granter's right of exclusion under the act governing public-private partnerships. The pre-emptive right of a public utility service provider is exercised in accordance with the regulations on the exercise of legal pre-emptive rights in bankruptcy proceedings. Separate regulation is also foreseen with regard to the continuing of operations of the bankruptcy debtor. That is, without prejudice to the regulations on the business activities of a bankruptcy debtor after the commencement of bankruptcy proceedings, a bankruptcy debtor that is a public utility service provider or that performs the functions of a public utility service provider under authorization from a public utility service provider is permitted to continue its activities as a public service or conduct other transactions required to ensure the uninterrupted provision of the public utility service. In the case of the example referred to above, the official receiver must ensure that public utility service functions are performed in full, which means that such decisions are therefore simply not left to his discretion.[200]

144. It is also worth noting that electricity undertakings, whatever their system of ownership or legal form, shall draw up, submit to audit and publish their audited annual accounts in accordance with the provisions of the act governing companies, unless otherwise provided by the EA-1 or some other act. In addition, such undertakings shall keep separate accounting records in accordance with accounting standards; their notes to the accounts shall show separate accounts for transmission and distribution activities, as required for the activities in question carried out by separate undertakings. In this sense this is the most basic form of (formal) unbundling (separation of accounts). Accordingly, it is not unreasonable for the act to impose additional liabilities or more intensive unbundling on certain electricity undertakings, such as electricity undertakings engaged in distribution or TSO activities.[201]

145. And last but not least, the EA-1B introduced a special section on management of capital investments in the energy sector. In accordance with the law governing companies, i.e. ZGD, the Government exercises the rights of the Republic of Slovenia as a shareholder in companies majority or fully owned by the Republic of Slovenia, which perform the activity of TSO,[202] system operator and distribution operator, and activity of the electricity market operator in the Republic of Slovenia. The ministry responsible for energy is responsible for monitoring these investments. Due to the ownership separation (unbundling) in the case of ELES d.o.o., SODO d.o.o., and Borzen d.o.o. the ZSDH, i.e. the legislative act which regulates the Slovenian State Holding and its operation, shall not be applied for capital investment in the aforementioned companies.[203]

---

200. *See* Arts 479–482 EA-1.
201. *See* for more in Arts 108–111 EA-1.
202. *See also* Art. 385a(2) EA-1.
203. *See* Art. 511 EA-1.

§5. OVERVIEW OF KEY REGULATIONS ON ELECTRICITY

146. The Slovenian energy sector and within it also the electricity sector have for over a decade been directly subordinated to EU law,[204] which has supremacy or primacy with respect to (other) Slovenian law and determines the external limits of Slovenian energy law and policy. Original Slovenian laws, regulations and other rules may not exceed these limits.[205]

147. The fundamental act in the field of electricity is the EA-1,[206] which is concretized by several secondary acts, which in terms of their content can be divided into several groups, i.e. secondary acts relating to: electricity as a product or societal good, a reliable supply of electricity, a support scheme for the production of electricity from renewable resources and high-efficiency cogeneration of heat and electricity, energy efficiency, energy permits, electrical energy infrastructure, government spatial and site plans for energy facilities, etc.

148. For practical reasons we specifically refer here only to selected regulations and other general legal acts on electricity, adopted on the basis of the EA-1,[207] as follows:

- Rules on support for electricity generated from RES and from high-efficiency cogeneration.[208]
- Rules on minimum technical requirements for the construction, operation and maintenance of low-voltage power lines.[209]
- Rules on the operation of the electricity market.[210]
- Decree on small installations for the production of electricity from RES or through high-efficiency cogeneration.[211]
- Decree on the self-supply of electricity from RES.[212]
- Regulation on the division of the 110 kV network into the distribution and transmission systems.[213]
- Regulation on the concession and on the method for the implementation of performing public service obligation relating to the activity of the electricity market operator.[214]

---

204. And consequently also the so-called European model of liberalization; as such it represents an integral part of the European or internal electricity market.
205. In accordance with the principle of supremacy, in the event of discordance between one set of regulations and the other, the regulations from the European Union system have priority.
206. *See* the above Introduction, Chapter 5.
207. Numerous regulations issued on the basis of the old law were repealed by the new law and are in effect until the issuance of new ones, so their practical value is substantially limited.
208. Official Gazette of the Republic of Slovenia, Nos 74/16 and 74/20.
209. Official Gazette of the Republic of Slovenia, No. 21/20.
210. Official Gazette of the Republic of Slovenia, Nos 74/18 and 62/19.
211. Official Gazette of the Republic of Slovenia, No. 14/20.
212. Official Gazette of the Republic of Slovenia, No. 17/19.
213. Official Gazette of the Republic of Slovenia, No. 35/15.
214. Official Gazette of the Republic of Slovenia, No. 39/15.

- Regulation on the method of determining and calculating the contribution for ensuring support for the production of electricity from high-efficiency cogeneration and RES.[215]
- Rules on the balancing of the electricity market.[216]
- Rules on technical conditions for the construction of overhead high-voltage lines of alternating current from 1 kV to 400 kV.[217]
- Legal Act on the methodology for determining the regulatory framework and the methodology for charging the network charge for electricity system operators.[218]
- Legal Act on the methodology determining prices of system services.[219]
- Legal Act amending the Legal Act on the rules for monitoring the quality of electricity supply.[220]
- Legal Act on the criteria for derogations from the requirements of EU regulations on connections to the electricity network.[221]
- Legal Act on the methodology for the preparation and evaluation of an investment plan of the electricity TSO.[222]
- Legal Act on the methodology for the preparation and evaluation of an investment plan of the electricity DSO.[223]
- Act laying down the mode of determining shares of individual production sources of electricity. and the manner of their presentation.[224]
- Act on Identification of Entities in Data Exchange among Participants in the Electricity and Natural Gas Markets.[225]
- Instruction on the management of the register of natural persons engaged in electricity generation.[226]
- Document determining the contribution for ensuring support for the production of electricity from high-efficiency cogeneration and RES.[227]
- Tariffs for network charges of electric-operators.[228]
- The decision on the appointment of the EELS d.o.o. the TSO of the electricity system.[229]

215. Official Gazette of the Republic of Slovenia, No. 46/15.
216. Official Gazette of the Republic of Slovenia, No. 97/14.
217. Official Gazette of the Republic of Slovenia, No. 52/14.
218. Official Gazette of the Republic of Slovenia, Nos 46/18, 47/18, 86/18, 76/19, 78/19 and 85/20.
219. Official Gazette of the Republic of Slovenia, Nos 15/18 and 20/19.
220. Official Gazette of the Republic of Slovenia, Nos 59/15, 23/18 and 62/19.
221. Official Gazette of the Republic of Slovenia, No. 86/18.
222. Official Gazette of the Republic of Slovenia, No. 97/14.
223. Official Gazette of the Republic of Slovenia, No. 97/14.
224. Official Gazette of the Republic of Slovenia, Nos 10/15 and 34/15.
225. Official Gazette of the Republic of Slovenia, No. 39/15.
226. Official Gazette of the Republic of Slovenia, No. 45/15.
227. Official Gazette of the Republic of Slovenia, No. 56/15.
228. Official Gazette of the Republic of Slovenia, No. 31/20.
229. Official Gazette of the Republic of Slovenia, No. 46/15.

Chapter 2. Production of Electricity

149. This chapter will primarily cover the conditions which must be satisfied in order for electricity to be produced.[230] This concerns obtaining the various consents and permits required to build and operate a power station or electricity production installation.[231] This chapter will also cover the technical conditions for building above-ground high-tension power lines and later also the method of providing lacking new capacities for electricity production.

150. At this point, it is worthy to emphasize that the legal (administrative and judicial) procedures regarding the relevant permits and consents are challenging as proved numerous times in real practice. As already discussed earlier in this monograph, numerous energy infrastructure projects were rejected, mainly due to the environmental concerns. Let us just briefly point out many unsuccessful attempts to build wind turbines (there are only few on the territory of Slovenia which seems to be indicative) and most recently also the rejection of hydro power plants (e.g., on river Mura). It seems recent legislative proposals which set additional conditions for interested persons[232] to have a right to participate in relevant administrative and judicial procedures have its roots in the aforementioned situation. Without any prejudice of individual cases, it seems that relevant procedures are too complicated since there is a real problem to build or modernize energy infrastructure. At the end of the day, there is no energy production which would be totally neutral as to the environment and nature. Yet, this is not to deny that different ways of production of energy generate different harmful effects and we have to choose those which are less detrimental with a due consideration of security of electricity supply since the latter is essential for normal functioning of the society (in case we want to keep 'business as usual').

230. Since the production of electricity is a commercial activity which is conducted on the free market, i.e., taking classical market mechanisms into account, in this chapter we will not pay special attention to this aspect.
231. Although it is not mandatory, it is preferable that before deciding to build electricity production installations, potential investors obtain:

   - site information which includes the measurements and conditions for the planned investment, as defined in currently valid spatial planning acts, data on protections, limitations and prohibitions in the adopted spatial planning measures, and data in connection with changes and amendments to spatial planning acts or planned drafting of new spatial planning acts;
   - an opinion on the possibility of connecting to a network issued by a (local) electricity distributor, taking account of the type, power and manner of connection of the production installation, the condition of the network and the disturbance tolerance;
   - an analysis of the suitability of the location;
   - design concept, project design and feasibility study which defines the optimal solution and subordinate solutions from the technical, economic and environmental point of view.

   For more on this see the document Useful advice for the construction of small-scale installations for the generation of electricity from renewable sources and the cogeneration of heat and power, Borzen d.o.o., and SODO d.o.o., 2012.
232. NGOs in particular.

§1. PERMITS AND CONSENTS SYSTEM

151. As noted above, the construction and operation of power plants or electricity production installations, which by their nature are substantial development projects in the broadest sense of the word, requires obtaining of various consents and permits from the competent authorities, which are intended to provide for the protection of the public interest. Below we present the typical consents and permits required for the construction of power plants or electricity production installations (such as in particular environmental protection consents or permits, consents for connecting to the electricity network, special permits with regard to the type and power of the production installation, energy permits and building permits) and their use or operation (use permit or operation permit). These consents and permits are issued within the framework of an administrative procedure, to which general rules (*lex generalis*) apply unless explicitly otherwise defined for an individual case by the EA-1 or other special act (*lex specialis*).

152. The investor which would like to build a facility for the production of electricity of rated electrical power greater than 1 MW, which is connected to the public network, must acquire a final energy permit issued by the competent minister. This permit must be acquired before carrying out any construction activity. In the case of construction of such facility, for which a building permit must be obtained, the investor may request the issuance of a building permit after obtaining a final energy permit.[233] Moreover, in the case of construction of a facility of national importance, the procedure for preparing a spatial plan can be introduced only after obtaining a final energy permit. It is also worthy to mention that the energy permit must be obtained for any reconstruction of discussed facilities, which changes the energy parameters of the facility and the scope of which is such that a construction permit must be obtained for the reconstruction intervention.[234] The energy permit shall specify: location and area to which the energy permit relates; type of facility, fuel, device to which the energy permit applies; manner and conditions of performing energy activity in the facility; conditions related to the facility, the device after the cessation of their operation; conditions relating to the use of a public good or public infrastructure; and the obligations of the holder of the energy permit in relation to the transmission of data to the minister responsible for energy.[235] The EA-1 provision on energy permit, i.e. Article 52, is further concretized by Rules on issuing energy permits.[236,237] The Rules define: conditions for energy permit; application for energy permit and its issue; and keeping the register of energy permits.

233. *See* Art. 52 EA-1.
234. *Ibid.*
235. *See* more in Art. 52 EA-1.
236. Official Gazette of the Republic of Slovenia, No. 19/16.
237. The Rules in question transpose the fifth and seventh paragraphs of Art. 14 of Directive 2012/27 / EU of the European Parliament and of the Council of 25 Oct. 2012 on energy efficiency, amending Directives 2009/125/EC and 2010/30/EU and repealing Directives 2004/8/EC and 2006/32 / EC (Official Journal of the European Union, L 315, 14.11.2012, p. 1).

153. Special category of permits depends on the type of power plant or electricity production installation, and to a certain extent on their planned capacity. The construction and operation of hydroelectric plants, for instance, is also conditioned by water rights, which constitutes a special right to use water as a public asset and is obtained on the basis of a permit for the direct use consumption of water for the production of electricity at a hydroelectric plant with an installed nominal capacity of less than 10 MW, or on the basis of a concession for water consumption for the production of electricity at a hydroelectric plant with an installed nominal capacity of 10 MW or more. The construction and operation of thermal power plants is therefore also conditioned, e.g., by a permit for emission of greenhouse gases (GHGs). The construction and operation of nuclear power plants is therefore also conditioned, e.g., by a consent which ensures nuclear safety.

154. Furthermore, the EA-1 also stipulates consents for connecting power plants or electricity production installations to the system for transmission or distribution of electricity. Such consents are important since they determine the connection point and conditions for connection. The final approval (consent) for connection shall be valid for two years, and within this time limit, the holder of the approval (consent) shall fulfil all the requirements stated in the connection approval (consent) and implement the connection. The period of validity of a connection approval (consent) may at the user's request be extended no more than twice, and on each occasion by no longer than one year. After the connection is installed, the connection approval (consent) conditions shall be valid until termination or until a change to the measurement point. The decision granting or rejecting the consent for connection is made under the mandate of public authority by the electricity system operator, in the form of a decision in an administrative procedure. The right to a connection is not absolute. In addition, when a prospective user of the system does not fulfil the prescribed connection conditions, the connection can also be rejected when all formal conditions are fulfilled, but where the connection would cause severe disruptions to the power supply, or where the electricity system operator would incur disproportionate costs due to the connection (except if the prospective system user covers the costs that exceed the proportionate costs). When the connection approval (consent) is final, the electricity system operator and the user of the system as the beneficiary of the connection approval (consent) shall enter into a connection contract which regulates all mutual relations regarding the connection and the connection procedure, and mutual relations regarding the maintenance of the connection. If the operational constraints contained in the connection approval (consent) are changed, the system user shall apply for a new connection approval (consent). Under certain conditions provided by the Act, a connection approval (consent) may be transferred to a legal or natural entity that has acquired facilities, devices or installations. Detailed conditions for connection approval (consent) shall be laid down in the Network Code and/or the relevant regulation.

155. There are, however, also several other permits and consents in other legislative acts. Let us begin with an assessment of impact on environment, in case it is needed,[238] and environmental protection consent is required for any planned development projects which could have a significant impact on the environment.[239] When it comes to environmental impact assessment, it is first appropriate to explain its meaning and purpose. It is a process which identifies and assesses the long-term, short-term, direct or indirect impacts of the intended environmental intervention on man, soil, water, air, biodiversity and natural values, climate and landscape, as well as on human immovable property and cultural heritage, and their mutual relations. In order to assess the impact on the environment, the holder of the intended intervention must provide the project[240] of the intended intervention in the environment as well as a report on the effects of the implementation of the intended intervention on the environment. The report in question is a fundamental basis for environmental impact assessment. It contains in particular the following issues: a description of the existing state of the environment, including existing pressures; a description of the intended intervention, including information on its purpose, location and size; a description of the measures envisaged to prevent, reduce and, where possible, eliminate significant adverse effects on the environment; data necessary for the identification and assessment of the main impacts of the intended intervention on the environment, the identification or assessment of the main impacts of the intended intervention on the environment and their evaluation; an overview of the most important alternatives considered by the operator, indicating the reasons for the chosen solution, in particular with regard to environmental impacts; identification of the

238. As stipulated in Art. 51 of the Environmental Protection Act (EPA-1, Official Gazette of the Republic of Slovenia, No. 39/06 – official consolidated text, 49/06 – ZMetD, 66/06 – odl. US, 33/07 – ZPNačrt, 57/08 – ZFO-1A, 70/08, 108/09, 108/09 – ZPNačrt-A, 48/12, 57/12, 92/13, 56/15, 102/15, 30/16, 61/17 – GZ, 21/18 – ZNOrg and 84/18 – ZIURKOE), for certain types of environmental interventions, due to their size, scope, location or other characteristics that may affect the environment, an environmental impact assessment is mandatory. Moreover, for certain types of interventions in the environment in which significant impacts on the environment may be expected due to the characteristics of the intended intervention or its location, the ministry shall carry out a preliminary procedure in which it checks whether the environmental impact assessment is needed also in such cases. In other words, in the first case the environmental impact assessment is mandatory and must always be carried out without any further discussion, while in the second case it is not certain if the discussed assessment is needed and for this reason a preliminary procedure as defined in Art. 51a of the Environmental Protection Act must be carried out. Since the delimitation between the discussed groups as defined in the EA-1 is blurred, the Government shall concretize the provision in question (*see* the Decree on environmental encroachments that require environmental impact assessments, Official Gazette of the Republic of Slovenia, Nos 51/14, 57/15 and 26/17). Regarding the environment impact assessment two further issues shall be pointed out. First, prior to the commencement of the environmental impact assessment procedure, the investor or holder of the intended intervention may request the Slovenian Environment Agency for information on the scope and content of the report on the effects of the implementation and operation of the intended intervention on the environment (*see* Art. 52 Environmental Protection Act). Second, in case the installation or facility for which a building permit is demanded has environmental impacts, the building permit issuance procedure and the environmental impact assessment procedure are merged (integrated procedure) and the building permit is issued by the Ministry of the Environment and Spatial Planning while the Slovenian Environmental Agency merely issues an opinion in an integrated procedure.

239. The concept of 'environment' has to be understood here in a broader context, since the procedure for issuing environmental protection consents takes account of regulations governing environmental protection, nature conservation, water management and cultural heritage.

240. The competent minister defines the concept of a project and its elements.

area in which the intended intervention causes environmental burdens that may affect human health or property; and a summary of the report that is easy to understand by the general public.[241] The said report is further concretized by the Decree on the method of drafting and on the content of the report on the effects of planned activities affecting the environment.[242] Both documents, i.e. the project and report, are needed for environmental consent. Namely, the holder of the intended intervention must apply to the Ministry for the issuance of an environmental consent with an application and shall enclose a project and a report on environmental impacts. In case the Ministry finds that the intended intervention is in obvious conflict with legal acts governing environmental protection, nature conservation, water management or protection of cultural heritage, and is therefore not permitted, it shall issue a decision rejecting the environmental consent (in this case the general public is not included, and competent foreign authorities, if there are cross-border effects, are not informed about the discussed procedure).[243] In case the obvious conflict is not detected by the Ministry, the latter continues the procedure according to Articles 57–65 EA-1. The environmental consent shall be distinguished from environmental permit for operation of installation which can cause great pollution (Articles 65–81 EA-1), environmental permit for operation of other installation and activities (Articles 82–85 EA-1), and environmental permit for operation of the facility (Articles 86–91 c EA-1).

156. And of course, when permits and consents in the field of energy are discussed, one cannot ignore the building permit and operation permit as regulated by the Building Act (BA).[244] Building permit is needed to begin a construction. The permit in question is a definitive administrative decision[245] which determines the specific conditions that have to be taken into account during construction. It is required for beginning construction of any installation or facility, unless it is a simple structure or object.[246] In general, the BA-1 defines simple object as object of such small dimensions that it cannot accommodate a large number of people, is structurally simple and spatially less perceptible.[247] More specifically, the Decree on small installations for the production of electricity from RES or through high-efficiency cogeneration, adopted at the basis of the EA-1, lays down the types, size and conditions for the installation and connection of installations for the production

241. *See* Art. 54(2) EA-1.
242. Official Gazette of the Republic of Slovenia, Nos 36/09 and 40/17.
243. *See* Art. 57(2) EA-1.
244. Official Gazette of the Republic of Slovenia, Nos 61/17, 72/17 and 65/20.
245. This includes reconstruction, where it is not a case of mere maintenance.
246. Moreover, a building permit is not required for maintenance of object and maintenance work in public interest, for a temporary object, and for implementation of a inspection measure; *see* Art. 4(1) BA.
247. *See* Art. 3(1)(4) BA. Moreover, *see also* Art. 8 of the Decree on the classification of structures (Official Gazette of the Republic of Slovenia, No. 37/18) and appendix to it. According to the latter all transmission electricity lines are demanding or complex object and the same is true for power plants and other energy facilities with electric power above 5 MW, all nuclear power plants, and photovoltaic power plants with electric power above 1 MW. Moreover, also distribution electricity lines are complex object in case they operate at 110 kV or more. On the other hand, however, distribution electricity lines can be treated as a simple object in case they operate at 1 kV.

of electricity from RES or by cogeneration of heat and electricity with high efficiency, which do not require a building permit.[248] The discussed Decree explicitly points out the facilities for building of which no building permit is needed, namely, installations producing electricity by cogeneration of heat and electricity, with a rated electrical power not exceeding 50 kW; installations producing electricity using solar energy, with a rated electrical power not exceeding 1 MW; and installations producing electricity using wind energy, with a rated electrical power of up to and including 50 kW.[249]

157. A use permit (or operation permit) is a permit for the beginning of the functional use of the facility[250] to which that permit relates, issued in the form of an administrative decision. In principle, this permit is required if a building permit was required in advance for the same facility (except for less complex objects).[251] The decision on issuing the use permit is made by the same authority that previously issued the building permit with respect to the construction of the facility in question. The decision is usually adopted on the basis of a definitive[252] building permit and the carrying out of a technical inspection (and a pilot test or test operation if necessary).

§2. Specificities of Building Above-Ground High-Tension Electrical Lines

158. Building (and design, maintenance and use) of above-ground high-tension AC electrical lines with a nominal voltage of from 1 kV to 400 kV in the Republic of Slovenia[253] must be carried out in accordance with the technical conditions defined by specific rules.[254] These conditions are intended to provide for safe and economical construction (and maintenance) and safe, reliable and uninterrupted operation or use of those lines, taking account of the safety of people and property and environmental protection.

159. The technical conditions for above-ground high-tension lines are the following:

- SIST EN 50341-1:2002 Above-ground electrical lines for alternating current above 45 kV – Part 1: General Requirements – Joint Provisions.

248. Yet, the Decree shall not apply to individual self-sufficiency devices.
249. *See* Art. 3 of the Decree on small installations for the production of electricity from renewable energy sources or through high-efficiency cogeneration.
250. The use or operation of technical equipment requires the obtaining of an special operation or work permit, for which the provisions of the use permit are applied, however, these provisions cannot be used in full extent, but with reasonable adjustments only (*mutatis mutandis*).
251. *See* Art. 6 of the BA.
252. In exceptional cases, where the facility is of national importance, also on the basis of a final building permit if the suitability of the facility is established.
253. Except for above-ground high-tension lines inside closed electricity facilities.
254. These are new rules (Rules on technical conditions for the construction of overhead high-voltage lines of alternating current from 1 kV to 400 kV), adopted in 2014 on the basis of the new EA-1.

- SIST EN 50341-3-21:2009 Above-ground electrical lines for alternating current above 45 kV – Part 3-21: National Normative Provisions (NNP) for Slovenia (on the basis of SIST EN 50341-1:2002).
- SIST EN 50423-1:2005 Above-ground electrical lines for alternating current between 1 kV and 45 kV inclusive – Part 1: General Requirements – Joint Provisions.
- SIST EN 50423-3-21:2009 Above-ground electrical lines for alternating current between 1 kV and 45 kV inclusive – Part 3-21: NNP for Slovenia (on the basis of SIST EN 50423-1:2005).[255]

160. In the territory of the Republic of Slovenia the highest nominal voltage, i.e. safe voltage with respect to the technical design and manufacture of equipment and networks, for above-ground high-tension lines is defined as 400 kV.

§3. Provision of Lacking New Production Capacities

161. Reliable electricity supply is one of the basic objectives of energy policy. In this respect, the Act explicitly states that in the event that the amount of capacity for electricity production for which a national spatial planning act was adopted, or for which a building permit was issued if the national spatial planning act is not binding, and measures for energy efficiency adopted on the basis of that Act, do not provide a reliable supply of electricity, the ministry responsible for energy or a market operator on its authority may carry out a public invitation to tender for new production capacities or the implementation of new measures for efficient consumption of electricity.[256]

162. The invitation to tender must be published in the Official Gazette of the Republic of Slovenia and the Official Journal of the EU, in order to ensure the required (international) publicity in accordance with the idea of the internal market. Only in this way can cross-border trade, i.e., the free flow of means of production and competition be achieved in this area. The deadline for submitting applications (tenders) must be no less than six months. The public procurement procedure, conditions for participation and selection criteria must be transparent and non-discriminatory.[257] Invitations to tender for new capacities or for the implementation of measures for EEU[258] must include a detailed description of the conditions of contract and the selection procedure, and a comprehensive list of the criteria that will

255. Article 5 of the Rules on technical conditions for the construction of overhead high-voltage lines of alternating current from 1 kV to 400 kV.
256. Before initiating the public procurement procedure, the ministry responsible for energy must establish whether a reliable supply of electricity can be ensured through measures for efficient energy use (Art. 53 EA-1).
257. In principle, all forms of discrimination are problematic, including discrimination based on nationality.
258. Candidates may instead of new production capacities offer electricity from existing production capacities, if the long-term provision, equal reliability of supply and environmental acceptability of electricity production is thereby ensured (Art. 53 EA-1).

be applied to the selection of tenderers, including the definition of the foreseen types of initiatives that the selected tenderers will participate in. The criteria must include a requirement that the new production facility must increase competitiveness on the electricity market, and that the conditions for participation of candidates in the invitation to tender must define the conditions that must be satisfied by the facility which is the subject of the public procurement procedure in order to obtain an energy permit.

163. The decision-making procedure on the selection of a candidate for new capacities is carried out according to regulations on public-private partnerships if a public-private partnership will be established between the investor and the Republic of Slovenia in connection with the new capacities.[259]

259. The provision of lacking new production capacities is regulated by Art. 53 EA-1 and is intended to implement Art. 8 of the aforementioned Directive 2009/72/EC.

Chapter 3. Exploitation of Electricity

164. Electricity has certain unique or special characteristics; it is not a natural resource and it is artificially produced, it cannot be effectively stored or accumulated and left to exploitation in a classical way, etc. Therefore, it would not be accurate to discuss the questions of exploitation of electricity in the same way as in the case of natural gas, petrol and coal. Of course, electricity can be exploited since it is an important form of energy used for various business and non-business activities; however, these aspects are covered in other parts or chapters of this monograph.

165. Namely, some general relevant information is already included in the Introduction of this monograph, and in the chapter Consumption of Electricity in Part I, while specific information concerning the production of electricity from coal and petrol is included in Part III of this monograph.

Chapter 4. Transport or Transmission of Electricity

166. This chapter discusses the transport of electricity through the transmission network or system.[260] First, the term transmission system is defined; this is followed by an overview of the fundamental characteristics of specific public law obligations relating to conducting activities as a TSO which is deemed a public service. The chapter then discusses the disintegration (separation) of the activity of the TSO from other activities in the electricity industry, and discusses the provision of system services, data confidentiality and select questions relating to the access to the system of third persons.

§1. Concept of the Transmission System and Related Concepts

167. Although the term transmission system is not explicitly defined in the new EA-1, its contents can be inferred from the legal definitions of other terms, such as: transmission, system and (transmission) system operator.[261]

168. Transmission means the transmission of electricity through a transmission system.[262]

169. System means electricity installations, plants and networks used for the function of electricity system operator.[263]

170. (Transmission) system operator means a natural or legal person who carries out the function of electricity (transmission) system operator and is responsible for operating, maintaining and developing the electricity transmission system in a given area and, where applicable, its interconnections with other systems, and for ensuring the long-term ability of the system to meet reasonable demands for the transmission of electricity.[264]

171. As follows from the legal definitions of the aforementioned terms and considering the legislation of the EU, a transmission system can be defined as special electricity installations, plants and networks operated, maintained and, if necessary, developed by a (transmission) system operator, in order to enable the transport of

260. For transparency purposes it should be highlighted that electricity is also transported through the distribution network or system discussed in a separate chapter (Part I, Chapter 4).
261. The EA-1 uses the term 'system operator', while Directive 2009/72/EC of the European Parliament and of the Council of 13 Jul. 2009 concerning common rules for the internal market in electricity and repealing Directive 2003/54/EC, Official Journal of the European Union, L 211 of 14 Aug. 2009, 55 uses the term 'transmission system operator' (TSO).
262. *See* Art. 36(31) EA-1 (compare Art. 2(3) of Directive 2009/72/EC).
263. *See* Art. 36(37) EA-1.
264. *See* Art. 4(33) EA-1 (compare Art. 2(4) of Directive 2009/72/EC).

electricity on the extra high-voltage (in principle 110 kV or more) and high-voltage interconnected system with a view to its delivery to final customers or (more likely) to distributors.[265]

§2. Public Services Obligations Attached to the Transmission of Electricity

172. In principle, the transmission system acts as a link between the producers of electricity on the one hand and distributors and customers on the other. The transmission system is thus one of the most significant integral parts of the electricity chain, which significantly impacts electricity supply in the Republic of Slovenia, which is a general (public) interest in this respect. It is precisely for this reason that the legislator opted not to leave the activities of TSOs to market whims, but to submit the activity to the special requirements of a public service, namely a special public law regime in the form of mandatory public services of general economic interest,[266] which ensures the following tasks are fulfilled in the desired manner:

– secure, reliable and efficient operation and maintenance of the transmission system;
– development of the system that takes into account the anticipated needs of system users, the requirements for safe and reliable system operation, and the guidelines from the development plan;
– long-term capacity of the transmission system to meet reasonable demands for connection to the system and energy transmission;
– control of electricity flows in the transmission system and provision of ancillary services;
– clearing of imbalances of consumption, delivery and cross-border transmissions in the system;
– provision of information to any other operator that is necessary to ensure the secure and efficient operation, coordinated development and interoperability of the interconnected system;
– provision of data necessary to effectively conclude supply contracts and for the exercise of the right to connection to system users and suppliers;
– non-discriminatory treatment of system users and suppliers;

265. The Decree on the energy infrastructure, which was derogated by the new EA-1 but still applies until a new decree is adopted regulating this area, provided that the electricity infrastructure comprises overhead and other multisystem lines of nominal voltages of 100 kV and more, substations, a dispatch centre and other buildings, devices and networks needed for ensuring public services of general economic interest in the field of electricity transmission, and parts thereof. The enclosure to the Decree enumerated these buildings, devices and networks which comprise the transmission system.

266. Since the activities are expressly designated as a state public service, regional or local authorities have no jurisdiction of this area. Only one (state) transmission network exists in the Republic of Slovenia, which is operated by ELES, d.o.o. (*see* Part I, Chapter 1 §1).

- electricity consumption and necessary energy sources forecasts through a comprehensive planning method, taking due account of savings measures taken by system users;
- collection of payments for congestion and of payments resulting from the inter-TSO compensation mechanism;
- purchase of electricity to cover shortfalls in the transmission system and the purchase of ancillary services in the transmission system by means of transparent, non-discriminatory and market-based procedures;
- quality of supply in accordance with the minimum standards.[267]

173. The Act requires the electricity TSO to perform its tasks in a manner that particularly promotes the integration of the electricity market. This opens the question of the other goals relating to activities carried out by TSOs, and whether these goals are necessarily subordinate to the integration of the electricity market (where the legislator has failed to clearly define whether this refers to the national or internal market). With respect to the first question, we believe that the activities carried out by TSOs should keep in mind the goals defined by the EA-1 (*see* Introduction, Chapter 5) which are sensible in the context of the relevant activity and which it would be inappropriate to statically rank. With respect to the second question, we believe that the integration of the internal electricity market should be nonetheless observed, as this is one of the main reasons for the legislative and other activities of EU institutions in this area. Among others, the obligations of the TSO concerning the cross-border exchange or transfer of electricity are also part of the context of the internal market integration.[268]

---

267. *See* Art. 54 EA-1. In this regard, the more general Art. 36 EA-1 should be highlighted, which provides that electricity undertakings shall, in the public interest, perform tasks that refer to the reliability, regularity, quality and price of supply and to environment protection, including the efficient use of energy, energy generated from renewable sources and climate protection; in addition, the electricity undertakings providing the services of general economic interest shall also ensure the following:

- permanent and uninterrupted system operation within the limitations set by the technical condition of equipment and quality supply standards;
- safe and reliable operation and maintenance of the system;
- system development;
- connection of system users in accordance with general and non-discriminatory conditions;
- a system that enables customers to freely choose their supplier and enables producers and suppliers to freely sell and purchase electricity;
- billing the use of the system;
- long-term planning of system development;
- provision of emergency supply to vulnerable users;
- provision of sustaining supply;
- other obligations specified in an act or some other regulation.

268. In this respect, the operator must act in accordance with Regulation (EC) 714/2009.

174. The activity of the TSO on the territory of the Republic of Slovenia may only be conducted pursuant to a (non-payable) concession, which is[269]granted to a natural or legal person for no more than fifty years in special proceedings, where the operator must have:

– transmission system;[270]
– an electricity TSO certificate;[271] and
– an electricity TSO designation.

175. Tasks of the TSO are funded from network charges and other revenues generated from providing services of general economic interest. If funding is provided any other way than through revenue generated from the relevant activities (by providing public funds to the TSO), EU rules concerning state aid, as well as other rules governing competition, must be observed. In contrast to transmission system management, any further distortion of competition and excessive trading on the internal market, which could arise as a result of channelling funds from regulated to unregulated activities, is practically impossible due to the so-called complete ownership unbundling outlined in the following section.

§3. Ownership Unbundling

176. As outlined in the previous section, the TSO must own the transmission system it operates. In addition, the Act provides that a legal or natural person that

269. The concession is granted after a tendering procedure or other competitive procedure determined by the regulations on public-private partnership, unless the concession is granted to an undertaking fully owned by the Republic of Slovenia that is not performing market energy sector activities. In the latter case, the concession shall be granted with the direct conclusion of a concession contract. When a competitive procedure is foreseen for granting a concession, the concession act shall determine transparent, non-discriminatory and proportional conditions that a legal or natural person must fulfil in order to be granted a concession. The ownership of a transmission system or part of it, an electricity transmission system operator certificate and an electricity transmission system operator designation shall not be conditions for obtaining a concession. The procedure for granting a concession by means of public tender shall be managed by the ministry responsible for energy. The decision on the selection of the concessionaire shall be issued by the Government. When the decision on the selection of the concessionaire becomes final, the grantor shall sign a concession contract with the concessionaire; *see* Art. EA-1.

270. In principle, only the transmission system operator can obtain a construction and utility (operating) permit for a building or device considered part of the transmission system (except in the event of new interconnectors that are entitled to exemption).

271. During certification proceedings, disintegration and ownership unbundling is verified, as explained below (Part I, Chapter 4 §3). After certification is obtained, the Energy Agency continuously verifies whether the legal conditions for certification continue to be fulfilled. In certain cases, the Energy Agency must, ex officio, begin proceedings for formal verification of the conditions.

owns a transmission system must perform the activity of an electricity TSO, and further, that a person other than an electricity TSO may not, in whole or in part, own the transmission system on which the electricity TSO performs TSO activity, unless otherwise provided by the Act.[272]

177. On the other hand, ownership of the transmission system and activities relating to such a system are 'isolated'. Due to the negative experience with vertically integrated incumbents which abused their market power stemming from the transmission system in order to improve their competitive position on the upstream or downstream market, these incumbents are now required by law to ensure ownership unbundling, as the same persons must not at the same time have direct or indirect control over[273] companies engaged in the production or supply of electricity and TSOs or owners, and vice versa[274] (this prohibition applies both to the electricity and natural gas segments). Since the mere prohibition or limitation on simultaneously controlling two or more aforementioned undertakings cannot prevent all undesired connections on the upstream or downstream market, the legislator also provided limitations to membership in the relevant bodies by prescribing that the same legal or natural person shall not simultaneously be a member of the administrative board, supervisory board or other body legally representing the undertaking, of an electricity TSO or a person owning a transmission system, or a representative related to the ownership management of an electricity transmission system or an electricity or natural gas transmission system, and a member of the administrative board, supervisory board or other body legally representing the undertaking performing the functions of production or supply of natural gas or electricity.[275]

178. It is appropriate to highlight that the strict interpretation of the above prohibition of simultaneous control of an electricity undertaking that performs an electricity production or supply activity and an entity acting as TSO, including the prohibition of simultaneous membership in the bodies of such undertakings, could practically inhibit or at least significantly impair the entrepreneurial activity of

272. The requirement from the preceding paragraph shall be deemed fulfilled when two or more legal or natural persons that own a transmission system establish a joint venture that acts as a system operator in two or more European Union Member States, where the Act also provides that no other undertaking may participate in such a joint venture; *see* Art. 60 EA-1.

273. In this respect, control means any rights, contracts or any other means which, either separately or jointly and having regard to the considerations of fact or law involved, confer the possibility of exercising a decisive influence on an undertaking, in particular by:

- ownership or the right to use all or part of the assets of an undertaking;
- rights or contracts which confer a decisive influence on the composition, voting or decisions of the bodies of an undertaking.

274. This limitation does not apply to undertakings who produce or supply electricity to third persons, either directly or via undertakings which they control, provided that they are, on an annual average, net consumers of electricity, and provided that the economic value of the electricity they sell to third parties is insignificant in proportion to their other business operations.

275. *See* Art. 61 EA-1.

Member States in the electricity sector;[276] thus the EA-1 provides that when two separate authorities of the Republic of Slovenia, a local community or another EU Member State exercise control as referred to above of an electricity TSO or transmission system and of an undertaking performing activities in the field of production or supply, they shall be deemed separate persons (and thus not subject to the prohibition).[277]

179. A legal or natural person controlling a TSO, an owner of the transmission system, the operators themselves or any person which is subject to the above limitation concerning the control and membership in certain electricity companies must prevent and remedy any non-conformities and inform the Energy Agency accordingly, which shall impose the relevant corrective measures as needed. The Energy Agency also pursues any such violations ex officio. If the measures are not implemented in a reasonable period of no less than one month and no more than six months from the day of notification of the reason, or in the period indicated by the Agency, the Agency shall, by way of a decision:

- prohibit the execution of voting rights or execution of proprietary entitlements pertaining to the management of less than half of the equity stake;
- impose the sale of the share in capital stock or an equity stake in the transmission system insofar as this exceeds half of the stock capital, or shares of, the undertaking;
- find that a member of the management board, supervisory board or other body representing the undertaking was appointed contrary to this act or that the person who represents the transmission system owner was authorized contrary to this act, and propose to the competent authority the commencement of a procedure for the dismissal or withdrawal of the authorization;
- prohibit the exercise of indirect or direct control.[278]

180. As a means of last resort, the Agency may initiate proceedings to test the conditions for the certificate if the aforementioned measures cannot remedy the violation.

181. The EA-1 also defines measures when the TSO becomes incapacitated or abandons the activity of TSO. Somewhat simplified, in such cases, a replacement operator can be appointed, while the initial operator must allow the replacement operator to perform its activity. If the owner or co-owners of the transmission system fail to ensure, within one year of the final decision appointing the replacement

276. Finally, this could trivialize Art. 345 of the TFEU, which provides that the Treaties should not impact ownership relationships in the Member States in any way whatsoever. Simplified somewhat, this provision concerning public undertakings is interpreted as meaning that Member States are formally free to establish, retain and abolish public undertakings, but are not completely free with respect to their management and market presence, as the latter two aspects are subject to the commercial law of the European Union.

277. Article 9(6) of Directive 2009/72/EC […] provides an essentially identical solution.

278. With consideration for the principle of proportionality, the Agency may, by means of a decision, impose one or more measures (Art. 66 EA-1).

operator, that the functions of electricity TSO are resumed in their transmission system by an electricity TSO that meets the relevant requirements, while the operation of this transmission system is necessary for a secure and reliable electricity supply in the Republic of Slovenia or a part of its territory, or in the case of an interconnector, the Agency shall propose to the Republic of Slovenia as the beneficiary of the expropriation that it initiate the expropriation procedure or procedure to restrict ownership rights. If this occurs, the expropriation or restriction of ownership rights shall be for the public benefit.[279]

§4. Provision of Mandatory Ancillary Services

182. Ancillary services are services which the TSO purchases on the market and which are necessary for providing the reliable and secure operation of transmission (and distribution) systems, such as secondary regulations with secondary reserve, reserve to the amount of the largest production unit, black start and voltage regulation when necessary.[280]

183. Due to the special importance of these services – which ensure balance between electricity consumed and generated, ensure the voltages achieve the agreed levels and ensure voltages can be re-established in the event of network failure[281] – the services can be provided mandatorily or by force if the operator fails to obtain them on the market or fails to obtain them under competitive conditions. Namely, following a request from the electricity TSO, the Agency may, without prejudice to concluded supply contracts, issue an administrative decision requiring one or several producers or customers of electricity that can, in view of technical and economic criteria, provide appropriate quantities of ancillary services on the most favourable terms, to conclude a contract immediately for the provision of ancillary services with the electricity TSO.[282]

184. This is not all, as the EA-1 provides that to the extent required in the interest of providing reliable ancillary services and conditioned by objective technical reasons, such as the technical limits of the transmission system or limits of cross-border lines, the electricity TSO shall provide reserve power from the reserve capacities available that are located within the control area for the secondary regulation of the transmission system of the Republic of Slovenia.

279. *See* Art. 73 EA-1.
280. In this regard, the EZ-1B included new provision, according to which TSO shall foster the advanced technologies and non-discriminatory approach when ensuring system services via the market; *see* Art. 74(1).
281. All this means that the absence of such services could result in the collapse of the electricity system with all the relevant impacts on the economy, transportation, healthcare, etc. The general/public interest is without a doubt present and should be considered in limiting the principle of contractual autonomy.
282. *See* Art. 74 EA-1.

§5. Protecting Data Confidentiality

185. Not only does data confidentiality refer to data explicitly labelled as confidential or as a business secret but it also refers to any commercially sensitive data whose disclosure to an unauthorized person would result in the undertaking the data refers to incurring significant damages. This of course does not apply to data which, by their very nature, cannot be deemed classified or a business secret or whose confidentiality could even be considered a crime. In any case, data confidentiality shall not be considered breached where the data is disclosed to the Energy Agency or other competent bodies conducting proceedings in line with their competencies, who need the relevant data in the pursuit of their activities. A TSO who is obligated to publish data needed for effective competition and market operations shall also not be deemed to have violated the obligation mentioned above.

186. An electricity TSO shall be obliged to preserve the confidentiality of commercially sensitive information obtained in the course of carrying out its business and shall be obliged to prevent the discriminatory disclosure of commercially advantageous information about its own activities; in particular, it shall not disclose commercially sensitive information to other parts of the undertaking that are not engaged in electricity TSO activities, except where and to the extent that this is strictly necessary to carry out a legal transaction. It should also be highlighted that the transmission system owner and, in the case of a combined operator, the electricity DSO and the other parts of the undertaking that are not involved in electricity TSO activities, must not use joint services which could allow unauthorized persons to obtain insight into confidential data, such as joint legal services, while they can generally use joint services for purely administrative or Information Technology (IT) functions.[283]

187. An electricity TSO must not, in the context of sales or purchases of electricity by related undertakings, misuse commercially sensitive information obtained from third parties in the context of providing or negotiating access to the system.[284]

188. After the EZ-1B introduced a special section on protection of personal data of system users, TSO must apply also some of the new provisions, i.e. Article 157 a–157 č.

283. *See* Art. 76 EA-1.
284. *See* Art. 77 EA-1.

§6. Access to the (Transmission) System

I. General

189. Since access to the transmission and distribution system,[285] as well as the system connection approval (consent) document,[286] are regulated mainly due to reasons that have already been elementarily presented in this monograph, we now mainly focus on the manner and contents of the relevant regulatory system in this area.[287]

190. The owner or operator of the electricity transport system cannot entirely freely decide if, who and under what conditions someone will be provided access to the system; in contrast, he must comply with the predefined regulatory framework, which he himself can additionally specify with the so-called Network Code,[288] which he is bound to and which requires transparency, objectivity and non-discrimination in allowing access to the transport system. On the other hand, third persons do not enjoy an absolute right to access or to connect to the system. By way of a justified decision,[289] the electricity system operator may refuse the connection to the transport system on account of lack of capacity or because the increased consumption and/or power delivery would prevent the operator from providing services of general interest.[290] If a dispute arises, the matter shall be settled by the Energy Agency,[291] which can either lay down the conditions for enhancing the system capacities or agree with the electricity system operator and refuse the request.

285. *See* Introduction, Chapter 1 §2.
286. *See* Part I, Chapter 2 §1.
287. Since the legislator has regulated access to the transmission and distribution system in the same chapter, we purposefully use the generic term 'transport system' below; this term refers both to the transmission and the distribution system, unless explicitly provided otherwise (e.g., Arts 121–130 and 134 EA-1, which are discussed in Part II, explicitly refer to the distribution system). General access regime is regulated in Arts 112 in 113 EA-1.
288. The Network Code shall regulate the operation and manner of managing transmission and distribution systems. The Network Code shall ensure the interoperability of systems and shall be transparent, objective and non-discriminatory. Prior to publishing the Network Code, the electricity system operator must obtain approval from the Agency and the Government.
289. The justification must be based on objective and technically and economically justified criteria.
290. An electricity system operator refusing a connection due to a lack of capacity or lack of connections shall be obliged to make necessary enhancements to the system upon the request of the person in question, and as far as it is economic to do so, or when this person is, alone or with other persons, willing to pay for such enhancements.
291. In this respect, we believe that the Energy Agency can be considered a court in the meaning of Art. 267 of the TFEU and can, where necessary, refer a preliminary question to the European Court of Justice. Even though administrative bodies and entities with public authority to pursue administrative tasks are not, in principle, considered a court in the meaning of the aforementioned provision, the situation here is specific as we believe that the condition that is not fulfilled in administrative proceedings – namely that the relevant bodies decides a dispute between two parties – is fulfilled in this instance. The Agency is therefore established by law for an undetermined period; it is bound by law and independently decides disputes between two parties (the relationship is thus at least between three persons). *See* more in Footnote 118.

II. Contractual Bases

191. Before the entity can provide electricity to the network, take electricity from the network or be connected to the system, the electricity system operator and system user must conclude a system use contract, which is subject to the maximum connection power and other operating limitations. With such a contract, the user undertakes to pay the relevant network charges, while the electricity system operator undertakes to allow the user to supply electricity to the system or take electricity from the system subject to the determined operational limitations. The electricity system operator defines the rules governing the conclusion and implementation of system use contracts and the manner of paying network charges in the aforementioned Network Code.[292]

192. In addition to the system use contract, before connecting to the system, the final system user shall conclude a so-called open contract that defines the balancing affiliation of the consumption point concerned. Such an agreement can only be concluded with a supplier that is a member of the balance scheme.[293]

III. Network Charges

193. Since network charges are paid for using the transport system, it is not insignificant[294] who defines them and how. As already mentioned,[295] the transformation of the closed and uncompetitive electricity markets of the Member States into open and (more) competitive markets, which should actually be integrated into one single market – the internal electricity market – would not have been possible or would have been much more difficult to achieve if owners of the essential infrastructure were allowed to determine network charges themselves, which would only be subject to general verification of their appropriateness in light of the rules of competition by the competition regulator.[296] It is for this reason that a different, more market-invasive approach was selected: namely pro-competitive (*ex ante*) regulation, which through the obligations imposed on the network owner or operator, provides interested companies not only with the formal option to access the network (which in itself would be devoid of any real value) but also with the actual ability to access the network by preventing the network owner or operator from charging exorbitant rates for using the network in question.

292. *See* Art. 114 EA-1.
293. With respect to the distribution system, the Act explicitly provides that only one open contract with one supplier may be in place for each consumption point at any one time. The system user may simultaneously conclude open contracts with several suppliers for a delivery point with a connected load exceeding 40 MW. In such a case, the balancing affiliation shall be distributed in advance among the suppliers (Art. 115 EA-1).
294. This is one of the sources the transport network operator uses to cover its eligible expenses.
295. *See* Introduction, Chapter 1 §2.
296. In this respect we would like to highlight that the so-called regulatory holidays (access holidays) approach was, in principle, rejected in Case C-424/07 [2009] I-11431.

194. Network charges are defined by the Energy Agency in the so-called regulatory framework (Articles 116–126 EA-1; these articles are here briefly presented as follows).[297] The regulatory framework is defined pursuant to the relevant decision (issued separately to the TSO and separately to the DSO, whereby the regulatory framework applicable to a DSO may be divided into individual areas of the distribution system). The Agency shall prescribe the methodology to set out the regulatory framework by means of a general act, based on the method of regulated annual revenue of the electricity system operator and its regulated network charges, which shall ensure that all eligible annual costs of the electricity system operator are covered. These costs include operating and maintenance costs, lost electricity costs, costs of ancillary services, depreciation costs and the regulated return on assets.[298] The electricity system operator's investment plan, which includes a financial evaluation of the investments under the applicable ten-year development plan to be carried out in the subsequent regulatory period, also serves as the basis to determine the operator's planned eligible costs. The method of establishing and specifying eligible costs shall encourage the cost-effective operations of the electricity system operator and enable it to attain a return higher than that set out in the regulatory framework if the eligible costs savings result from the operator's endeavours to increase its cost-effectiveness. If the electricity system operator incurs costs exceeding the eligible costs, the difference shall be offset against the regulated return on assets. In setting out the eligible costs, the Agency shall bear in mind the electricity system operator's obligation to improve its performance by a factor set by the Agency in a general act, taking account the planned general economic productivity and the efficiency of the electricity system operator based on comparative efficiency analyses.

195. Network charges are intended as payment for services the electricity system operator is obligated to provide. The Energy Agency must define categories of system users and the ratio of tariff items charged to them in a manner reflecting the costs individual users or categories of users cause when using the electricity system, as well[299] as in a manner than encourages the efficiency of electricity system operators and system use. Network charges include the following items:

- network charges for transmission system (earmarked to cover the electricity TSO's expenditure on maintenance, operation and develop the system, as well as earmarked to cover the electricity TSOs' expenditure on ancillary services of power oscillation damping in the system, voltage and reactive power regulation, and the procurement of black-start services);

297. Regulatory framework means a specification of the amount of planned eligible costs of the electricity system operator by individual year of the regulatory period, planned network charges, planned other revenue from performing the function of electricity system operator, and network surplus or deficit from previous years.
298. Part of the regulated return can depend also on the efficiency of using the transport system.
299. Due to the uncontested significance of so-called green electricity and related economic challenges, the Act explicitly provides that tariff rates for producers using renewable energy sources must take account of the tangible cost-based benefits derived from the integration of the power plant into the network.

- network charges for distribution system (earmarked to cover the electricity DSO's expenditure on maintenance, operation and developing the system);
- network charges for connected load (earmarked to cover the electricity system operator's expenditure on maintenance, operation and development of the system);
- network charges for excessive reactive power consumption (earmarked to cover the electricity system operator's expenditure on providing network voltage conditions and to simultaneously encourage users to take measures to reduce reactive power consumption).[300]

196. That said, additional charges may occur in practice, which are subject to regulation imposed by the Energy Agency. The prices of other services not covered by network charges and charged to system users by the electricity system operator are set by the Energy Agency, taking account of the actual costs thereof.

197. The essence should not be overlooked in the magnitude of the aforementioned, which is that the purpose of determining the regulatory framework by administrative decision is, on the one hand, to determine conditions for the electricity system operator's unhindered operations, and, on the other hand, to protect customers in terms of supply and network use charges.[301] Considering the above, it is no surprise that the legislator paid special attention to monitoring the implementation of the regulatory framework (which on the one hand means that the operator must monitor itself and report on its findings to the Energy Agency, who, on the other hand, also conducts active supervision) as well as to measures adopted in the event of any deviation from the planned regulatory framework,[302] as any deviation by its very nature presents the risk of the aforementioned goals remaining unfulfilled, which could have severe adverse impacts on the wider society.

198. It is also worth noting that determining network charges is a complex and demanding task, which requires both knowledge and tact, since excessive network charges inhibit competition which achieves the goals of liberalization, thus jeopardizing the basic goal of introducing liberalization and casting into doubt the legitimacy of the entire related operations. However, excessively low network charges discourage network investments, which can also result in the aforementioned undesirable scenario. This shows that in terms of price regulation, one is constantly between two unavoidable risks.

300. *See* Arts 132–138 EA-1.
301. The Act specifically focuses on the revenue from the congestion management of cross-border lines. The provisions concerning revenue from the congestion management of cross-border lines are more stringent on the system operator compared to Regulation (EC) No. 714/2009 […] since revenue from the congestion management of cross-border lines represents a significant source of covering the eligible expenses of the system operator; *see* Art. 117(3–7) EA-1.
302. *See* Art. 120 EA-1.

§7. Selected Topics

199. Since well-maintained and appropriately geographically located electricity infrastructure is a *conditio sine qua non* for fulfilling the energy policy goals, the Act provides a special exemption applicable to new major infrastructure, i.e. new direct current interconnections or significant increase in capacity in existing interconnectors.[303] Notwithstanding the provisions of the act governing general administrative procedure, the Agency shall ex officio repeat the procedure for issuing a decision granting exemption within one month of receiving a decision by the European Commission requesting the Agency to amend or annul the decision granting exemption.

200. In the conclusion of this section we would like to highlight protective measures that apply to crisis situations occurring in the electricity system. Should this happen and endanger the health of people, the value of the equipment or the integrity of the electricity network, the system operator of the electricity transmission network may introduce measures by means of which it limits the supply of electricity to defined categories of customers, specifies the order of precedence of restrictions, and specifies the means of electricity consumption and the obligatory production of electricity. The electricity TSO shall implement measures in cooperation with the electricity DSO in a manner that causes the least possible disturbance in the functioning of the internal electricity market and must not be wider in scope and longer in duration than is strictly necessary to remedy the consequences of the shortage and to restore the normal operation of the system.[304]

303. This exemption is subject to Art. 16(6) and/or Art. 17 of Regulation (EC) No. 714/2009.
304. *See* Art. 146 EA-1.

Chapter 5. Distribution of the Electricity

201. This chapter discusses the transport of electricity through the distribution network or system. First, the term distribution system is defined; this is followed by an overview of the fundamental characteristics of specific public law obligations relating to conducting activities as a DSO which is deemed a public utility. Chapter 4 then discusses the unbundling (separation) of the activity of the DSO from other activities in the electricity sector, and discusses the closed distribution system, select questions relating to the access to the system of third persons and leasing a significant part of the distribution network.

§1. Concept of the Distribution System and Related Concepts

202. Although the term distribution system is not explicitly defined in the new EA-1, its contents can be inferred from the legal definitions of other terms, such as: distribution, system and (distribution) system operator.

203. Distribution means the distribution of electricity through a distribution system.[305]

204. System means electricity installations, plants and networks used for the function of electricity (distribution) system operator.[306]

205. DSO means a natural or legal person who carries out the function of electricity DSO and is responsible for operating, maintaining and developing the electricity distribution system in a given area and, where applicable, its interconnections with other systems, and for ensuring the long-term ability of the system to meet reasonable demands for the distribution of electricity.[307]

206. As follows from the legal definitions of the aforementioned terms and considering the legislation of the EU, a distribution system can be defined as special electricity installations, plants and networks operated, maintained and, if necessary, developed by a DSO, in order to enable the transport of electricity on high-voltage, medium-voltage and low-voltage (in principle 110 kV or less) distribution systems with a view to its delivery to customers.

305. *See* Art. 36(3) EA-1.
306. *See* Art. 36(37) EA-1.
307. *See* Art. 4(7) EA-1.

§2. Public Services Obligations Attached to the Distribution of Electricity

207. As already said for the transmission system, in principle, the distribution system acts as a link between the producers of electricity (or the transmission network operator) on the one hand and customers on the other. The distribution system is thus one of the most significant integral parts of the electricity chain, which significantly impacts electricity supply in the Republic of Slovenia, which is a general (public) interest in this respect. It is precisely for this reason that the legislator opted not to leave the activities of DSOs to market whims, but to submit the activity to the special requirements of a public service, namely a special public law regime in the form of mandatory public services of general economic interest,[308] which ensures the following tasks are fulfilled in the desired manner:

(1) secure, reliable and efficient operation and maintenance of the distribution system;
(2) development of the distribution system, taking into consideration:
  (a) anticipated needs of system users;
  (b) requirements concerning safe and reliable system operation; and
  (c) guidelines from the development plan of the electricity DSO;
(3) long-term ability of the distribution system to meet reasonable demands for connection to the system and energy distribution;
(4) security of energy supply through adequate capacity and network reliability;
(5) the management of electricity flows in the system and ancillary services;
(6) data that must be provided to system users and suppliers to enable them to effectively conclude supply contracts and exercise the right to connection;
(7) forecasts of electricity consumption and necessary energy sources by means of a comprehensive planning method, taking due account of saving measures taken by consumers;
(8) provision of information to any other operator necessary to ensure the secure and efficient operation, coordinated development and interoperability of the interconnected system;
(9) quality of supply in accordance with minimum standards;
(10) purchase of electricity to cover losses, and ancillary services in the distribution system in transparent, non-discriminatory and market-based procedures.[309]

208. These tasks are funded from network charges and other revenues generated from providing services of general economic interest.

209. When planning the development of the distribution system, the electricity DSO shall consider energy efficiency and consumption-side management measures or distributed generation that might eliminate the need to upgrade or replace electricity capacity.

308. These can be ensured within the entire territory or within a part thereof.
309. *See* Art. 78 EA-1.

210. In this regard it is worth noting that upon prior approval (consent) by the Government, the electricity DSO may temporarily transfer these tasks to a natural or legal person that has appropriate staff and technical equipment to carry out the transferred tasks, provided that this entity does not carry out the activities of electricity supply or generation.[310] This entity shall ensure the electricity DSO direct and permanent access to all data used and obtained for the purpose of carrying out electricity DSO tasks.

211. A person who:

- obtains a (non-payable) concession to provide this public service from the Government; and
- owns or leases a distribution system, can act as a DSO.

212. Owning a distribution system is thus clearly not a requirement as the absence of ownership can be remedied through a lease. Such a solution is needed in Slovenia mainly because the former and current DSO does not own the distribution system, which is mainly owned by five companies, with other smaller parts owned by other companies. The Act defines such a lease in detail.[311]

§3. Legal Unbundling

213. In contrast to the position of a TSO, which must not be vertically integrated (and where ownership unbundling is prescribed), a DSO can be vertically integrated, providing it is functionally independent in terms of its legal form, organization, decision-making and IT system from other activities not related to distribution.[312] For this purpose, it shall ensure the implementation of at least the following measures:

- is organized as a legal person and does not pursue an activity belonging to the upstream or downstream market;
- the persons responsible for the management of the electricity DSO shall not participate in the company structures of the integrated electricity undertaking responsible, directly or indirectly, for the day-to-day operation of the production, transmission or supply of electricity;

310. This shows that in contrast to the electricity transmission system operator, no ownership unbundling is needed with respect to electricity distribution system operators. *See* below for more on this.

311. *See* Art. 82 EA-1.

312. The requirement relating to the legal separation or unbundling does not apply to distribution system operators with less than a thousand customers. It should also be mentioned that the Slovenian act permits so-called combined systems under certain circumstances, where the same person carries out the activities of transmission and distribution system operator. This is per se not especially problematic from the point of view of both activities, which are subject to similar legal regimes, but can be problematic if such a company is related to a company active on the upstream or downstream market, and the power from such closed markets could follow through onto markets with open competition.

- the professional interests of the persons responsible for managing the electricity DSO shall be taken into account in a manner that ensures their ability to act independently;
- independently of the integrated electricity company, the DSO must be actually able to adopt decisions on the funds needed for network operations, maintenance and development.[313]

214. Since, when the DSO is vertically integrated, there is a real risk of this connection being abused, the Energy Agency and Competition Protection Agency must monitor the electricity DSO's activities, ensuring it does not abuse the vertical integration in a manner that would distort competition both in terms of restrictions of competition and of unfair competition or unfair business practices (e.g., brand communication and marketing activities must not create confusion as to the separate identity of the part of a vertically integrated company engaged in supply).

§4. Closed Distribution Systems

215. Closed distribution system means a network isolated from the public distribution network which, under the conditions provided by this Act, is intended for the distribution of electricity within a geographically confined industrial, commercial or shared services site and, as a rule, does not supply household customers and is directly connected to the transmission system. Currently, there are four closed distribution systems of electricity in the Republic of Slovenia. The concept of closed distribution system is regulated in Articles 89–96 EA-1; these articles are here briefly presented as follows.

216. The distribution of electricity within small and closed electricity distribution systems, which have acquired the status of a closed distribution system,[314] is not deemed a service of general economic interest performed by the DSO.

217. An electricity distribution system with a single network supply point directly connected to the transmission system distributing electricity within a geographically confined industrial, commercial or shared services site, and as a rule not supplying household customers, shall obtain the status of a closed distribution system subject to the Agency's approval (permit), if:[315]

- due to specific technical or safety reasons, the operations or the production process of the final customer of that system are integrated; or
- the system distributes electricity primarily to the owner or operator of the system or their related undertakings (this requirement shall be considered as satisfied

313. *See* Art. EA-1.
314. This status is conveyed through an Agency decision for the maximum period of ten years.
315. *See* Art. 90 EA-1.

when the owner and its related undertakings make at least 80% of the total yearly electricity consumption and production).[316]

218. Subject to certain conditions, the electricity TSO shall provide to the closed DSO access to the transmission system. A closed DSO shall enjoy the same rights, duties and responsibilities as stipulated for the 'classical' DSO, except in case of exceptions as approved by a decision of the Agency. The status of closed distribution system shall not preclude a final customer located within the geographically confined site from requesting and being granted access to the distribution or transmission system in accordance with this act (*see* Article 92(3) EA-1).

219. In principle, the closed DSO may transfer the authorization of the closed distribution system status to another person if the conditions are violated. If the conditions needed for the existence of a closed distribution system cease to exist, the status shall be revoked.

§5. Leasing a Significant Part of the Distribution System

220. Although the concept of distribution system is not identical to the transmission system, both concepts are similar in many aspects. It is thus no surprise that many of the provisions are the same. Thus, the EA-1 contains many general common provisions that have been presented above, and which are thus not presented in Chapter 3, but merely referred to. Notwithstanding the above, it is worth mentioning special provisions which apply to distribution system network access. Below we do not go into all the details and merely refer to Articles 112–138 EA-1 (some issues regulated by these provisions are presented directly below).

221. It occurs in practice that an electricity DSO is not the owner of the whole or a significant part of the distribution system[317] in which it carries out its activity and leases a significant part or the whole of the distribution system from the owner or other legal or natural person managing or holding it and/or uses it on a legal basis

316. Incidental use by a small number of households having an employment or other relationship with the owner of the system shall not preclude the electricity distribution system referred to in the preceding paragraph from obtaining the status of a closed distribution system.
317. A significant part of the distribution system shall mean a part of the system that meets the following conditions:

- it had at least 1,000 final customers connected on any one given day in the calendar year preceding the year in which the network charges for the subsequent regulatory period were set; and
- the electricity transmitted across this network in the calendar year preceding the year in which the network charges for the subsequent regulatory period were set represented at least 5% of the total electricity transmitted through the distribution system in the Republic of Slovenia.

other than pursuant to an ownership right.[318] The special provisions of Articles 121–126 EA-1 apply to these special cases (concerning the setting of the regulatory framework if the electricity DSO is not the owner of a significant part of the distribution system or the main tasks of the electricity DSO are carried out by another person) shall apply in addition to general provisions of Articles 116–120 EA-1 (concerning a regulatory framework) and Articles 127–130 EA-1 (concerning regulation through quality)[319] in setting out the regulatory framework for such a distribution system, in establishing deviations from the regulatory framework and in calculating network charges. Put more simply, owners of significant parts of the distribution system, who are not also operators of the distribution network, are in principle subject to the same provisions on keeping separate accounts, on providing the relevant data to the Energy Agency, and similar, as the DSO. We aim to establish a similar position as if the DSO owned a certain significant part of the network or itself performed certain tasks, which should also be reflected in the lease amount. The maximum lease payment or payments for essential tasks relating to maintaining and operating the distribution system must be defined in a manner as if the DSO was the owner of the network or completed all the relevant tasks himself.

---

318. This reflects the situation established in the Republic of Slovenia in terms of electricity distribution. SODO, sistemski operater distribucijskega omrežja z električno energijo, d.o.o., which provides the public utility of acting as the electricity distribution system operator in the territory of the Republic of Slovenia (for voltages of 0.4, 10, 20 and 35 kV–110 kV only by exception), does not own the (entire) distribution system (which is mainly owned by Elektro Celje, d.d., Elektro Gorenjska, d.d., Elektro Ljubljana, d.d., Elektro Maribor, d.d., and Elektro Primorska) and has concluded agreements on the lease of electricity distribution infrastructure and services agreements (such as for maintaining the electricity infrastructure and organizing on-call services, managing and operating the electricity distribution network, developing, planning and investing in the electricity infrastructure, drafting and managing investments, monitoring and determining the quality of supply, electricity metering, ensuring access to the distribution network and other services for users, as well as providing other services needed by SODO).
319. In setting the eligible costs for the purpose of setting out the regulatory framework for an electricity distribution system, the EA-1 provides that the Agency shall also take into account the regulation of electricity supply quality within the framework of electricity distribution system operator activity. Somewhat simplified, this is a special, even more advanced manner of regulation, where the sector regulator does not engage in assessing the necessity of individual investments and costs, but only assesses qualitative indicators of the quality of the (desired) electricity supply, where the measures and investments used to improve these indicators lie within the domain of the distribution system operator itself.

Chapter 6. Consumption of Electricity

222. This chapter deals with the consumption of electricity. This chapter mainly focuses on the protection of final electricity consumers and especially on the protection of (vulnerable) household electricity consumers and emergency electricity supply. It is worth pointing out that the latter two actually concerns the provision of the so-called universal service.

§1. General Protection of Final Electricity Customers

223. At the outset, we would like to highlight the fact that the EA-1 distinguishes between final electricity customers, which are defined as any natural or legal person buying energy for his own final consumption, and household electricity customers, which are defined as a customer purchasing electricity for his own household consumption, excluding consumption for performing commercial or professional activities.[320] This clearly shows that the concept of final customer is broader than the concept of household customer (each household customer is also a final customer, but not vice versa). This section deals with the general protection of final consumers,[321] while special protection of household customers is discussed in the next section of this chapter. The just mentioned issues are regulated in Articles 39–51 EA-1 as follows.

224. Final customers of electricity shall have the right to an electricity supply on the basis of an open contract on supply with a supplier[322] regardless of the EU Member State in which the supplier is registered. In other words, a final customer

320. In addition, the EA-1 also distinguishes between:

- a 'customer', which is defined as a supplier or a final customer of electricity (all customers shall be eligible customers);
- a 'business customer', which is defined as a customer purchasing electricity, which is not for household use, for their own use;
- a 'small business customer', which is defined as a customer at low-voltage connection that is not a household customer and whose maximum consumption power does not exceed 41 kW;
- an 'eligible customer', which is defined as a customer who is free to purchase electricity from the supplier of his/her choice.

321. Consumer protection regulations apply in the absence of more specific provision (at least to a certain degree) to questions relating to the protection of final customers not dealt with in the EA-1 or another specific law, especially when dealing with household customers.
322. Open supply contract means a legal transaction in the electricity market determining the balancing affiliation of delivery points and not determining the exact quantity supplied. A supply agreement concluded with a Slovenian final customer is always interpreted according to Slovenian law, regardless of where the agreement was concluded.

of electricity in the Republic of Slovenia shall have the right to conclude an electricity supply agreement with any supplier from the EU who fulfils the legal requirements for supplying electricity in the Republic of Slovenia.[323] Accordingly, interested supplies from the EU should be given access to Slovenian final customers regardless of their place of registration.

225. Prior to connection to the system, the electricity DSO shall notify the customer of his or her rights and obligations in connection with the choice of supplier and in connection with the sustaining or emergency supply.[324]

226. Since final customers are not directly involved in the electricity market, as they are only retail customers, from their point of view, a liberalized electricity market means they have the right to freely choose their supplier (as already mentioned above); however, it is appropriate to add that this right does not extinguish upon the customer's single choice, but rather extends to the right to switch suppliers in a quick,[325] effective and free-of-charge manner. In principle, all a final customer who wishes to switch suppliers needs to do is communicate a request for the change to the electricity system operator of the system to which the customer is connected. Alternatively, the new supplier may communicate the request on behalf of, and for the account of, the final customer on the basis of an authorization.

227. Final customers are also protected through free and periodic information on their actual electricity consumption, the characteristics of such consumption and on efficient use of electricity, with sufficient frequency to enable them to regulate their own electricity consumption. In addition, an electricity system operator shall enable customers using the system on which it performs the function of an operator to access their consumption data; this information shall be given within a sufficient time frame which takes account of the capability of customer's metering equipment, the electricity product in question and the cost-efficiency of such measures.[326]

228. At the same time, the protection of final customers is ensured through a transparent invoice, which clearly discloses all elements of the final price,[327] and through the provision of additional clarifications to reasonable questions. A special form of protecting final customers (even though this measure is also aimed at fulfilling other energy goals) is also the obligation of electricity undertakings to ensure

323. That said, the conditions must be consistent with the laws of the European Union, otherwise the conditions cannot apply.
324. *See* Art. 39(3) EA-1.
325. The transfer should be concluded within twenty-one days of lodging a complete request. The final account is made within six weeks from the commencement of receiving the electricity supply from the new supplier.
326. An electricity system operator shall also enable access to data to other legal or natural persons that enclose with a request for access to data on a customer's consumption the customer's authorization for each case separately or for all future cases until such authorization is revoked. Although this service can be charged, the price must comply with the direct costs of the operator's service.
327. The relevant data must also be provided through promotional materials and on the website.

maximum energy efficiency by optimizing, in accordance with the Agency's recommendations, the use of electricity, especially by providing electricity use management services, developing innovative pricing formulas and introducing intelligent metering systems or networks when appropriate.

§2. Special Protection of Certain Groups of Final Customers

229. The EA-1 provides special protection of certain groups of final customers, namely household customers (consumers in the narrow sense of the term) and especially those who, due to their financial circumstances, income and other social circumstances and living conditions, are unable to obtain an alternative source of energy for household use that would incur the same or smaller costs for essential household use, and small business customers. These groups of final customers are subject to special benefits ensured by the supplier or DSO. Of course, both may decide to provide these benefits to other final customers, subject to them observing the principle of equal treatment.

230. The EA-1 thus explicitly provides in Articles from 45 to 50 that household customers must be ensured:

- a single point of access to information on their rights, valid regulations and general acts for the exercise of public authority and the methods for handling complaints;
- an energy checklist;
- special mandatory protective provisions concerning the supply contract, including the general terms and conditions;
- intelligent metering systems;
- a transparent, simple and inexpensive out-of-court procedure for handling complaints.[328]

231. In addition to all the above benefits, the Act additionally provides in Article 51 that the most vulnerable household customers are provided protection against their electricity supply being cut-off or restricted, if, in view of the circumstances (season, temperatures, place of residence, health condition and other similar circumstances) such an action could jeopardize the life and health of the vulnerable household customer and persons living in his household.[329] The costs of such necessary supply shall be eligible costs of the DSO.

---

328. This kind of disputes, i.e. disputes between the household user (consumer) and supplier, shall not be confused with the disputes with the operator as regulated in Art. 413 EA-1 (*see also* Footnotes 118 and 291). Namely, the latter are not settled by alternative dispute resolution institutions but rather by the Agency.

329. Prior to disconnection, the electricity distribution system operator shall notify the customer of the possibilities of emergency supply and of the evidence to be provided by the customer in order to be approved for emergency supply by the operator, and of the time limits within which such evidence must be submitted. Detailed conditions and the price of emergency supply that covers the costs of the purchase of energy shall be prescribed by the operator in the Network Code referred

232. The Act provides the following benefits to small business customers:

- single point of contact;
- special mandatory protective provisions concerning the supply contract, including the general terms and conditions;
- intelligent metering systems.

§3. Emergency Supply

233. Emergency supply represents a concretization and is one of the forms of the so-called universal service. Article 44 EA-1 provides that the DSO must automatically and without transfer periods guarantee supply to customers connected to its system if the validity of their supply contract is terminated as a result of measures which are the consequence of insolvency or illiquidity of the supplier, in accordance with the regulation governing the operation of the electricity market. The DSO must immediately inform the customer of the termination of validity of the contract and the commencement of provision of emergency supply.

234. The price of the supply must be made public and must be higher than the market price for supply to a comparable customer, but may not exceed it by more than 25%.[330] If the electricity DSO does not set the price or sets it contrary to the upper threshold, according to Article 44(4) EA-1, the price shall be set by the Energy Agency.

to in Art. 144 of the Act in accordance with the rules and criteria prescribed by the Energy Agency. The EZ-1B brought additional provision according to which the operator of distribution system automatically offers a contract in case all conditions for necessary supply are met. In case the conditions are not met, the operator informs an user about its finding and continues with the disconnection activities (new Art. 51(4)).

330. The price of electricity for emergency supply shall be set by the distribution system operator at a level that covers the long-term price of the purchase of electricity and the costs of guaranteeing and providing emergency supply. The conditions of emergency supply shall be detailed in the Network Code.

Part II. Regulatory Framework Concerning Gas

235. The first part of the contents deals with the regulatory framework concerning gas. It is comprised of the following six chapters.

236. Chapter 1 (General Introduction), which serves as an introduction to the regulatory framework concerning gas, presents the main properties and characteristics of the gas sector in the Republic of Slovenia and provides an overview of Slovenian energy policy. This is followed by a presentation of the legal framework applicable to gas infrastructure and a discussion of certain special characteristics in the operations of energy companies. In the end, some key acts and other regulations governing the sector and which constitute the main Slovenian legal acts in the field of natural gas are presented.

237. Chapter 2 (Production) discusses in particular the conditions that need to be fulfilled for natural gas production to take place. That encompasses above all various approvals or consents and permits which an entity needs to obtain prior to launching a refinery or any other facility or installation related to natural gas.

238. Chapter 3 (Exploitation) presents the relevant provisions of the ZRud-1, which provides conditions for acquiring the concession for exploiting natural gas and the process for abandoning production, as well as permits for conducting natural gas research.

239. Chapter 4 (Transport) discusses the transport of natural gas through the transmission network or system.

240. Chapter 5 (Distribution) discusses the transport of natural gas through the distribution network or system.

241. Chapter 6 (Consumption) discusses the consumption of gas. This mainly highlights the general protection of (final) natural gas customers, the special protection of certain groups of customers, including the most vulnerable natural gas customers, and ensuring the reliability of natural gas supply.

242. Let us point out that the EA-1C, adopted on 29 April 2020, transposed Directive (EU) 2019/692 of the European Parliament and of the Council of 17 April

2019 amending Directive 2009/73/EC concerning common rules for the internal market in natural gas.[331] In other words, the core mission EA-1C was to adjust the EA-1 to the demands of the new gas directive.

331. Official Journal of the European Union, L 117, 3.5.2019, 1.

Chapter 1. General Introduction

243. This chapter is designed as an introduction to a discussion of the regulatory framework for gas.[332] This chapter first presents the main properties and characteristics of the gas sector in the Republic of Slovenia and provides an overview of the Slovenian energy policy. This is followed by a presentation of the legal framework applicable to gas infrastructure and a discussion of certain special characteristics in the operations of energy companies (these two topics are mainly presented by reference to the relevant text in Part I). In the end, some key acts and other regulations governing the sector and which constitute the main Slovenian legal acts in the field of natural gas are presented.

§1. Gas Sector in the Republic of Slovenia

244. Using selected figures such as those for domestic production, imports and consumption of natural gas, data on the transmission and distribution systems, and data on market structure, the natural gas sector in Slovenia was presented in the introduction to this monograph, in Chapter 1 §2 General Information about the Slovenian Energy Sector, but for practical reasons certain additional useful information and explanations relating to individual sectors and markets within the Slovenian natural gas sector are given here.

245. In the technical sense, the Slovenian natural gas sector is by its very nature comparable to the natural gas sectors of other EU Member States, and can be similarly divided into several mutually reliant branches that together form a complementary whole. This refers to the pumping or production, trading,[333] transport via gas transmission and distribution networks, supplying and storing natural gas and managing terminals for liquefied natural gas (LNG).[334]

246. The new EA-1 provides that the activity of the natural gas TSO is an obligatory national service of general economic interest,[335] and provides that the activity of the natural gas DSO is an optional local service of general economic

332. Although primary focus is on natural gas, we would like to highlight that everything applicable to natural gas in this monograph in principle also applies to biogas and other types of gas which can be technically feasible and safely introduced into the natural gas system and be transferred through such a system.

333. Trading with natural gas is currently governed by a regulation that has been derogated by the new EA-1; however, the new act at the same time provided that the regulation shall apply until the issue of a new regulation governing trading with natural gas in the Republic of Slovenia. In light of the above, we do not present the current regulation, which will soon be revised.

334. Undertakings performing at least one of these activities shall be considered as natural gas undertakings. All natural gas undertakings shall, in the public interest, perform tasks that refer to the reliability, regularity, quality and price of supply and to environment protection, including the efficient use of energy, energy generated from renewable sources and climate protection. In addition to these general obligations, natural gas undertakings entrusted with the operation of services of general economic interest in the sense of the Art. 106(2) TFEU shall perform special tasks (*see infra*).

335. *See* Art. 177 EA-1.

interest.[336] Natural gas undertakings performing a service of general economic interest in the sense of Article 106(2) TFEU shall provide the following:

- permanent and uninterrupted operation of the system within the limitations set by the state of the art and supply quality standards;
- safe and reliable operation and maintenance of the system;
- connection of system users on general and non-discriminatory terms;
- access to the system on general and non-discriminatory terms;
- charging for access to the system at the regulated access tariff;
- long-term planning of system development;
- other obligations under this Act or other regulations;
- system enabling customers to freely choose their supplier, and producers and suppliers to freely sell and purchase natural gas.[337]

247. The ministry responsible for energy shall notify the European Commission once every two years of new measures adopted for public service obligations, including consumer and environmental protection, and of their possible effect on national and international competition.[338]

248. Immediately below we first briefly explain some basic characteristics of the aforementioned activities relating to gas.

249. Natural gas pumping or production is inseparable from the corresponding infrastructure and devices, which in terms of technical matters, safety, environmental protection and planning are such important facilities that they require a special system of permits to ensure that the principal risks are managed. In the Republic of Slovenia, minute quantities of natural gas are produced, meaning that natural gas supply nearly entirely depends on imports.[339]

250. The transport of gas is undertaken along the gas transmission and distribution networks. The following entities ensure the transport of natural gas in the Republic of Slovenia:

- one natural gas TSO, namely Plinovodi, operater prenosnega sistema zemeljskega plina, d.o.o.; and
- thirteen (regional) natural gas DSOs, namely: Energetika Ljubljana, d.o.o., Plinarna Maribor, d.d., Adriaplin, d.o.o., Energetika Celje, d.o.o., Petrol, d.d., Domplan, d.d., Istrabenz plini, d.o.o., Javno komunalno podjetje Slovenj Gradec,

336. *See* Art. 216 EA-1.
337. Of course, in addition to these general obligations such undertakings are also bound to fulfil specific public services obligations.
338. *See* Art. 160 EA-1.
339. *See supra*, Introduction, Chapter 1 §2.

d.o.o., Javno podjetje plinovod Sevnica, d.o.o., JEKO-IN, d.o.o., Javno komunalno podjetje Vrhnika, d.o.o., Komunalno podjetje Velenje, d.o.o., and ENOS, d.d.[340]

§2. Slovenia's Natural Gas Sector Policy

251. Slovenia's policy with regard to the natural gas sector can be inferred from the new EA-1, which is the fundamental and systemic regulation for the natural gas and energy sector in general, and can also be inferred from the various strategic documents and decisions in individual cases made by national bodies and authorities responsible for the natural gas sector. An awareness of policy in this area is the key to understanding and correctly interpreting the relevant laws and other regulations, as only in this way are the public objectives and measures revealed, in short, the national vision and strategy for the natural gas sector in a specific period. The fundamental main goals of the currently applicable energy policy, which of course also apply to the natural gas sector, are defined in the new EA-1, while their further division and specification, as well as connections to existing measures, are anticipated in special long-term planning documents. Since the above has already been presented in this monograph (*see* Part I, Chapter 1 §2), below we only refer to certain key highlights of the draft national energy policy, which relate to the strategy applicable to the natural gas sector.

252. The aforementioned strategy considers natural gas as part of the fuel supply and in terms of sustainable use and local energy supply.

253. When discussing fuel supply, the question of the natural gas market and the question of natural gas supply are specifically dealt with. The natural gas market is expected to gradually converge with the neighbouring markets and be more significantly integrated into the internal market, while natural gas is expected to be traded on open public markets in the region and the competitiveness of the Slovenian natural gas market is expected to increase. In terms of natural gas supply, additional infrastructure is expected to be built and existing infrastructure is expected to be appropriately maintained. Development until 2030 is expected to ensure the reliable supply of existing and new natural gas customers including the use of natural gas for producing electricity and heat, developing transfer capacities, especially through inclusion in international projects in order to additionally diversify supply routes to existing and new natural gas sources and storage capacities in order to improve the reliability and competitiveness of supply. At the same time, Slovenia is expected to become a regionally important state in terms of natural gas transit. A support environment ensuring the optimum development and investments in natural gas transmission networks is expected to be ensured, along with the effective marketing of capacities in order to ensure high utilization of the transit and distribution capacities. Decisions concerning project implementation are expected to continue to be

340. The fields of operation of these companies are apparent from the following website: https://www.giz-dzp.si/clani.

based on demand for transit capacities and the economic feasibility of investments. Infrastructure projects which ensure sufficient transit capacities and convergence with the N-1 infrastructure standard, the elimination of bottlenecks in the network, bidirectional flow to and from neighbouring transmission networks, connecting new customers and electricity-generating units, co-production of heat and electricity, and providing gas to as yet unsupplied parts of the country as well as supplying existing customers, inclusion in international projects aimed at constructing gas pipeline connections, ensuring connections to LNG terminals in the region and access to newly available storage capacities in the region, are expected to be realized. The viability of storing natural gas in Slovenia is also expected to be explored.

254. In terms of sustainable use and local energy supply relating to natural gas, more support to using compressed natural gas in the transport sector, mainly as engine fuel used in means of transport, shall be provided.

§3. Gas Infrastructure

255. Gas infrastructure comprises facilities, installations and lines which are part of the natural gas pumping, production and storing system, the natural gas transfer and distribution system, and the LNG system. All these cases concern public economic infrastructure pursuant to the act governing the construction of buildings. Among other things, this means that construction in their vicinity is very limited and subject to special permits and approvals or consents. In addition, the ownership rights to plots and real estate in the vicinity may be subject to limitations, including expropriation and legal servitudes in the public interest, if such measures are needed in order to construct and maintain gas infrastructure, observing the principle of proportionality.

256. Since, by its very nature, gas infrastructure is part of the energy infrastructure, some important aspects of which have already been presented in this monograph (*see* Part I, Chapter 1 §3), we will only deal with the special provisions governing gas infrastructure further below.[341]

257. Protected and safety zones of natural gas systems are defined for safety reasons. Other facilities, installations and lines may only be built in the natural gas system protected zone and works that might affect the network operation may only be carried out under specific conditions and at a certain distance from pipelines and facilities of this network depending on their type and purpose, while other facilities, installations and lines may not be planned and constructed or work carried out in the safety zone of a natural gas transmission system unless this is urgently required

341. We do not discuss the technical details and solutions provided by two regulations (one applicable to pipelines with an operating pressure exceeding 16 bars and one applicable to pipelines with an operating pressure up to and including 16 bars) which the new EA-1 has derogated and at the same time provided they still apply until new regulations in this field come into effect.

for the construction, reconstruction, operation, supervision or maintenance of infrastructure or a public utility service under the regulations on construction, where the investor or contractor of works obtains the approval (consent) of the operator of this transmission system prior to the commencement of works.[342]

258. The protected zone for a natural gas transmission system is a 65-m-wide belt of land on both sides of a transmission system gas pipeline measured from its axis, and a belt of land 65 m from the fence of the measurement-regulation station and other facilities of the transmission system, with the exception of compressor stations.[343] The protected zone of a natural gas transmission system is also a belt 100 m from the fence of the compressor station. The safety zone for a natural gas transmission system is a 5-m-wide belt of land on both sides of a gas pipeline measured from its axis.[344] The protected zone for a natural gas distribution system is a 5-m-wide belt of land on both sides of a gas pipeline measured from its axis.[345]

259. The Act provides for security reasons (in order to ensure the relevant transparency enabling control and the relevant actions) that operators and natural gas distributors shall provide for:

- an infrastructure register comprising a survey cadastre of lines and connections and a list of the elements and devices incorporated in the system;
- a report on the infrastructure scope and location to a concession provider and to the consolidated cadastre of public infrastructure.

260. We would like to draw attention to the fact that the Act on basic safety of transport via oil and gas pipelines also governs the safety aspects of transporting natural gas;[346] however, this Act is fairly general and also outdated in some parts. In addition, the new EA-1 also impacts certain questions dealt with by this act, which is why it is not presented separately in this monograph.

---

342. *See* Art. 469(2) in 469(5) EA-1.
343. *See* Art. 469(1) EA-1 (If additional safety activities or measures which a transmission securities operator is obliged to carry out as part of the provision of the public utility service of natural gas transmission system operator have to be carried out as a result of the construction of a facility, installation or line or the performance of other work at a greater distance from the natural gas transmission system than the protected zone of the transmission system in order to ensure an acceptable level of risk to a gas pipeline or other parts of the transmission system, the costs of these activities or measures shall be eligible costs of the provisions of this public utility service; *see* Art. 469(3) EA-1).
344. *See* Art. 469(19) and 469(4) EA-1.
345. *See* Art. 469(1) EA-1.
346. Official Gazette of the Republic of Slovenia, No. 64/73.

§4. Selected Special Features in the Operations of Natural Gas Undertakings

261. In light of the clear general interest of ensuring activities needed for the desired supply of natural gas, the EA-1 restricts enforcement against gas infrastructure, restricts the bankruptcy of concessionaires and restricts industrial action at concessionaires or providers of public services. Since the Act deals with these questions in the same way as is prescribed for the energy industry in general (including the natural gas industry), in order to avoid repetition, we direct readers to Part I, Chapter 1 §4 for more detailed insight into certain special features in the operations of natural gas undertakings.[347]

§5. Overview of Key Regulations Governing Natural Gas

262. The Slovenian energy industry, and the natural gas industry as one of its parts, has been for more than ten years subject to the legislation of the EU,[348] which prevails over (other) Slovenian law and defines the external boundaries of the Slovenian energy policy and law. Slovenian laws and other regulations cannot exceed these boundaries.[349]

263. The EA-1, which has been specified by several regulations, is the basic law governing the field of natural gas. Due to practical reasons, we highlight below only certain select regulations governing gas, as adopted pursuant to the new EA-1,[350] as follows:

- Act determining the methodology for charging for the network charge for the gas distribution network.[351]
- Act determining the methodology for setting out the regulatory framework of the gas DSO.[352]
- Act on rules for monitoring the quality of natural gas supply.[353]
- Act on mandatory content of the system operating instructions for the natural gas transmission network.[354]

---

347. However, the EA-1 does not regulate transparency issues with common provisions for natural gas and electricity undertaking. Namely, transparency of natural gas undertakings is regulated separately in Arts 234–237 EA-1.
348. In addition, consequently also the so-called European liberalization model, which represents as such an integral part of the European (internal) natural gas market.
349. In accordance with the principle of primacy, in the event of collision between the laws, the rules belonging to the legal system of the European Union shall prevail.
350. The new act has derogated several of the regulations issued on the basis of the old act. However, at the same time, the new act provides that such regulations shall apply until new regulations are adopted, resulting in the practical value of old regulations being fairly limited.
351. Official Gazette of the Republic of Slovenia, No. 21/18.
352. *Ibid.*
353. Official Gazette of the Republic of Slovenia, No. 28/15.
354. Official Gazette of the Republic of Slovenia, Nos 17/15 and 66/17.

- Act determining the methodology for preparation and evaluation of an investment plan of the gas TSO.[355]
- Act determining the methodology for preparation and evaluation of an investment plan of the gas DSO.[356]
- Act on the preventive action plan for natural gas supply.[357]
- Act concerning the method of electronic data reporting for valid regular tariffs comparison of electricity and natural gas suppliers for household and small business customers.[358]
- Regulation on the emergency plan for natural gas supply.[359]
- Network code for the natural gas distribution system.[360]
- Act on the mandatory content of the Network Code for the natural gas distribution system.[361]
- Decree on the operation of the natural gas market.[362]
- Rules on access to data on household consumption of natural gas.[363]
- Act on the methodology for determining network charges for the natural gas transmission system.[364]

355. Official Gazette of the Republic of Slovenia, Nos 9/15 and 16/18.
356. Official Gazette of the Republic of Slovenia, No. 9/15.
357. Official Gazette of the Republic of Slovenia, No. 97/20.
358. Official Gazette of the Republic of Slovenia, No. 69/14.
359. Official Gazette of the Republic of Slovenia, No. 97/20.
360. Official Gazette of the Republic of Slovenia, Nos 55/15 and 80/17.
361. Official Gazette of the Republic of Slovenia, No. 61/15.
362. Official Gazette of the Republic of Slovenia, No. 61/16.
363. Official Gazette of the Republic of Slovenia, No. 10/17.
364. Official Gazette of the Republic of Slovenia, Nos 20/19, 8/20 and 85/20.

Chapter 2. Production of Gas

264. This chapter discusses in particular the conditions that need to be fulfilled for natural gas production to take place. That encompasses above all various approvals or consents and permits which an entity needs to obtain prior to launching a refinery or any other facility or installation related to natural gas.

265. As already mentioned, the quantities of natural gas produced in Slovenia are minute. In 2012, domestic natural gas accounted for 0.18% of consumption, while the estimated figure for 2013 and 2014 stands at 0.35%.[365] Nowadays, this share is even smaller, i.e. around 0.2%. As a result, Slovenia satisfies most of its natural gas needs through imports (mainly from Austria since the import of natural gas from Austria amounts 88% of all imported natural Gas).

266. Natural gas and oil has been produced in the depression near Murska Sobota continuously since 1943. Some 590 million sm^3 of natural gas has been produced since then. More than 160 wells have been drilled in this time, while fracking was attempted as early as in 1956. Fracking has been performed a few dozen times since then, and no negative environmental impacts have been noted.

§1. General Overview

267. The most important environmental acts gas producers within the territory of Slovenia must, *inter alia*, comply with the following legislative acts:

- Environmental Protection Act (ZVO-1).[366]
- Waters Act (ZV-1).[367]
- Nature Conservation Act (ZON).[368]
- Mining Act (ZRud-1).[369]
- All regulations relating to the aforementioned acts (many decrees conveying mining rights for exploiting minerals in various parts of Slovenia; decrees on mining concession fees and rehabilitation; workplace health and safety regulations and technical measures; other classification and categorization regulations, and technical decrees).

---

365. The most recently published Energy Balance of the Republic of Slovenia provides that domestic production reached 1.6 million sm^3, while the forecast for 2013 is 3.0 million sm^3 and the forecast for 2014 2.9 million (Energy Balance of the Republic of Slovenia for 2014, Ministry for Infrastructure and the Environment, 25).
366. Official Gazette of the Republic of Slovenia, No. 39/06 – official consolidated version, 49/06 – ZMetD, 66/06 – odl. US, 33/07 – ZPNačrt, 57/08 – ZFO-1A, 70/08, 108/09, 108/09 – ZPNačrt-A, 48/12, 57/12, 92/13, 56/15, 102/15, 30/16, 61/17 – GZ, 21/18 – ZNOrg and 84/18 – ZIURKOE).
367. Official Gazette of the Republic of Slovenia, Nos 67/02, 2/04, 41/04, 75/08, 57/12, 100/13, 40/14, 56/15 and 65/20.
368. Official Gazette of the Republic of Slovenia, Nos 56/99, 31/00, 119/02, 22/03, 41/04, 96/04, 46/14, 21/18, 31/18 and 82/20.
369. Official Gazette of the Republic of Slovenia, Nos 61/10, 62/10, 76/10, 57/12, 111/13, 4/14 and 61/16.

268. It should also be highlighted that since July 2014, environmental activities are regulated by the Decree on the categories of activities for which an environmental impact assessment is mandatory (Official Gazette of the Republic of Slovenia, Nos 51/14, 57/15 and 26/17), which has made environmental impact assessments significantly more stringent. The new decree introduces even more strict criteria governing fracking compared to the European Commission recommendations.

269. New wells can only be drilled within a concession area for the exploitation of minerals (hydrocarbons) and in compliance with environmental regulations, which focus heavily on environmentally sensitive areas, the protection of waterways and health protection.

270. When extracting from a well is no longer economically feasible, the well is closed and must be rehabilitated in compliance with all the requirements outlined in the ZRud-1. The closure is performed in accordance with established practices in the oil and natural gas production industry – which, *inter alia*, includes installing cement plugs which prevent the pollution of waterways with hydrocarbons or other substances which could potentially pass through the well.

271. All links to environmental protection have been presented in Part IV. Interaction between Energy Law and Environmental Law. This section, however, focuses on presenting the most important permits needed for natural gas production.

§2. System of Approvals or Consents and Permits for Natural Gas Production

272. In addition to environmental regulations, the EA-1 is also relevant to natural gas production, as it simplifies the procedures regarding the development of natural gas infrastructure in terms of the number of permits required. Thus, a special energy permit for natural gas production is no longer required (as opposed to power production where such permit is still needed for the development of certain types of power plants – *see* Part I, Chapter 2 §1 Permits and Consents System), and neither is a licence to perform an energy activity.[370]

273. This section does not include detailed descriptions of the permits and consents which have already been introduced in the section on power generation, but rather refer the reader to Part I, Chapter 2 §1 Permits and Consents System.

370. On the date of entry into force of the EA-1, the Decree on the conditions and procedure for issuing and revoking a licence to perform an energy activity (Official Gazette of the Republic of Slovenia, Nos 21/01, 31/01 and 66/05) was revoked (Art. 549 of EA-1) and all licence issuing procedures initiated prior to the entry into force of EA-1 were terminated.

274. Natural gas undertakings, as provided for in Article 158 EA-1, who engage, among other things, in natural gas production, must perform their duties in the public interest.

275. The infrastructure for the production of natural gas comprises gas pipelines from the gas-producing wells to a central gas station, the lines from the respective station to consumers, and the pipelines from producing wells to a gathering unit, and their constituent parts.[371]

276. Energy infrastructure, which includes, among other things, the facilities for natural gas production (along with gas transmission and distribution system, and natural gas storage) shall be designed and built cost-effectively and in line with state-of-the-art technology and must be maintained so as to ensure the best possible technical operation and cost-effectiveness.[372] The owners of such energy infrastructure must provide for routine and major maintenance works as well as adequate damage insurance. The work must be performed in compliance with the provisions of the act governing the construction of buildings. There are two sets of rules that govern the technical specifications for the construction, operation and maintenance of gas pipelines.[373]

277. The construction of a new energy facility or installation for natural gas production can begin once a final building permit has been obtained (Article 4 of the BA), which also provides for the exceptions when the construction can be initiated without a permit (simple objects and other cases as stipulated in Article 5 of the BA).

278. The inspectorate responsible for energy (i.e., energy inspectorate) shall supervise the implementation of technical requirements in the construction, operation, and use of facilities for natural gas production. Persons liable shall ensure undisturbed inspection (allow free access to any facilities or networks, and make available all required information and reports) by the energy inspector who must have relevant knowledge and training.

279. An energy facility for the production of natural gas which has been built based on a building permit can start operating once an operating permit has been obtained (Article 6 of the BA).

371. This is provided for in Art. 6 of the Decree on the energy infrastructure (Official Gazette of the Republic of Slovenia, No. 22/16).
372. *See* Art. 462 EA-1.
373. This concerns two regulations the application of which has been extended based on Art. 554 EA-1, namely, Rules on specifications for the construction, operation and maintenance of pipelines of operating pressure up to and including 16 bar (Official Gazette of the Republic of Slovenia, Nos 26/2002 and 54/2002); Rules on specifications for the construction, operation and maintenance of pipelines of operating pressure over 16 bar and on conditions for spatial intervention in their protected zones (Official Gazette of the Republic of Slovenia, Nos 12/10 and 45/11).

280. A special permit of the Energy Agency is required for the development of a direct line which is provided for by Directive 2009/73/EC concerning natural gas supply, as a right of undertakings and (final) consumers in the territory of a Member State. Gas supply via a direct line is only permitted in cases when access to the system has been refused or if the necessary system does not exist.[374]

281. All energy facilities and installations must be built in accordance with Spatial Planning Act,[375] whereby the ministry responsible for energy, as the holder of spatial planning activities concerning the energy industry, shall provide guidelines and opinions to intermunicipal and municipal spatial planning documents. As regards gas infrastructure projects, the planners and the municipalities are advised to refer directly to the national TSO, that is, the company Plinovodi d.o.o.,[376] concerning mandatory guidelines governing this particular area.

282. Natural gas production is necessarily associated with the exploitation of mineral resources at a specific extraction site, the permit for which is granted based on a preliminary mining concession (discussed in more detail in Chapter 3 §1 Award of Concession for Natural Gas Exploitation).

283. Further down, this section includes all permits and approvals or consents related to environmental protection which are required for natural gas production and the way they interact with each other.

I. Environmental Approval or Consent and Environmental Permit

284. In line with Slovenia's Environmental Protection Act (EPA-1) and its implementing regulations, which concretize more specifically individual statutory requirements, in the field of environmental protection a natural gas-producing entity needs two administrative acts, that is, an environmental approval (consent) as well as an environmental permit.

285. It needs to be underlined at this point that the environmental approval (consent) and the environmental permit need to be applied for prior to the construction permit. The latter cannot be awarded or is considered null and void in cases where

374. *See* Art. 267 EA-1.
375. Official Gazette of the Republic of Slovenia, Nos 33/07, 70/08 – ZVO-1B, 108/09, 80/10 – Siting of Spatial Arrangements of National Importance Act (ZUPUDPP), 43/11 – Agricultural Land Act (ZKZ-C), 57/12, 57/12 – Siting of Spatial Arrangements of National Importance Act (ZUPUDPP-A) (109/12), 76/14 – decision of Constitutional Court, 14/15 – Act Regulating Measures Aimed at Fiscal Balance of Municipalities (ZUUJFO) and 61/17 – ZUreP-2.
376. General Guidelines for Energy Industry, Ministry of Infrastructure and Spatial Planning, No. 350-139/2017-213, 1 Jun. 2018, 15.

an environmental approval (consent) or an environmental permit should have been issued but were not. Moreover, operation of the installation or facility depends on the discussed documents.[377]

286. An environmental approval (consent) is required prior to any encroachment that might have a significant impact on the environment, and therefore requires an assessment of the effects on the environment,[378] which is provided for in the Decree on the categories of activities for which an environmental impact assessment is mandatory.[379] It is an institute resulting from the transposition of European directives into the legislation of the Republic of Slovenia.

287. In line with Annex 1 to the Decree on the categories of activities for which an environmental impact assessment is mandatory,[380] the activities affecting the environment which require environmental impact assessment and environmental approval (consent) include mining, listed under B, or more specifically:

- natural gas production, providing the volume of extracted gas exceeds 500,000 standard cubic metres (sm^3) a day;
- storages for liquid gas, natural gas and other explosive gases, and gas terminals with a capacity of at least 25.000 t;
- pipelines with dimensions above 800 mm and 40 km.

288. In addition, there are also cases in which environmental impact assessment is not automatically mandatory but is checked in a preliminary procedure according to Article 51a of the EPA-1. The following activities in the field of natural gas are subject to the said regime:

- production of natural gas which does not meet the criteria as mentioned above; i.e., the volume of extracted gas does not exceed 500,000 standard cubic metres (sm3) a day;
- surface gas extraction;
- storages for liquid gas, natural gas and other explosive gases, and gas terminals with the capacity between 150 t and 24.999 t.

289. An investor allocating capital to energy facilities or installations shall, in line with paragraph 3 of Article 7 of the Decree on the categories of activities for which an environmental impact assessment is mandatory, submit the following documents along with the application to initiate the preliminary procedures:

377. *See* Art. 51a(7) EPA-1; Art. 61(7) (non-applicable according to Art. 125(4) BA) EPA-1; Art. 69 EPA-1.
378. *See* Art. 50 EPA-1.
379. Official Gazette of the Republic of Slovenia, Nos 51/14, 57/15 and 26/17.
380. Modes of interventions in the environment for which environmental impact assessment is always mandatory are stipulated by Art. 2 of the discussed Decree.

- mining project for the acquisition of an exploration permit in line with the rules governing the mining industry, providing they concern the exploration of mineral resources; or
- proposal for a mining concession act in line with the rules governing mining industry, provided they concern the exploration of mineral resources.

290. Furthermore, the EPA-1 stipulates that a polluter shall have an environmental permit for an installation where an activity is carried out which may pollute the environment due to emissions.[381] Such a permit is also a prerequisite for the operation of a plant or a facility (environmental operating permit).[382] In line with item 1.2. of Annex 1 to the Decree on the categories of activities and facilities that might cause environmental pollution on a wider scale,[383] the respective activities include, among other things, refining of natural gas.

291. Notwithstanding that the procedures for the issue of both instruments (environmental approval or consent and environmental permit) are conducted in line with the requirements for each instrument separately, certain activities (e.g., public presentations)[384] shall be performed, whenever possible, simultaneously for both.[385]

292. Slovenia, as noted earlier on in this chapter, produces relatively small volumes of natural gas. In 2014 and 2015, there was a strong opposition of the civil initiative as well as local environmental organizations against the expansion of the local refinery and natural gas production in the Lendava area (the Mura Depression on the Petišovci Field), mostly on environmental grounds. The procedure for the environmental approval (consent) or, as the case may be, the environmental permit which was started in June 2015 is still 'open'. The main point of the opposition to natural gas production and a new natural gas treatment plant, i.e., refinery in the Mura Depression is the conviction of the stakeholders (local residents and environmentalists) that the new system would be used to produce gas by means of hydraulic fracturing, which is a rather contested procedure from the point of view of the environmentalists. This thesis has been negated throughout the procedure by the investors since they defended a rather opposite thesis, namely, that the planned hydraulic fracturing is safe. There were some procedural events so far, but for practical reasons we only focused on the latest events as follows. In 2019, the Slovenian Environment Agency issued a decision according to which environmental impact assessment is needed as well as environmental approval. The investors lodged an appeal to the competent Ministry; however, the latter rejected the appeal which means a confirmation of the Agency's decision. Since the investors were not satisfied with the administrative decision, they lodged a lawsuit before the Administrative Court of the Republic of Slovenia. In 2020, the Court issued a judgment in which it also rejected the investors' claims. There is a real chance that the dispute

381. *See* Art. 17 EPA-1.
382. Adrijana Viler-Kovačič, Okoljevarstveno dovoljenje, Pravna praksa 2006, Nos 19–20, 6–9.
383. Official Gazette of the Republic of Slovenia, No. 57/15.
384. *Ibid.* Adrijana Viler-Kovačič, Okoljevarstveno soglasje, Pravna praksa 2004, No. 30, 15–18.
385. In fact, in some cases there was an option to merge both procedures according to Art. 92 of the Environmental Protection Act; however, as of 2016 the said article is derogated.

will be settled before the International Centre for Settlement of Investment Disputes, except in case the Republic of Slovenia will pay a claimed damages compensation to the investors or in case investors will accept the discussed procedural outcome (which seems to be less likely). On the other hand, however, the Slovenian Environment Agency issued a positive decision as to the natural gas refinery (which seems to be of limited importance without the right to pump gas).

II. Nature Conservation Approval or Consent and Permit

293. Nature conservation approval (consent) is provided for encroachments in the form of a construction or building of objects in those areas which are considered to have a special status, based on the regulations governing nature conservation.[386] The objective is to verify whether an activity fosters environmental protection and nature conservation in accordance with the provisions of the Nature Conservation Act and other nature conservation rules (e.g., the rules concerning the protection of the Triglav national park).[387] The activities in such areas need to be planned and implemented so as to prevent damage to nature, whereby it is necessary to decide for the option that has the least impact on the environment while having more or less equivalent effects.

294. Since (or when) natural gas production requires environmental approval (consent), the Nature Conservation Act enables, for reasons of procedure optimization, the assessment determining whether an encroachment is admissible or not, to be conducted as part of the procedure for issuing an environmental approval (consent).[388] In this case, a special nature conservation approval is not awarded. Instead, its contents are incorporated in the environmental approval. Naturally, this procedure involves also the Institute of the Republic of Slovenia for Nature Conservation, which provides its opinion. The environmental approval can be awarded providing that the concerned encroachment is judged positively; if a positive evaluation of the impact of the encroachment is conditioned by the implementation of mitigating measures, the latter must be included in the environmental approval (consent). If, however, the encroachment receives negative evaluation, the issue of the approval needs to be refused. At this point, it is worthy to point out, however, that in some cases the nature conservation permit or better to say the permit to encroach in the nature is needed.[389] In general, this kind of permit is needed in cases where interventions or encroachments in nature may endanger biodiversity, natural value or a protected area and for which it is not necessary to obtain a permit under spatial planning laws and regulations as well not under other laws and regulations.

386. *See* Art. 105 and 105a NCA.
387. Nature Conservation Act (NCA), Official Gazette of the Republic of Slovenia, No. 96/04 – official consolidated text, 61/06 – Societies Act (ZDru-1), 8/10 – National Farmland and Forest Fund Act (ZSKZ-B), 46/14, 21/18, 31/18 and 82/20.
388. *See* Art. 105(7) NCA.
389. *See* Art. 104 and 104a NCA.

III. Water Approval or Consent and Water Permit

295. Water approval (consent) is an administrative act, governed by the Waters Act (WA),[390] which stipulates, in Article 150, that an encroachment in physical space that could permanently or temporarily affect the water regime may only be carried out on the basis of a water approval (consent).

296. In line with item 7 of paragraph 2 of Article 150 of the WA, a water approval is required also for mining activities.

297. It should be noted that in natural gas production, the producing entity needs a water approval along with an environmental approval (consent).[391]

298. A water permit must be obtained by a gas company for the types of direct use of water that exceed general use, such as for the private supply of drinking water provided as a commercial public service, for technological purposes and other types pursuant to paragraph 1 of Article 125 of the WA, which exceed general use of water.

299. A water permit must be obtained prior to the permit for an encroachment in physical space pursuant to regulations on spatial planning and the construction of buildings.[392]

IV. GHG Emissions Permit

300. In line with paragraph 1 of Article 118 of the Environmental Protection Act, the operator of an installation where an activity causing GHG emissions takes place must obtain, from the ministry responsible for the environment, a GHG emissions permit prior to the commencement of the operation of the installation or any parts thereof.

§3. Conditions Governing Ownership Unbundling in Gas Sector Undertakings Performing Natural Gas Production Functions

301. An additional condition that needs to be considered with regard to natural gas production undertakings carrying out any of the functions of gas production is the ownership unbundling requirement applying to the TSO, the objective of which is to prevent interaction and conflict of interests. Thus, a gas-producing undertaking (as well as power trading undertaking) can neither hold a majority stake in nor have

---

390. Official Gazette of the Republic of Slovenia, Nos 67/02, 2/04 – Health Inspection Act (ZZdrl-A), 41/04 – Environmental Protection Act (EPA-1), 57/08, 57/12, 100/13, 40/14, 56/15 and 65/20.

391. *See* Art. 151a(4) WA.

392. Article 125(5) WA.

any control over the TSO in question.[393] They have however the right to dividends in case of minority shareholding. The person that exercises control over a TSO cannot exercise control over an undertaking performing any of the functions of natural gas or electricity production or supply.[394] By this, the provisions from the items (b) and (c) from the first paragraph of Article 9 Directive 2009/73/ES have been transposed into the legislation of the Republic of Slovenia.

302. Furthermore, to prevent interaction and conflict of interests, it is prohibited for a person to be simultaneously a member of the supervisory board, the administrative board or bodies legally representing the TSO and those representing the undertaking performing any of the functions of gas or power production and supply.

303. A simplified implementation of ownership unbundling is enabled in case of (partial) state ownership in the undertakings. The EA-1 provides for the state – being the owner of the undertaking performing the function of gas or power production or supply and the owner of TSO – to fulfil the requirement of ownership unbundling already by exercising control over both entities through two separate public authorities.[395]

304. In the event of a violation of the provisions concerning ownership unbundling, a person in relation to whom a reason arises that constitutes a violation shall be obliged to take all necessary measures to eliminate the violation and notify of its occurrence the Energy Agency, which supervises the carrying out of the prohibitions concerning ownership unbundling and acts in the event that violations have not been eliminated.

305. For the purpose of promoting and facilitating the development of new energy infrastructure, gas infrastructure may be exempted from the provisions related to ownership unbundling in case of new transmission pipelines, i.e. transmission systems, or facilities concerning the functions of an LNG terminal operator or storage facilities.[396] A time-limited exemption shall only be granted in the case and to the extent required to carry out investments above all for the purpose of economic risk management and in case the investment fulfils the stipulated conditions which include enhanced competition in gas supply and enhanced security of supply.

393. Article 183 EA-1.
394. Control means any rights, contracts or any other means which, either separately or in combination and having regard to the considerations of fact or law involved, confer the possibility of exercising a decisive influence on an undertaking, in particular by (a) ownership or the right to use all or part of the assets of an undertaking; and (b) rights or contracts which confer a decisive influence on the composition, voting or decisions of the bodies of an undertaking (item 17 of Art. 159 EA-1).
395. Article 186 EA-1.
396. The exemption refer may also be granted for significant increases in capacity of existing infrastructure and for modifications of such infrastructure which enable the development of new sources of natural gas supply (Art. 261(3) EA-1).

Chapter 3. Exploitation

306. This chapter presents the relevant provisions of the ZRud-1, which provides conditions for acquiring the concession for exploiting natural gas and the process for abandoning production, as well as permits for conducting natural gas research.

§1. Granting the Concession to Extract Natural Gas

307. A concession for extracting minerals within a certain area can be obtained pursuant to the mining concession document, which must be issued prior to the concession, and pursuant to the tender conducted to select the holder of the mining rights to extraction. In the special cases defined in paragraph 2 of Article 34 of the ZRud-1, no public tender is required.

308. The Government shall issue the relevant mining concession document at the proposal of the ministry responsible for mining. The Ministry shall propose the Government issue the relevant mining concession document:

- based on the assessment that the need to extract a certain mineral within a certain area exists; or
- based on the application of a natural or legal person interested in obtaining mining rights to extract a certain mineral within a certain area.

309. Article 35 of the ZRud-1 defines the contents of the application for granting mining rights and the conditions for the issue of the mining concession document.

310. When mining rights are conferred pursuant to a public tender and two or more applicants provide their complete applications, the selection of the holder of mining rights to extraction shall be conducted as an auction, at which eligible applicants shall compete to obtain the status of holder of mining rights to extraction with their bids on the amount of mining concession fee they are prepared to pay per unit of mineral in its original state. The auction is governed by Article 42.a of the ZRud-1.

311. The selected holder of mining rights to extraction must conclude a concession agreement with the ministry responsible for mining. The concession agreement shall be concluded at the initiative of the entity holding the decision on the selection of the mining rights holder. In accordance with Article 44 of the ZRud-1, the entity must attach to the initiative two copies of an audited mining project for the purposes of obtaining an extraction concession and proof of the right to mine on the land in question.

312. In accordance with indent 1 of paragraph 2 of Article 101 of the ZRud-1, the mining project for the purposes of obtaining the extraction concession should comply with the provisions of the Spatial Planning Act governing mining. In this respect, Article 151 of the ZRud-1 explicitly provides that those acts which, under the Spatial Planning Act (ZPNačrt),[397] define a certain area as reserved for extraction of a certain type of mineral, shall be considered as the Spatial Planning Act governing mining. In accordance with Article 106 of the ZRud-1, the mining engineer responsible is also responsible for the compliance of the mining project with the Spatial Planning Act.

313. The conclusion of a concession agreement for acquiring the right to perform mining works on land may be suspended for up to two years, and for a further two years at the request of the selected holder of mining rights. After expiry of this period the mining rights shall extinguish.

§2. Authorization to Research Natural Gas

314. Authorization to research a certain mineral within a certain research area for a certain period of time can only be issued pursuant to a prior public tender. The ministry responsible for mining shall decide to hold a public tender:

- based on the established interest to extract a mineral economically and feasibly; or
- based on the application filed by a particular interested legal or natural person with the ministry responsible for mining.

315. Article 25 of the ZRud-1 defines the contents of the application and the conditions for organizing a public tender for the issue of a research authorization.

316. It is worth mentioning that when two or more justified applicants apply to a research authorization tender, the selection of the holder of mining rights to research shall be conducted as an auction, at which the candidates shall compete to obtain the status of holder of a research authorization with their bids on the amount of mineral research fee they are prepared to pay. The auction is governed by Article 25.a of the ZRud-1.

317. If the holder of mining rights to extraction opts to abandon mining works either in full or in part, regardless of the reason, it must comply with the relevant provisions of the concession agreement.

§3. Authorization to Abandon Mining Works

318. The holder of mining rights to extraction must report its intent to abandon mining works either in part or in full to the competent mining inspection authority

397. Official Gazette of the Republic of Slovenia, Nos 33/07, 70/08, 108/09, 80/10, 43/11, 57/12, 109/12, 76/14, 14/15 and 61/17.

no more than fifteen days before the works are to end and at the same time file an application with the ministry responsible for mining for the issue of an authorization to abandon mining works.

319. If, after verifying the mining concession fees have been paid and the rehabilitation funds have been reserved, the ministry responsible for mining finds that there are no impediments to issuing the authorization to abandon mining woks, it shall issue a resolution appointing a technical inspection committee and determining the date of technical inspection; otherwise, it shall reject the application. There shall be no appeal against the aforementioned resolution.

320. The technical inspection committee is responsible for conducting a field inspection and determining the reasons for abandoning mining works, the stocks or sources of minerals and determining whether the conditions for abandoning works are fulfilled. The holder of mining rights to extraction shall provide the committee with the mining and technical documentation pursuant to which mining works took place and pursuant to which the decision to abandon the extraction of minerals was taken.

321. If the ministry responsible for mining determines, based on the technical inspection committee's minutes, that the conditions for abandoning mining works are fulfilled, it shall issue an authorization for abandoning mining works; in the opposite case it shall reject the application.

322. The decision issued in proceedings relating to the issuing of the authorization to abandon mining works shall be served to the holder of mining rights to extraction in person and delivered to the mining inspection and the local community where the mine lies.

323. After the authorization for abandoning mining works becomes final, the holder of mining rights to excavation shall begin closing works, finally rehabilitate the environment and reverse the impacts of conducting the mining works. In areas where the consequences cannot be entirely rehabilitated or reversed, the holder of mining rights to excavation shall take measures necessary to eliminate any risk to human or animal life and health, any potential environmental pollutants and any foreseen damage to buildings and the environment.

324. Closing works can only be conducted pursuant to a confirmed environmental rehabilitation project.

325. Only after the closing works have been completed and the environment rehabilitation finalized can the holder of mining rights to extraction file with the ministry responsible for mining an application for issuing the decision on the termination of rights and obligations relating to the mining rights to extraction.

326. After receipt of the application with the relevant documentation and prescribed evidence, the ministry responsible for mining shall determine the date of the technical inspection, during which the committee ascertains whether the environmental rehabilitation has been completed and whether the measures implemented are sufficient.

327. If it is ascertained at the technical inspection that certain mining structures have not been removed, such structures can be preserved if the holder of mining rights to extraction submits the written position of the authority of the relevant self-governing local community that the authority does not object to such structures being preserved and that it will include the structures in its planning documents. If a construction permit is obtained for such a structure, no fees for spatial degradation and usurpation shall be levied notwithstanding the provisions of regulations governing construction.

328. If, during the technical inspection, the committee finds deficiencies, it shall notify the holder of mining rights to extraction in the relevant minutes and determine the timeframe in which the deficiencies must be remedied. The holder of mining rights to extraction must inform the ministry responsible for mining whether it has remedied the deficiencies within the timeframe and provide proof thereof.

329. After performing the technical inspection, the ministry responsible for mining shall issue the decision terminating rights and obligations or shall reject the issue of such a decision if it determines that the rehabilitation of the environment has such deficiencies that it represents a risk to the life and health of humans, traffic, neighbouring buildings or the environment, and that the deficiencies cannot be remedied.

330. The holder of mining rights to extraction whose application to issue the decision terminating rights and obligations has been rejected shall be entitled to re-file such an application once it has remedied the deficiencies established during the technical inspection and completed rehabilitation in accordance with the relevant regulations. Until such a decision is issued, it must ensure that maintenance and other works are conducted in the mining area so as to prevent any risk to human or animal life or health and any potential environmental pollutants.

331. The decision issued in proceedings relating to the termination of rights and obligations shall be served to the holder of mining rights to extraction in person and delivered to the mining inspection and the local community where the mine lies.

§4. Termination of Rights and Obligations and the Consequences Thereof

332. The rights and obligations of the holder of mining rights to extraction shall extinguish when the decision terminating the rights and obligations becomes final.

333. Such a decision is a condition for the holder of mining rights to extraction being stricken from the mining register ex officio by the ministry responsible for mining.

334. Before sticking the holder from the register, the holder of mining rights to extraction shall provide the mining plans, metering logs and other documentation on the condition of mining works to the Geological Survey of Slovenia so that the latter can obtain the data it needs to draft state geological maps and to determine which material represents material that must be held indefinitely in accordance with the regulations governing archives.

335. As of the date the holder of mining rights to extraction is stricken from the mining register, the mine in which the mining works were performed before being stricken, shall be deemed closed.

336. After the holder of mining rights to extraction is stricken from the mining register, the mining inspector's jurisdiction over the site of the closed mine shall also extinguish.

Chapter 4. Transport or Transmission of Natural Gas

337. This chapter discusses the transport of natural gas via the transmission network and system.[398] First the term transmission system is defined; this is followed by a discussion of the fundamental attributes of specific public law obligations relating to the pursuit of activities as a TSO, which is deemed a public utility. The chapter then discusses the de-integration (separation) of the activities of the TSO from other activities in the gas sector, including the separate arrangements with regard to an independent transmission operator, and discusses access to the (transmission) system and other selected issues.

§1. Concept of the Transmission System and Related Concepts

338. Although the term transmission system is not explicitly defined in the new EA, the concept can be inferred from the legal definitions of other terms, such as transmission, system and TSO.

339. Transmission means the transport of natural gas through a network which mainly contains high-pressure pipelines with a view to its delivery to customers, but not including supply. Transmission does not mean transport through an upstream pipeline network[399] and it also does not mean (downstream) high-pressure pipelines primarily used in the context of the local distribution of natural gas.[400]

340. System means transmission networks, distribution networks, LNG facilities and/or storage facilities owned or operated by a natural gas undertaking, including linepack and its facilities supplying ancillary services and those of related undertakings needed to provide access to transmission, distribution and LNG.[401]

341. TSO means a natural or legal person who carries out the function of transmission and is responsible for operating, ensuring the maintenance of, and, if necessary, developing the transmission system in a given area and, where applicable, its interconnections with other systems, and for ensuring the long-term ability of the system to meet reasonable demands for the transport of gas.[402]

342. From the legal definitions of the aforementioned terms, and with regard to EU legislation, a transmission system can be defined as the transmission pipeline

398. For transparency purposes it should be noted that natural gas is also transported through the distribution network or system, which is discussed in a separate chapter (Part II, Chapter 5).

399. Upstream pipeline network means any pipeline or network pipelines operated or constructed as part of an oil or gas production project, or used to convey natural gas from one or more such projects to a processing plant or terminal or final coastal landing terminal (Art. 159(40) EA-1).

400. *See* Art. 159(39) EA-1 (c.f. Art. 2(3) of Directive 2009/73/ES).

401. *See* Art. 159(48) EA-1.

402. The EA-1 does not contain an explicit definition of gas transmission system operator; it does not, however, contain numerous provisions in accordance with Art. 2(4) of Directive 2009/73/ES.

network, compressor stations, a dispatch centre, metering stations and other facilities necessary for providing the public utility in the transmission of natural gas, and the components thereof.[403] It is operated, maintained and, if necessary, developed by a (transmission) system operator, in order to enable the transport of natural gas in high-pressure pipelines (at more than 16 bars) with a view to its delivery to customers.

§2. Public Utility Obligations Attached to the Transmission of Natural Gas

343. In principle, the natural gas transmission system is the intermediary between the natural gas producers on one side and the distributors and consumers on the other. It is thus one of the integral links in the chain of the gas sector, which has a significant impact on the supply of natural gas in Slovenia, an indication of the general (public) interest in this respect. It is precisely for this reason that the legislator opted not to leave the activities of TSOs to market whims, but to make the activities subject to the special requirements of a public utility, namely a special public law regime in the form of a mandatory national public utility for the entire territory of Slovenia, which in accordance with Article 177(2) EA-1 encompasses:

- the execution of transmission;
- the safe, reliable[404] and efficient[405] operation and maintenance of the transmission system;
- the development of the system, having regard for the anticipated needs of system users, the requirements of the safe, reliable operation of the system and the guidelines of the development plan of the TSO;
- the provision of long-term capacity in the transmission system to facilitate reasonable requests for connection and access to the system;
- the assurance of the reliability of the supply of natural gas with the requisite system capacity and reliability;
- the provision of system services;
- the determination and accounting of the balancing of deviations in consumption and delivery of natural gas from the forecasts;
- the forwarding of sufficient information to any other TSO, storage system operator, LNG system operator or DSO to ensure the transmission and storage of natural gas that is compatible with the safe, effective operation of a connected system;

403. The regulation on energy infrastructure, which was repealed by the new EA-1 is still applied until new secondary legislation is adopted to regulate this area, gives a definition of the individual elements that make up the transmission system.

404. To this end the transmission system operator must *inter alia* put in place sufficient cross-border capacity for inclusion in the European transmission infrastructure, tailored to all the economically justifiable and technically feasible requirements for capacity, having regard for the reliability of the natural gas supply.

405. Transmission system operators supply energy that they need to pursue their business activities, under transparent, non-discriminatory and market-based procedures.

- the prompt provision of the requisite information to system users to enable them to effect access to the system;
- the establishment and supervision of mechanisms for managing flows and balancing deviations in the network, as defined in the system operating guidelines of the natural gas transmission network;
- forecasts of consumption of natural gas and requisite resources by means of an integrated planning method, having regard for energy-saving measures at system users;
- the non-discriminatory treatment of individual system users or types of system users, and in particular the non-favouring of their affiliates;
- other tasks set out by law, regulations and by-laws for the exercise of public authorizations;
- the organization of the balancing market in natural gas.[406]

344. The aforementioned public utility is provided by a concessionaire,[407] i.e. the TSO, who has obtained the concession[408] and meets the following conditions:

- it is the owner of a transmission system;[409]
- it has TSO certification;[410]

---

406. Detailed rules on the method of implementation of all the aforementioned public utility obligations are set out by the Government via a decree.
407. At the moment the concessionaire in Slovenia is Plinovodi d.o.o., but it should also be noted that with regard to the possibility of obtaining the concession to pursue the activities in question the EA-1 works on the principle of non-discrimination, or the equal treatment of all EU entities.
408. The concession may be awarded for a maximum of thirty-five years, and no exclusive or special rights may be awarded for the concession. The concession is awarded according to the rules governing public utilities and public-private partnership, except where stipulated otherwise by the EA-1. In accordance with Art. 179 EA-1, the concession act published in the Official Gazette of the Republic of Slovenia sets out transparent, non-discriminatory and proportionate conditions that a legal or natural person must meet to be awarded the concession. The ownership of a transmission system or a part thereof, transmission system operator certification, and designation as a transmission system operator are not conditions for obtaining a concession. Should the concession-granter allow the concessionaire to acquire property rights on real estate under government ownership or other benefits in connection with the implementation of the concession, it must offer these benefits to every concessionaire under the same terms. The awarding of the concession is decided on by the Government via a ruling, at the request of a party to the procedure. A public tender procedure or another form of competitive procedure set out by the regulations on public-private partnership is not carried out for the award of the concession. The law governing services in the internal market also apply to the procedure for issuing the ruling referred to in this paragraph. The ministry responsible for energy must inform the European Commission of the reasons for a refusal to award the concession within thirty days of the finality of the ruling by virtue of which the award of the concession was refused. After the ruling on the award of the concession becomes final, the concession-granter and the concessionaire sign a concession agreement.
409. If the owner of a transmission system does not meet the conditions for pursuing the activities of a transmission system operator, it must meet the conditions within one year of the operating permit for the transmission system entering into force, otherwise measures will be taken to terminate the pursuit of the activities of a transmission system operator as set out by Art. 210 EA-1.
410. The certification process is regulated by Arts 204–208 EA-1, and begins with the submission of a complete application for a certificate by the owner of the transmission system or the transmission system operator. The European Commission is informed without delay of the Agency's decision or the presumption of the issue of certification, together with the information relating to the decision.

– it has been designated a TSO.[411]

345. When TSO procures the energy (natural gas) it has to act in transparent, non-discriminatory and market-based fashion.

346. TSO must take care of sufficient cross-border connections which means access to transmission networks of other countries. In this regard, it can conclude contracts (covering technical issues concerning the operation of interconnections)[412] not only with the Member States but also with third countries. Yet, this is only possible in a way that EU rules as well as national rules are respected. Moreover, the decisions of the Agency shall be respected.[413]

347. The activities of a TSO are financed from network charges and other revenues for the provision of a public utility, whereby the latter include revenues from auctions for reason of congestion in cross-border pipelines (although this option may not be abused, it is necessary to consistently strive to create the conditions for sufficient cross-border capacity, taking the relevant technical, physical and economic aspects into account).

§3. Unbundling of Transmission Systems and TSOs

I. Ownership Unbundling

348. As outlined in the previous section, in principle, the TSO must own the transmission system that it operates. The law also stipulates that a legal or natural person that owns a transmission system must pursue the activities of a TSO, and furthermore that no person other than a TSO may own all or part of the transmission system on which the TSO pursues the activities of a TSO,[414] unless stipulated otherwise by the law, having regard for European gas legislation (*see* the explanations

The decision takes effect as of the issue of an opinion by the European Commission or after the deadline set out in Art. 3(1) of Regulation (EC) No. 715/2009 passes.

411. If after the ruling on the issue of certification becomes final or after the establishment of the presumption of the issue of certification (which arises when the Agency fails to issue a ruling on the issue of certification within the mandated deadline period of four months) the candidate is the owner of a transmission system, at the Agency's proposal the Government designates the candidate as a transmission system operator via a resolution published in the Official Journal of the European Union and the Official Gazette of the Republic of Slovenia, and forwards it to the European Commission.

412. The interconnections are considered as a transmission pipeline crossing or connecting the border between the Republic of Slovenia and another Member State due to the connection of national transmission networks of those countries, or a transmission pipeline between the Republic of Slovenia and a third country to the territory of the Republic of Slovenia or the territorial sea.

413. For a greater transparency, TSO has to inform the relevant ministry and the Agency latest in eight days after concluding of such contract about its content; *see* Art. 177(6) EA-1.

414. The aforementioned requirement is deemed to have been met when two or more legal or natural persons that own a transmission system establish a joint venture that acts as a system operator in two or more European Union Member States, whereby it is essential that no other undertaking participates in the joint venture. *See* Art. 182(2) EA-1.

below with regard to exemptions for a company that is certified as an independent transmission operator). However, according to the intention of the legislator (supranational and consequently national), ownership of the transmission system and the activities relating to the system are 'isolated'. Given the negative experience with vertically integrated incumbents that abused their market power stemming from the transmission system in order to improve their competitive position on the upstream or downstream market, these incumbents are now explicitly required by law, according to Articles 183 and 184 EA-1, to ensure ownership unbundling, as the same persons may not at the same time have direct or indirect control[415] of undertakings engaged in the production or supply of natural gas and TSOs or owners, and vice versa (this prohibition also applies to cross-ownership of the electricity and natural gas sectors). Since the mere prohibition or restriction of the simultaneous (capital) control of two or more aforementioned undertakings cannot prevent all undesirable links on the upstream or downstream market, the legislator also stipulated restrictions with regard to membership of governing bodies by prescribing that the same person may not simultaneously be a member of the management board, the supervisory board or any other body that acts as the statutory representative of a TSO or a person owning a transmission system, or a representative in connection with the ownership governance of a natural gas transmission system or an electricity or natural gas transmission system, and a member of the management board, supervisory board or any other body that acts as the statutory representative of an undertaking pursuing the activity of production or supply of natural gas or electricity (*see* Article 185 EA-1). In this regard, it should be noted that the strict interpretation of the above prohibition of simultaneous control of the aforementioned undertakings and the prohibition of simultaneous membership of the governing bodies of such undertakings could practically prevent or at least significantly impair the free enterprise of Member States in the gas sector and the energy sector in general,[416] for which reason Article 186 EA-1 explicitly stipulates that when two separate bodies of the Slovenian state, its local authorities or another EU Member State exercise control in the aforementioned sense of a TSO or a transmission system and of an undertaking pursuing activities in production or supply, they are deemed separate persons (and thus not subject to the prohibition).

415. In this respect control means rights, contracts or any other means that, either separately or jointly, and having regard for the relevant de facto or de jure circumstances, allow a decisive influence to be exerted on an undertaking, in particular by means of:

- ownership or the right to use all or part of the assets of an undertaking;
- rights or contracts that confer a decisive influence on the composition, voting or decisions of the governing bodies of an undertaking; *see* Art. 159 (17th indent) EA-1.

416. Finally, this could undermine Art. 345 TFEU, which stipulates that the Treaties should not prejudice property ownership arrangements in the Member States in any way whatsoever. Simplified somewhat, this provision concerning public companies is interpreted as meaning that Member States are formally free to establish, retain and dissolve public companies, but are not completely free with respect to their governance and their actions on the market, as the latter two aspects are subject to the commercial law of the European Union.

349. A legal or natural person that controls a TSO, the owners of the transmission system, the operators themselves or any person that is subject to the above restriction concerning the control and membership of the governing bodies of the aforementioned undertakings must prevent and remedy any non-conformities and inform the Energy Agency accordingly. The Energy Agency imposes corrective measures as necessary (and also pursues any such breaches ex officio). If the measures are not implemented within a reasonable period of no less than one month and no more than six months from the day of notification of the grounds, or within the period indicated by the Agency, the Agency issues a ruling to:

- prohibit the exercise of the voting rights or proprietary entitlements in connection with the governance of a participating interest of less than half;
- order the sale of a share of the share capital or participating interest in the transmission system insofar as this exceeds half of the undertaking's nominal capital or shares;
- establish that a member of the management board, supervisory board or another body acting as the statutory representative of the undertaking was appointed in contravention of the law or that the person who represents the transmission system owner was authorized in contravention of the law, and propose to the competent authority the initiation of proceedings for dismissal or the withdrawal of the authorization;
- prohibit the exercise of indirect or direct control.[417]

II. Independent Transmission Operator

350. As stated in the introduction to this section, the requirement for ownership unbundling is not absolute, as there is an exemption for the case of an independent transmission operator. The Slovenian legislator exploited the option envisaged by the European legislator, whereby the transition to a new organizational model for the gas sector could of necessity be gradual, without necessitating rapid market reorganization and restructuring of (vertically integrated) gas undertakings, which has certain advantages compared with ownership unbundling (and weaknesses, of course),[418] but is still (sufficiently) effective from the perspective of preventing conflicts of interest and abuse of a dominant position in the manner described in the previous section.

417. Having regard for the principle of proportionality, the Agency may impose more than one measure via a ruling. As a last resort, the Agency may initiate proceedings to test the conditions of certification if the aforementioned measures cannot remedy the breach (*see* Art. 188 EA-1).

418. The draft of the new EA-1 cited the following advantages and weaknesses compared with ownership unbundling in the explanation of the section on the independent transmission operator:

- advantages: a vertically integrated undertaking generally has more capital and a better rating than a de-integrated undertaking, which improves its negotiating options with banks and other business partners and its market position in general; sufficient time for a measured de-integration; the avoidance of potential reviews of the constitutionality of interventions in

351. A vertically integrated undertaking that owned a transmission system as at 3 September 2009 and meets the special legal conditions presented below may be an independent transmission operator. It should be organized as a company pursuant to the Companies Act, albeit not just in any form, as the new EA-1 stipulates only three options. An independent transmission operator may only be organized as a public limited company (joint-stock company), a limited liability company or a limited partnership, although irrespective of the choice it is essential by law that the company has the governing bodies typical of a public limited company, and the rules on public limited company governing bodies apply to the role, duties and responsibilities of the independent transmission operator's (ITO's) governing bodies. In addition to these general provisions, the law specifically stipulates that the ITO should have a supervisory body that performs the function of a supervisory board in a two-tier governance system, having regard for the EA-1 and EU legislation.[419] A TSO therefore may not have a single-tier governance system in the sense of the law governing companies, and its partners may not directly govern the undertaking or manage its operations.

352. The activities of the system operator encompass the following tasks:

- representing the TSO in legal transactions and in any communications with the Agency, other regulatory authorities and third parties;
- representing the TSO in the European network of TSOs for natural gas;
- deciding on access to the system and taking the actions necessary for its implementation, where it should not discriminate against individual system users or types of system user, and in particular may not favour its own affiliates;
- collecting all payments in connection with the transmission system;
- operating, maintaining and developing a safe, reliable and economical transmission system;
- planning investment to provide long-term capacity in the system, to satisfy reasonable demand and reliability of supply;
- establishing appropriate undertakings, including those established with one or more TSOs, natural gas exchanges and other relevant stakeholders, to make progress in the creation of regional markets or to facilitate the liberalization process;
- providing collective services, including legal, accounting and information services; and
- performing other tasks set out for the TSO by the law.[420]

---

property rights, particularly in the context of the fundamental principle of proportionality, when it is considered that European legislation allows for solutions that do not prejudice property rights;

- weaknesses: a vertically integrated undertaking is more exposed to conflicts of interest than a de-integrated undertaking, which requires more intensive supervision; the possibility of unforeseen measures imposed by the European Commission; complications in any privatization process.

419. *See* Art. 196 EA-1.
420. *See* Art. 190(2) EA-1.

353. Given that these are important tasks in the public interest, it is no surprise that the legislator stipulated logical obligations with regard to human resources (the requisite personnel for carrying out the activities or the aforementioned tasks must be employed directly by the operator itself, and part of a vertically integrated undertaking may not provide personnel for another part, provide services for it, hire personnel employed at another part of the undertaking, or provide services provided by another part of the undertaking)[421],[422] technical resources and other material resources (the operator must fully own the transmission system and the other resources necessary to pursuing the activity of natural gas transmission; no other person may fully or partly own the transmission system on which the TSO pursues the activities of a TSO, and the law further stipulates explicitly that the operator may not share systems or IT equipment, premises or secure access systems with another part of the vertically integrated undertaking or use them together therewith, and may not have the same consultants or external providers for IT systems or equipment and secure access systems), and financial resources (the operator must at all times have sufficient financial resources at its disposal to ensure its activities are pursued properly and effectively and to develop and maintain an effective, safe and economical transmission system).[423] Furthermore, with the objective of ensuring the requisite independence for the effective implementation of the imposed obligations, and for effective competition on the market or for its general development, the law regulates the commercial, financial and capital relations between operators and the vertically integrated undertaking of which the operator is part.[424] In general, the aforementioned relations must be in accordance with the market conditions, whereby the law further stipulates special measures that on the one hand should ensure the appropriate availability of assets on the part of the operator and should prevent the uncontrolled flow of assets between the operator and the vertically integrated undertaking or affiliates, which could harm the aforementioned requirement for financial resources and also impair the independence of the operator. In accordance with the above, a vertically integrated undertaking must, e.g., make adequate financial resources available to the TSO for investment projects and for the replacement of existing assets in sufficient time and at the TSO's request, and the TSO must have the power to obtain money on the capital market, in particular by borrowing and by raising capital.[425] The operator must have the de facto right to take decisions, independently of the vertically integrated undertaking, in connection with the

421. However, in certain cases an absolute prohibition on cooperation would be disproportionate, for which reason Art. 191(5) EA-1 stipulates that a transmission system operator may provide services for a vertically integrated undertaking if the provision of the services is not discriminatory towards system users, the services are available to all system users under the same terms, and the terms do not restrict, distort or prevent competition in production or supply, and if the Agency approves the terms for the provision of services before provision commences.

422. Article 195 EA-1 contains specific provisions with regard to ensuring the independence of members of an operator's governing bodies.

423. *See* Arts 191 and 192 EA-1.

424. *See* Arts 192 and 193 EA-1.

425. Notwithstanding the law governing companies, decisions to raise loans or to issue debt securities are taken by the transmission system operator's management board, while decisions to increase its capital are taken by its supervisory body; *see* Art. 192(4) EA-1.

resources needed for operating, maintaining and developing the system.[426] By contrast, the TSO is not allowed to make loans to a vertically integrated undertaking. From the financial/capital perspective it is now significant that subsidiaries of a vertically integrated undertaking that pursues activities of production or supply may not directly or indirectly own shares or participating interests in a TSO, and a TSO may not directly or indirectly own shares or participating interests in a subsidiary of a vertically integrated undertaking that pursues activities of production or supply and may not receive dividends from such an undertaking or enjoy any other financial benefits from such an undertaking. From the commercial/financial perspective it is, e.g., significant that a TSO must keep records of commercial and financial relations with a vertically integrated undertaking or with affiliates, and must grant the Agency access to the relevant documents at its request. Furthermore, the TSO must submit commercial and financial contracts or agreements with the vertically integrated undertaking to the Agency for approval (consent); otherwise the legal transactions are null and void.

354. With regard to ensuring the operator's independence from a vertically integrated undertaking, the EA-1 also contains provisions on the governance structure and the company's memorandum or articles of association, which in simple terms prevent interference in the decision-making processes on the TSO's governing bodies,[427] while the law also requires the TSO, with the aim of ensuring its independence, to draw up a special compliance programme that sets out targets and measures to prevent discriminatory behaviour, and sets out obligations for employees in meeting these targets. The programme requires the approval (consent) of the Agency, which also supervises its implementation. In addition, to expand supervision, the law further stipulates that supervision in this connection is also conducted by a compliance officer, who is appointed by the TSO's supervisory body, although the decision requires the Agency's approval (consent).[428]

§4. Access to the Transmission System

I. General

355. Since access to the transmission and distribution system is regulated mainly due to reasons that have already been elementarily presented in this monograph at the industry level,[429] further in this section we mainly focus on the manner and contents of the relevant regulatory system in this area.[430]

---

426. Without prejudicing the supervisory body's decisions, decisions in connection with the resources needed for operating, maintaining and developing the system are taken by the transmission system operator's management board independently within the framework of its powers and responsibilities. Article 192(5) of the EA-1.

427. *See* Art. 194 EA-1.

428. *See* Arts 198 in 199 EA-1.

429. *See* Introduction, Chapter 1 §2.

430. Since the legislator has regulated access to the transmission and distribution system in the same chapter, we purposefully use the generic term 'transport system' below; this term refers both to the

356. The owner or operator of the natural gas transport system cannot entirely freely decide if, who and under what conditions someone will be provided access to the system; in contrast, he must comply with the predefined regulatory framework, which *inter alia* requires him to provide objective and non-discriminatory access to the system to persons who have a justified interest and fulfil the relevant statutory conditions[431] and/or to system users. That said, the aforementioned persons of course do not have an absolute right to the system or to be connected to the system. A gas system operator can issue a justified decision[432] refusing access to the system due to the lack of necessary capacity when access to the system prevents the implementation of public service obligations or in the event of serious economic and financial difficulties with 'take-or-pay' contracts of natural gas undertakings.[433] If a dispute arises, the matter shall be settled by the Energy Agency,[434] which can either lay down the conditions for enhancing the system capacities or agree with the operator and refuse the request for system access.[435] In cross-border cases, one shall apply the rules of the country which is competent for the relevant pipeline and refuses access to it. In case more countries are competent, they have to consult each other.[436]

357. Before we discuss the provisions relating exclusively to access to the natural gas transmission system, it is worth first presenting the fundamental characteristics of the natural gas market and supply contracts, which is regulated by a common provision (Article 240 EA-1) which applies to both the transmission and the distribution system. First, it should be pointed out that an individual natural or legal person may join the balance scheme through a single balancing contract or a single compensation agreement.[437] The supplier and the system user shall conclude a gas supply contract; however, it should be noted that only a supplier that is a member of the balance scheme may conclude an open contract with the system user. It

---

transmission and the distribution system, unless explicitly provided otherwise (e.g., Arts 247–249 EA-1, which are discussed in Part II, Chapter 5, explicitly refer to the distribution system).

431. For example, a gas transmission system operator shall, if necessary for the purpose of carrying out their functions in relation to the cross-border transmission of natural gas into/from Slovenia, have access to the network of other gas transmission system operators, while the gas distribution system operator shall have the right of access to the transmission system (to exit points of consumption which are connected to the distribution system where it performs gas distribution system operator functions).

432. The justification must be based on objective and technically and economically justified criteria.

433. An operator refusing a connection due to a lack of capacity or lack of connections shall be obliged to make necessary enhancements to the system upon the request of the person in question, and as far as it is economic to do so, or when this person is, alone or with other persons, willing to pay for such enhancements.

434. *See* the Footnotes 118 and 291.

435. The aforementioned concerning refusal of access to the system shall also apply to access to the LNG system and upstream pipeline networks, except for the parts of such networks and facilities which are used for local production operations at the site of a field where the gas is produced and in other special circumstances defined by Art. 246 EA-1.

436. This is so also in case a third country is competent; *see* Art. 246(2).

437. Balance scheme membership shall cease upon cessation of validity of the balancing contract or the compensation agreement.

should also be pointed out that with regards to final users, the Act specifically provides that they cannot conclude closed contracts and must have an open contract that defines the balancing affiliation of the consumption point concerned (only one open contract with one supplier may be in place for each consumption point at any one time).[438] The gas TSO shall lay down detailed rules for the implementation and/or notification of natural gas supply contracts in the Network Code, while the Government shall lay down by means of a decree detailed rules for the operation of the natural gas market, imbalance clearing for the consumption and supply of natural gas, change of supplier and for other elements concerning the operation of the natural gas market.

II. Contractual Bases

358. The system operator provides access to the transmission system through concluding transmission agreements at entry points of the transmission system (i.e., points at which the transmission system of the Republic of Slovenia is linked with the transmission systems of neighbouring countries, other transmission systems in the Republic of Slovenia or delivery sources, storage facilities and LNG terminals in the Republic of Slovenia) and exit points of the transmission system (i.e., all consumption points and all points at which the transmission system of the Republic of Slovenia is linked with the transmission systems of neighbouring countries, other transmission systems in the Republic of Slovenia or storage of natural gas).[439] Subject to the condition that the transmission system technical capacities and the technical capacity limits of individual entry or exit point allow for it, transmission system users may conclude an individual transmission contract for one or more entry points, and/or an individual transmission contract for one or more exit points of the transmission system. Individual transmission contracts concluded by system

438. By exception, there may be several open contracts with different suppliers for any consumption point where the consumer's annual consumption exceeds 2 million sm^3. However, in such a case, the customer shall notify the gas system operator and suppliers of the relationship between balancing groups at the consumption point for each accounting interval separately; otherwise, the gas system operator shall take into consideration the last relationship notified.

439. The technical capacity of individual entry and exit points of the transmission system and their limits shall be defined and published daily by the gas transmission system operator on its web site. The transport of natural gas between entry and exit points shall be carried out considering the technical capacity of the transmission system and in compliance with the provisions of Regulation (EC) No. 715/2009. Relevant points as defined and published by the gas transmission system operator in compliance with Regulation (EC) No. 715/2009 shall be approved by the Agency after consulting with network users. All transactions with natural gas, irrespective of the entry or exit point, shall be deemed to have been carried out at the virtual point (i.e., a notional point located between the entry and exit points in a transmission system, at which it is considered that natural gas undertakings and final customers in the Republic of Slovenia have conducted all trading in volumes of natural gas). For all transactions at the virtual point, the gas transmission system operator shall ensure that all market participants are subject to the same transparent and non-discriminatory conditions, while users of the virtual point shall pay to the gas transmission system operator the costs of registration of participation and the costs of individual transactions. The remuneration for the virtual point services shall be defined by the gas transmission system operator following the prior approval of the Agency.

users for entry or exit points may be concluded for different transmission capacities and for different periods of time. This allows for the greater liquidity and competitiveness on wholesale natural gas markets.[440] Of course, over a certain period or accounting interval, the deviations that occur in practice should be balanced, which is done through concluding a balancing agreement or including the consumption point in a balancing group by concluding an open contract.[441]

359. Transmission contracts at exit points of the transmission system in the Republic of Slovenia to which final customers are connected shall be concluded by the final customer connected to the transmission system or by the natural gas supplier on behalf of, and for, the account of the final customer. Transmission contracts at exit points of the transmission system in the Republic of Slovenia to which the distribution system is connected shall be concluded only by the operator of such distribution system. The transmission contract may refer to the total capacity of several exit points of the distribution network.[442]

III. Network Charges

360. Since network charges are paid for using the transport system, it is not insignificant[443] who defines them and how. As already mentioned,[444] the transformation of the closed and uncompetitive natural gas markets of the Member States into open and (more) competitive markets, which should actually be integrated into one single market – the internal natural gas market – would not have been possible or would have been much more difficult to achieve if owners or the operators of the essential infrastructure were allowed to determine network charges themselves, which would only be subject to general verification of their appropriateness in light of the rules of competition by the competition regulator.[445]It is for this reason that a different, more market-invasive approach was selected: namely pro-competitive (*ex ante*) regulation, which through the obligations imposed on the network owner or operator, provides interested companies not only with the formal option to access the network (which in itself would be devoid of any real value), but also with the actual ability to access the network by preventing the network owner or operator from charging exorbitant rates for using the network in question.

---

440. Natural gas can be traded regardless of its (current) location in the system (the actual contractual routes are unimportant).
441. More detailed rules on the balancing of deviations are provided in Art. 243 EA-1 and the Network Code adopted by the operator.
442. The gas transmission system operator shall prescribe procedures for transmission system capacity allocation, congestion management and trading of capacities in the secondary market in compliance with Regulation (EC) No. 715/2009, subject to the prior approval of the Agency. In doing so, it shall provide for measures and activities to prevent speculative practices by system users; *see* Art. 242 EA-1.
443. This is one of the sources the transport network operator uses to cover its eligible expenses.
444. *See* Introduction, Chapter 1 §2.
445. In this respect we would like to highlight that the so-called regulatory holidays (access holidays) approach was, in principle, rejected in Case C-424/07 [2009] I-11431.

361. Network charges, which represent payment for mandatory system operator services pursuant to the EA-1, are defined in the so-called regulatory framework,[446] which is adopted by the system operator pursuant to the methodology defined by the Agency[447] and with the Agency's approval (consent).[448] The regulatory framework provides a quantitative definition of the planned eligible costs[449] of a system operator by individual years of a regulatory period, the planned network charge, other revenue from system operator activities, and surpluses or shortfalls from previous years. If the regulatory period is longer than one year, a regulatory framework shall also refer to the balancing of the tariff items for the purpose of preventing sharp fluctuations in the network charge in individual years of the regulatory period. The gas system operator shall identify the deviations from the regulatory framework for single years, shown as surplus or deficit from network charges, and shall disclose the established deviations in the notes to the accounts.

---

446. The method of determining the network charges is presented in the continuation of this monograph.
447. The general act used to define the methodology must contain:

   - the types, determination criteria and method of calculating elements of the regulatory framework;
   - the types of eligible costs, including the regulated return, criteria for identifying costs and method to determine costs;
   - the method for including incentives for having acquired European funds;
   - the duration of the regulatory period;
   - the contents of the request to consent to the regulatory framework to be submitted by the gas system operator;
   - the type, form and method of submission of information necessary to set out the regulatory framework;
   - detailed rules and the method to establish deviations from the regulatory framework;
   - parameters of individual quality dimensions, their reference values, and method and standards for their calculation;
   - minimum quality standards for various services of the gas system operator;
   - the amount of compensation and time limits for payment of compensation in the event of a violation of the guaranteed level of quality of service.

   When establishing the methodology, the Agency shall use the method of the gas system operator's regulated annual revenue and regulated network charges, ensuring that all eligible annual costs incurred by the gas system operator are covered, including the regulated return, unless the Act provides for the coverage of eligible costs for a longer period; *see* Art. 250 EA-1.
448. To enable the establishment of the regulatory framework, the gas system operator shall prepare an investment plan containing a financial evaluation of investments under the applicable ten-year development plan to be carried out in the subsequent regulatory period (however, no investment plan need be drawn up if a ten-year network development plan has been drafted). The gas system operator's investment plan is regulated in Art. 252 EA-1.
449. Eligible costs are regulated in Art. 251 EA-1, while we highlight that the method of establishing and specifying the eligible costs must encourage the cost-effective operations of the gas system operator and enable it to attain a return higher than that foreseen in the regulatory framework where savings on eligible costs result from its endeavours to increase its cost-effectiveness. If the gas system operator incurs costs exceeding the eligible costs, the difference shall be offset against the regulated return on assets.

362. In accordance with Article 256 EA-1, the Agency shall specify the methodology for calculating network charges in the relevant general act,[450] which shall provide separate charges for using the transmission system (separately for entry and exit points), using the distribution system, system services (own use for system functioning, balancing any differences), measurements and other services.

363. In the aforementioned general act, the Agency shall specify:

– tariffs and tariff rates representing classes of system users in terms of system use characteristics within certain maximum value ranges;
– the services that may be charged to system users in addition to network charges by the gas system operator within the framework of the service of general economic interest;
– method of calculating network charges;
– method of calculating network charges and cost of services.

364. Tariffs and tariff rates for network charges shall be objective, transparent and non-discriminatory, and shall encourage the consumption of gas from renewable sources.[451] In compliance with the aforementioned methodology, the gas system operator shall set tariff rates so that the revenue from network charges envisaged for the planned use of the system is equal to the amount of regulated revenue from network charges in the regulatory period, while taking care not to discriminate against remote regions. The prices of other services not covered by network charges and charged to system users by the gas system operator shall be set by the system operator in agreement with the Agency, account being taken of actual costs thereof.

IV. Ensuring the Quality of the Natural Gas Transmission System

365. The quality of service relating to the gas transmission system is (also) ensured through so-called quality monitoring, which is the responsibility of the gas system operators, and the supervision of such monitoring is performed by the Agency.[452] Quality monitoring refers to user access to services and consumer satisfaction. This mainly relates to the following issues:

– the duration and frequency of system operation disruptions;
– the time required to repair the system;
– the time required to deal with complaints and transmit information;
– the time required for connection to the network;
– other quality aspects of services, as provided for in the Agency's general act.

450. This must be done in a manner that encourages the efficiency of system operators and system use.
451. The gas system operator shall publish tariff rates in Uradni list Republike Slovenije and on the operator's webpage.
452. *See* Arts 258–260 EA-1.

366. The Agency shall specify the reference value of the parameters of quality dimensions for each natural gas system operator and/or individual areas of the natural gas system so that these values provide a realistic target for the quality of supply, taking into account the condition of the system, the performance of the function to date and the operation of the system. Minimum quality standards are defined and guaranteed in a sense that if they are not achieved, the operator shall be liable to pay the user a certain compensation which has a similar function to liquidated damages; if the actual damages exceed the amount of compensation, the user shall have the right to claim full damages according to the general rules of the laws of tort.

V. Special Treatment of New Infrastructure

367. Special treatment of major new infrastructure, i.e. the interconnection pipeline, LNG and storage facility is reflected in the fact that it may, upon request, be temporarily exempted from the provisions of Articles 182 through 186 (ownership unbundling), 238 (principle of regulated access to the system), 242 (transmission contracts), 246 (specific provision for LNG systems, upstream pipeline networks and storage facilities), and Articles 250 through 257 (regulatory framework) EA-1. Such an exemption can be granted when the following conditions are met:

- the investment must enhance competition in gas supply and enhance the security of supply;
- the level of risk attached to the investment must be such that the investment would not take place if an exemption were not granted;
- the infrastructure must be owned by a natural or legal person which is separate at least in terms of its legal form from the gas system operators in whose systems said infrastructure will be built;
- charges must be levied on users of said infrastructure; and
- the exemption must not be detrimental to competition on relevant markets on which investment will most likely affect in one way or another, nor to the effective functioning of the internal market in natural gas, nor to the efficient functioning of the gas systems to which the infrastructure is connected, nor to security of supply with natural gas in the EU.[453]

368. The granting of the exemption covering all or part of the capacity of the new infrastructure, or of the existing infrastructure with significantly increased capacity shall be decided by the Agency at the request of the infrastructure owner or the investor. As of its receipt, the Agency shall transmit to the European Commission a copy or the request for exemption, as well as inform it of the outcome, as explained below. Before the Agency can take a decision, it has to consult national regulatory authorities of relevant countries (Member States or third countries). In case regulators of those countries are not responsive and do not reply in three months, the Agency can take the decision.

453. Article 261 EA-1.

369. In deciding to grant an exemption, consideration shall be given to the need to impose conditions regarding the duration of the exemption and non-discriminatory access to the infrastructure. The Agency shall take into account in particular the additional capacity to be built or the modification of existing capacity, the time horizon of the project and national circumstances in relation to gas supply.

370. The Agency shall decide on a request for exemption within six months of receiving the request, except in cases when decision-making on the new infrastructure is being carried out in several Member States.[454] The Agency shall publish the decision on exemption on its webpage no later than one month after the approval by the European Commission. The Agency shall immediately inform the Commission of the provisions of the preceding Article and submit information providing detailed reasons on the basis of which the Agency granted or refused the exemption, including the financial information justifying the need for the exemption; the analysis undertaken of the effect on competition and the effective functioning of the internal market in natural gas; the reasons for the time period and the share of the total capacity of the gas infrastructure in question for which the exemption is granted; if the exemption relates to an interconnector, the result of the consultations with the regulatory authorities of neighbouring countries; the contribution of the infrastructure to the diversification of natural gas supplies. Notwithstanding the provisions of the act governing the general administrative procedure, the Agency shall ex officio repeat the procedure for issuing the decision granting the exemption after receiving the decision by the European Commission requesting that the decision granting the exemption be amended or annulled. In a repeated procedure, the Agency shall issue the decision without a special fact-finding procedure, but shall give the party the opportunity to make a statement on the facts and circumstances relevant to making a decision. On the basis of data collected in the repeated procedure, the Agency shall abrogate or annul the decision granting exemption in accordance with the European Commission decision within one month of receiving the Commission's decision, and notify the European Commission thereof. A decision granting an exception approved by the European Commission shall lose its effect two years from the Commission's approval of the Agency's decision in the event that construction of the infrastructure has not yet started, and five years from its adoption in the event that the infrastructure has not become operational, unless the Commission decides that any delay is due to major obstacles beyond the control of the person to whom the exemption was granted.[455]

454. If the new infrastructure is located in several Member States, the Act provides that when all the regulatory authorities of the 'involved' Member States agree on a request for exemption within six months, they notify ACER thereof. The Agency shall not perform any tasks in connection with the granting of an exception when the regulatory authorities referred to in the first paragraph of this Article fail to agree within a period of six months from the date on which the request for exemption was received by the last of the aforementioned regulatory authorities, or upon a joint request from the regulatory authorities referred to in the preceding paragraph to perform tasks in connection to granting exemption by ACER (Art. 265 EA-1).

455. *See* Arts 263 in 264 EA-1.

§5. SELECT ISSUES

I. Development of the (Transmission) Network

371. Within nine months of the adoption of the national energy development plan, the TSO and DSOs must draw up development plans for the system, subject to the approval of the minister responsible for energy.[456] Development plans should be formulated for at least ten years, and be in accordance with the national energy development plan, and should be adopted every two years.

372. Notwithstanding the above, the TSO must draw up a ten-year network development plan: after consulting with all the relevant interested parties, by 1 June each year it adopts a ten-year network development plan[457] and submits it to the Agency, which decides whether to approve it.[458] For the first three years of the plan, the TSO must also enclose an investment plan.

II. Storage System Operators and LNG System Operators

373. The owner(s) of a storage system or an LNG system is/are obliged to designate at least one storage system operator or LNG system operator before commencing operation.[459] Storage system operators and LNG system operators are required to operate with safe, reliable and efficient transmission and storage equipment or LNG plants, to maintain and develop their equipment with regard to the economic situation and having regard for environmental protection, and to make use of appropriate methods to perform the obligations of their services. These operators may not discriminate against system users or types of system user, and in particular may not favour their affiliates, and must forward information to the TSO, other storage system operators, other LNG operators or the DSO to ensure the transmission

456. The development plan should define the principal infrastructure for the transmission of natural gas (and electricity) and for the distribution of electricity that needs to be built or upgraded in the next ten years for the reliable supply of natural gas (and electricity), the safe operation of networks (and adaptation to further evolution in the production of electricity from renewables), in the context of the introduction of intelligent network services and the provision of storage facilities. In so doing it should proceed from forecasts of natural gas (or energy and power) received, and from forecasts of coverage of natural gas (or energy and power) received. The development plan should contain an assessment of the possibility of increasing the energy efficiency of gas (and electricity) infrastructure by means of load balancing and interoperability, connectivity with energy production plants, including micro-production, and should set out a timetable and a financial evaluation of the planned investments and actual measures to make cost-effectiveness improvements in network infrastructure; *see* Art. 30 EA-1.

457. The mandatory content of the plan is set out by Art. 200 EA-1.

458. If approval is granted, the Agency must then monitor and assess the implementation of the plan, taking measures as appropriate in accordance with Arts 201 and 203 EA-1.

459. The period for which a storage system operator or an LNG system operator is designated is stipulated by the Agency at the request of the owner(s) of the storage system or LNG system via a ruling, taking account of an assessment of efficiency and economic balance; *see* Art. 211 EA-1.

and storage of natural gas in a manner compatible with the safe and effective operation of connected systems. In addition, they must provide users with the information that they require for effective access to the system.[460]

374. Here the separation of storage system operators should also be noted. A storage system operator whose facilities are technically or economically vital to ensuring effective access to the system for reason of supply to consumers and that is part of a vertically integrated undertaking must be independent of other activities that are unrelated to transmission, distribution and storage, particularly with regard to formal legal status, organization and decision-making. A storage system operator must ensure that the following measures at least are taken to ensure its independence in organization and operation:

– the persons responsible for managing the storage system operator may not participate in the governing bodies of an integrated gas undertaking that are directly or indirectly responsible for the day-to-day production and supply of natural gas;
– the professional interests of the persons responsible for managing the storage system operator must be taken into account in a manner that allows them independence of action;
– the storage system operator must have the right to decide, independently of an integrated gas undertaking, on the resources required for operating, maintaining and developing storage facilities.[461]

III. Data Protection

375. As was outlined in the section on electricity,[462] data protection and the prevention of data misuse is also important in the gas sector, and is regulated by law. The TSO, storage system operators, LNG system operators and the owner of the transmission system are obliged to safeguard the confidentiality of sensitive data obtained during the pursuit of their business activities, irrespective of whether it is classed as a trade secret. They are obliged to prevent the discriminatory disclosure of commercially advantageous information about their own activities; in particular they may not disclose commercially sensitive information to other parts of the undertaking that are not engaged in TSO activities, or storage system operator activities or LNG system operator activities, except where and to the extent that this is strictly necessary to execute a legal transaction.[463] This does not prejudice the duty to disclose information for the needs of the exercise of public powers.

376. The aforementioned persons may not in any case misuse commercially sensitive information obtained from third parties in the context of providing or negotiating access to the system. The law also stipulates that they are obliged to publish

460. *See* Art. 212 EA-1.
461. For more, *see* Art. 213(3–5) EA-1.
462. *See* Arts 76 and 77, and 157 a–157 č EZ-1.
463. Here, there is also a prohibition on joint departments and the use of shared workers.

the information necessary for effective competition and the successful functioning of the market, with the exception of the commercially sensitive information as defined earlier in this text.[464]

IV. International Treaties

377. International treaties concerning natural gas shall be concluded according to the Act on External Affairs[465] and to Article 281a EA-1.[466] The ministry competent for energy shall inform the European Commission about the country's intention to negotiate with a third country about the international treaty concerning natural gas at least five months before the start of the negotiations, and it asks the European Commission for confirmation in case the treaty in question fully or partly relates to: common rules on transmission, distribution, supply and storage of natural gas; organization and operation of natural gas sector; access to market; and criteria and procedures which apply for decision regarding approval for transmission, distribution, supply, storage and the operation of the systems. Slovenia can continue with negotiations only after it receives approval from the European Commission. Moreover, the country has to respect all guidelines and demands of the European Commission when negotiating with third country. During the negotiations, the country informs the European Commission of the progress and also about the outcome of the negotiations. In this regard, it provides the European Commission with the draft agreement which must be approved by the European Commission. After the country receives the approval, it can continue with actions needed for conclusion and ratification of the international agreement. Of course, the same logic applies in case of modification of any such international agreement concerning natural gas.[467] The provision in question reveals decisive power of the European Commission in the field of international agreements of Member States with third countries. In other words, Member States depend on EU approval. This way the EU can effectively avoid disturbances made by bilateral agreements.

378. Let us point out again that the Agreement between the Government of the Republic of Slovenia and the Government of the Russian Federation on Cooperation in Construction and Operation of the Gas Pipeline on the Territory of the Republic of Slovenia[468] shall be modified according to the discussed provision, i.e. Article 281a EA-1.

464. *See* Art. 215 EA-1.
465. Official Gazette of the Republic of Slovenia, No. 113/03 – official consolidated version, 20/06 – ZNOMCMO, 76/08, 108/09, 80/10 – ZUTD, 31/15 and 30/18 – ZKZaš.
466. Article 281a EA-1 is new provision introduced by the EA-1C in 2020.
467. Article 281a(9) EA-1.
468. Official Gazette of the Republic of Slovenia (International Treaties), Nos 4/10 and 14/12.

Chapter 5. Distribution of Natural Gas

379. This chapter discusses the transport of natural gas through the distribution network or system. First the term distribution system is defined; this is followed by an overview of the fundamental characteristics of specific public law obligations relating to conducting activities as a DSO which is deemed a public utility. The chapter then discusses the unbundling (separation) of the activity of the DSO from other activities in the natural gas sector, and discusses the closed distribution system, as well as select questions relating to the access to the natural gas distribution system.

§1. Concept of the Distribution System and Related Concepts

380. Although the term distribution system is not explicitly defined in the new EA, its contents can be inferred from the legal definitions of other terms, such as: distribution, system and (distribution) system operator.

381. Distribution means the transport of natural gas through local or regional pipeline networks with a view to its delivery to customers, but not including supply.[469]

382. System means distribution networks, LNG facilities and/or storage facilities owned or operated by a natural gas undertaking, including linepack and its facilities supplying ancillary services and those of related undertakings needed to provide access to transmission, distribution and LNG.[470]

383. DSO means a natural or legal person who carries out the function of distribution and is responsible for operating, ensuring the maintenance of, and, if necessary, developing the distribution system in a given area and, where applicable, its interconnections with other systems, and for ensuring the long-term ability of the system to meet reasonable demands for the distribution of gas.[471]

384. As follows from the legal definitions of the aforementioned terms and considering the legislation of the EU, a distribution system can be defined as special installations, plants and networks operated, maintained and, if necessary, developed by a DSO, in order to enable the transport of natural gas on low-pressure pipelines (namely, at 16 bars or less) with a view to its delivery to customers.

469. Article 159(6) EA-1.
470. Article 159(48) EA-1.
471. The EA-1 does not contain an explicit definition of gas distribution system operator, however, it contains numerous provisions accordant with Art. 2(6) of Directive 2009/73/EC.

§2. PUBLIC SERVICES OBLIGATIONS ATTACHED TO THE DISTRIBUTION SYSTEM

385. As already said for the transmission system, in principle, the distribution system acts as a buffer between the producers of natural gas (or the TSO) on the one hand and customers on the other. It is thus one of the integral links in the chain of the gas industry, which has a significant impact on the supply of natural gas in Slovenia, which is an indication of the general (public) interest in this respect. This is most clearly evident in the concept of a service of general economic interest, with respect to which the legislator has prescribed that the activity of a TSO is only an optional local service of general economic interest, while the activity of a TSO is an obligatory national service of general economic interest. It follows from the above that, first, local communities have a decisive role in organizing the aforementioned services of general economic interest, which can organize such an activity on their entire territory or on a part thereof, and that second, market-oriented (local) distribution is possible in accordance with the applicable regulations in the Republic of Slovenia. However, even though distribution does not represent a service of general economic interest, the activity is not entirely free of any regulation since the EA-1 provides that all natural gas undertakings shall, in the public interest, perform tasks relating to the security, regularity, quality and price of supply, and environmental protection, including energy efficiency, energy from renewable sources and climate protection. The Act (as *lex specialis*) also provides for the following additional public service obligations of a company performing services of general economic interest as DSO:

- safe, secure and efficient operation and maintenance of the distribution system under acceptable economic conditions, with due regard for the environment and energy efficiency;
- development of the distribution system, while also taking into account the anticipated needs of system users and the requirements concerning safe and reliable system operation;
- long-term ability of the distribution system to meet reasonable demands for connection and access to the system;
- security of natural gas supply through adequate capacity and network reliability;
- provision of necessary information to system users to enable them to effectively exercise the right to access the system and its use.[472]

386. The functions of a gas DSO may be carried out by a legal or natural person which:

- has the right to perform the service of general economic interest;
- is the owner or leaseholder of a distribution system allowed to operate in accordance with the relevant regulations;[473] and

472. *See* Art. 216 EA-1 (compare Art, 160 EA-1, which generally, as *lex generalis*, defines the obligations of natural gas undertakings carrying out a service of general economic interest).

473. When the gas distribution system operator is neither the owner of the system nor a part thereof, the gas distribution system operator and the owner shall conclude a contract regulating all the issues

– has been designated as a gas DSO.[474]

387. As already mentioned, the local community has a key role in this respect. The gas DSO's service of general economic interest may be provided by a local community within a part or throughout its territory, in any case in the manner stipulated by the act governing services of general economic interest, and the act governing public-private partnerships. It is, e.g., important to note that an exclusive right can be granted for a period of thirty-five years, which allows the holder of this right to, in the relevant area covered by the right, be the exclusive provider of system access to end users and prevent all other companies from providing system access in the relevant area (however, the above-mentioned does not apply to a closed distribution system).[475]At the same time, in the organization and implementation of the public service, the local community has to take into account various other rules, including the rules of the EU which also include very restrictive rules on state aid, which, in practice, the public authorities grant to undertakings in order to protect the general or public interest. With respect to the funding of the gas DSO's service of general economic interest, the Act provides generally that the gas DSO activity shall be funded from network charges and other revenue for the provision of the service of general economic interest.[476]

388. The distribution system shall, as a rule, have at least one connection to the transmission system. The distribution system may be connected to another distribution system only on the basis of the prior approval of the Agency when this involves

---

regarding the use of the network concerned, in order for the gas distribution system operator to perform the tasks of a gas distribution system operator.

474. A person meeting the statutory conditions shall, on its own request, be designated by way of a decision of the Agency as a gas distribution system operator. In setting the period for which the gas distribution system operator is to be designated, the Agency shall take into account the efficiency and economic balance assessment, whereby such a period if the concession is granted, shall be equal to the duration of the concession. The longest period for which the Agency may designate a relevant gas distribution system operator shall be thirty-five years. The Agency shall annul the Act on the designation of a gas distribution system operator if it determines that any of the conditions has not been met, and when any such condition cannot be expected to be met within a reasonable time, and when the gas distribution system operator violates certain obligations. In such circumstances the Agency designates a gas distribution system operator in the Republic of Slovenia or any other European Union Member State to temporarily undertake the functions of the gas distribution system operator in the distribution system and lays down the conditions under which the owner or co-owners shall be obliged to lease the distribution system for use to the gas distribution system operator envisaged to undertake the activities and the time limit for complying with this obligation. If the owner or co-owners of the distribution system fail to ensure, within one year of the final decision referred to above, that the functions of the gas distribution system operator are resumed in their distribution system by the gas distribution system operator which meets the statutory requirements, the local community as beneficiary of the expropriation, shall initiate the expropriation procedure or procedure to restrict ownership rights. *See* Arts 219 and 220 EA-1.

475. Closed distribution system means a distribution system in the local community that is separated from the distribution system intended for the distribution of natural gas within a geographically confined industrial, commercial or shared services site and, as a rule, does not supply household customers in this area and is directly connected to the transmission system through an exit point. *See* Art. 159(63) EA-1.

476. *See* Art. 217 EA-1.

the same gas DSO. In issuing the approval, the Agency shall take into account the ten-year gas network development plan and the distribution network development plan, and shall give its approval provided that the interconnecting distribution system is reasonable in terms of costs and development, and adequate safety and reliability of operation of all relevant distribution systems have been provided for.[477]

§3. Legal Unbundling

389. A distribution network operator can be vertically integrated as the law does not require separation in terms of ownership unbundling, although it must be independent from other activities not relating to distribution, at least as regards its legal form, organization and decision-making.[478] That said, the aforementioned does not preclude the operation of a combined transmission, LNG, storage and DSO, provided it meets the ownership unbundling requirements as specified for the activity of gas transmission (*see* Part II, Chapter 4 §3).

390. Since the Act does not provide for ownership unbundling even though this is the most effective measure for preventing the distortion of competition on upstream and downstream markets, the Act attempts to compensate for this shortcoming (in addition to the aforementioned legal unbundling) with the explicit requirement that the vertically integrated natural gas DSO shall refrain from discriminating between individual system users or types of users, particularly in favour of its related undertakings, while natural gas DSOs shall not, in their communication or branding, create confusion in respect of the separate identity of the supply branch of the vertically integrated undertaking. In addition, the Act also envisages strict monitoring performed by the Agency.

§4. Closed Distribution Systems

391. A natural gas distribution system with a single network supply point directly connected to the transmission system distributing natural gas within a geographically confined industrial, commercial or shared services site, and as a rule not supplying household customers, shall obtain the status of a closed distribution system subject to the Agency's approval, if:

- due to specific technical or safety reasons, the operations or the production process of the final customer of that system are integrated; or

477. *See* Art. 216(6) in 216(7) EA-1.

478. In practice, however, even this kind of separation is rather relativized, as the Act provides that the aforementioned separation or legal unbundling obligation does not apply to natural gas undertakings to which fewer than 100,000 end customers are connected.

- the network distributes natural gas primarily to the owner or operator of the system or their related undertakings (this requirement shall be considered as satisfied when the owner and its related undertakings make at least 80% of the total yearly natural gas consumption).

392. Closed distribution systems are not organized as a service of public economic interest mainly due to their individual aim to service individual companies (rather than household customers).[479]

393. According to our information, in the Republic of Slovenia there are no closed distribution systems of natural gas at the moment, since all proceedings are still pending; however, at the end of the day, we do not expect a great number of such systems (not only because of factual reasons but also because of the (too) narrow or at least ambiguous wording of certain legislative provisions). Issues relating to the approval for obtaining the status of closed distribution system and the cessation of this status, and other issues related to the closed distribution system of natural gas are regulated in Articles 226–233 EA-1.

§5. Access to the Natural Gas Distribution System

394. In the EA-1, access to the distribution system is regulated through general and specific rules. The general rules governing access to the natural gas transmission and distribution system, including network charges, have already been presented in the chapter discussing the transmission of natural gas (*see* Part II, Chapter 4 §4). Therefore we only focus on those special rules on access to the distribution system provided for in Articles 247–249 EA-1.

395. The gas DSO shall ensure access to the transmission system at the transmission system exit points where the transmission system is connected to the distribution system on which it functions as DSO to all distribution system users (persons other than the DSO may not by themselves gain direct access).

396. Connection to the distribution system gives the final customer access to the system in compliance with the connection conditions, the Network Code and the contract on access. The final consumer may conclude a contract on access for a capacity that is lower than the technical capacity of the connection. The final consumer may authorize the natural gas supplier to conclude a contract on access to the distribution system with the gas DSO on behalf of, and for the account of, the final consumer.

---

479. However this does not apply absolutely to household users since the Act provides that incidental use by a small number of households having an employment or other relationship with the owner of the system shall not preclude the electricity distribution system from obtaining the status of a closed distribution system. *See* Art. 227(2) EA-1.

397. The gas supplier can issue a single bill for natural gas supplied and for the use of the system. The gas DSO shall allow the supplier to issue a single bill for natural gas supplied and for the use of the system for those consumptions points for which the supplier obtained approval by the final customer.[480]

480. The gas distribution system operator and the supplier shall conclude an agreement on the single bill to be issued by the supplier in compliance with the form published by the Agency on its website within one month following the receipt of the supplier's request for the conclusion of such agreement. The operator may refuse to conclude the agreement or may withdraw from the agreement on the single bill if the supplier fails to provide appropriate insurance to cover the assumed liability. The Agency defines parameters for appropriate ensurance in modes of ensurance; *see* Art. 249(2) and (3) EA-1.

Chapter 6. Consumption of Gas

398. This chapter deals with the consumption of gas and thus mainly highlights the general protection of (final) natural gas customers, the special protection of certain groups of customers, including the most vulnerable natural gas customers, and ensuring the reliability of natural gas supply.

§1. General Protection of Natural Gas Customers

399. At the outset, we would like to highlight the fact that the EA-1 defines various groups of natural gas customers (defining different regimes applicable to such customers), as follows:

- customer means a wholesale or final customer of natural gas or a natural gas undertaking which purchases natural gas;[481]
- final customer means a customer purchasing natural gas for his own use with a concluded gas supply contract;[482]
- non-household customer means a customer purchasing natural gas which is not for his own household use;[483]
- household customer means a customer purchasing natural gas for his own household consumption, excluding consumption for performing commercial or professional activities;[484]
- vulnerable customer means a household customer that, due to financial circumstances, income and other social circumstances and living conditions, is unable to provide itself with an alternative source of energy for heating that would incur the same or lower costs for residential heating space;[485]
- small business customer means a non-household natural gas customer whose estimated average annual consumption does not exceed 10,000 sm^3;[486]
- wholesale customer means a natural or legal person, other than a gas TSO or a gas DSO, that purchases natural gas for the purpose of resale inside or outside the system in which he is established;[487]
- eligible customer means a customer who is free to purchase gas from a supplier of his own choice.[488]

400. This section deals with the general protection of (final) customers as provided for in Articles 161–165 EA-1, while the special protection of vulnerable customers and household customers in general, as well as the protection of small business customers, is dealt with in the next section in this chapter. Before going

481. Article 159(28) EA-1.
482. Article 159(15) EA-1.
483. Article 159(19) EA-1.
484. Article 4(13) EA-1.
485. Article 159(43) EA-1.
486. Article 159(16) EA-1.
487. Article 159(55) EA-1.
488. Article 159(57) EA-1.

into further detail, we would like to highlight that Article 161 EA-1, which deals with the right to conclude an agreement with a natural gas supplier, refers to customers in general,[489] while Articles 162–165 EA refer to final customers.[490]

401. The EA-1 enables natural gas customers connected to the transmission or distribution system to have their gas provided by a supplier pursuant to the relevant agreement, regardless of the EU Member State in which the supplier is registered.[491] In other words, a customer in the Republic of Slovenia, who fulfils the above condition, shall have the right to conclude a natural gas supply agreement with any supplier from the EU who fulfils the legal requirements for supplying natural gas in the Republic of Slovenia. Accordingly, interested supplies from the EU should be given access to Slovenian natural gas customers regardless of their place of registration.

402. The free choice of one's supplier is not exhausted once the natural gas supply contract is concluded, but is preserved even after. The Act allows the final customer to change his choice of supplier or subsequently chose a new supplier after initially selecting his supplier. In principle, a final customer can freely change suppliers, which actually increases the competitive pressure on suppliers and thus enhances market efficiency. In light of this, the final customer must not only be legally able to change suppliers, but such a change should also be quick, effective and free-of-charge. In principle, all a final customer who wishes to switch suppliers needs to do is communicate a request for the change to the system operator of the system to which the customer is connected. Alternatively, the new supplier may communicate the request on behalf of, and for the account of, the final customer on the basis of an authorization.

403. Final customers are also protected through free and periodic information on their actual natural gas consumption, the characteristics of such consumption and on efficient use of energy, with sufficient frequency to enable them to regulate their own natural gas consumption.

404. A special form of protecting final customers (even though this measure is also aimed at fulfilling other energy goals) is also the obligation of natural gas undertakings to ensure maximum energy efficiency by optimizing, in accordance with the Agency's recommendations, the use of natural gas, especially by providing energy use management services, developing innovative pricing formulas and introducing intelligent metering systems or networks when appropriate. Finally, the Act

489. In contrast to the comparable provision (Art. 39 EA-1) that applies to the electricity industry.
490. Consumer protection regulations apply in the absence of specific regulations (at least to a certain degree) to questions relating to the protection of final customers not dealt with in the EA-1 or another specific law, especially when dealing with household customers.
491. Prior to connection to the system, the natural gas distribution system operator shall notify the customer connected to the system in the Republic of Slovenia of his or her rights and obligations in connection with the choice of supplier and in connection with the emergency supply, in accordance with the Act. If such a supply agreement is concluded, it is always interpreted according to Slovenian law, regardless of where the agreement was concluded. Article 161 EA-1.

also provides as a benefit to final customers that natural gas suppliers shall be obliged to send to all of their final customers an energy checklist established by the European Commission on the basis of the twelfth paragraph of Article 3 of Directive 2009/73/EC […], including the instructions for its use.

§2. Special Protection of Certain Groups of Final Customers

405. The EA-1 provides special protection of certain groups of final customers, namely household customers (consumers in the narrow sense of the term) and especially those household customers who are especially vulnerable, as well as small business customers. These groups of final customers are subject to special benefits ensured by the supplier or DSO. Of course, both may decide to provide these benefits to other final customers, subject to them observing the principle of equal treatment.

406. The EA-1 thus explicitly provides in Articles from 170 to 176 that household customers must be ensured:

- a single point of access to information on their rights, valid regulations and general acts for the exercise of public authority and the methods for handling complaints;
- special mandatory protective provisions concerning the supply contract, including the general terms and conditions;
- notification and access to data on their consumption;
- intelligent metering systems;[492]
- a transparent, simple and inexpensive out-of-court procedure for handling complaints.[493]

407. In addition to all the above benefits, the Act additionally provides that the vulnerable household customers are provided protection against their natural gas supply being cut-off or restricted, if, in view of the circumstances (season, temperatures, place of residence, health condition and other similar circumstances) such an action could jeopardize the life and health of the vulnerable household customer and persons living in his household. The costs of such emergency supply, which is deemed part of the universal service, shall be eligible costs of the operator.

408. The EA-1 provides the following benefits to small business customers:

- single point of contact;
- special mandatory protective provisions concerning the supply contract, including the general terms and conditions;

492. This should actually be provided to all system users.
493. This kind of disputes, i.e. disputes between the household user (consumer) and supplier, shall not be confused with the disputes with the operator as regulated in Art. 413 EA-1. Namely, the latter are not settled by alternative dispute resolution institutions but rather by the Agency.

– intelligent metering systems.

§3. Ensuring the Security of Natural Gas Supply

409. Reliable supply of natural gas is ensured pursuant to Regulation (EU) 2017/1938 of the European Parliament and of the Council of 25 October 2017 concerning measures to safeguard the security of gas supply and repealing Regulation (EU) No 994/2010.[494] In the Republic of Slovenia, the sector regulator – the Energy Agency – is responsible for this area, while the state must cooperate with other Member States of the EU in order to ensure reliable supply of natural gas. In fact, the EA-1 introduced the concept of solidarity aid or cooperation between Member States according to Regulation 2017/1938.[495]

410. The reliable supply of natural gas is ensured through preventive and curative measures. Preventive measures include the obligation of a supplier that supplied natural gas to final customers in the Republic of Slovenia to ensure that the supply of natural gas in the current calendar year is provided from at least two different sources of supply, on the condition that the largest supply source does not exceed 70% of the volumes supplied by the same provider for final customers in the Republic of Slovenia. However, the obligation of gas system operators to, if due to the scope and duration of exceptional circumstances or other circumstances that endanger the security of natural gas supply and/or for a longer period cause a serious supply disruption in the Republic of Slovenia, and suppliers are unable to ensure a supply of natural gas to protected customers in sufficient volumes by means of the measures set out in the Emergency Plan, take all steps to enable customers transmission and distribution for the supply of natural gas within the framework of safe operation of natural gas network, can be considered a curative measure. If, due to the scope and duration of exceptional circumstances, the aforementioned emergency measures cannot ensure a secure supply of natural gas to protected customers, gas system operators shall – regardless of their contractual obligations to their suppliers, users and customers under the Emergency Plan – reduce or interrupt the consumption of natural gas at consumption points of individual types of customers or their appliances. The sequence of reducing or interrupting the consumption of natural gas to types of customers and their appliances shall be laid down by the Agency in the Emergency Plan, taking into consideration the manner of use of natural gas by individual types of customers, the need to consume natural gas with the aim of ensuring the life and health of people, and the type and scope of damage which may be caused to individual types of customers by a reduction or interruption in the consumption of natural gas.[496] In short, in such circumstances, protected customers enjoy a privileged position compared to other customers.

494. Official Journal of the European Union, L 280, 28.10.2017, 1.
495. *See* Art. 169(10), (11) and (12) EA-1.
496. *See* Art. 169 EA-1.

411. As already said, all the measures discussed above are regulated in favour of the so-called protected customers, i.e. household customers connected to a gas distribution system, distributors of heat for remote heating,[497] as well as essential social services connected[498] to a gas distribution or transmission system (except education institutions and public administration offices).[499]

497. In case they cannot use nothing else as natural gas and supply household users and social services (except education institutions and public administration); *see* Art. 168(1) EA-1.

498. The essential social services referred to in the preceding paragraph shall be providers of:

- health care services, including rehabilitation and care;
- educational and care activities;
- educational activities, including student residence halls and university libraries;
- social welfare services; *see* Art. 168 EA-1.

499. The essential social services are defined in Art. 168(2) EA-1.

Part III. Regulatory Framework Concerning Petrol and Coal

412. The purpose of Part III of this monograph is the presentation of regulation and basic characteristics in the area of petrol and coal in the Republic of Slovenia.

413. Chapter 1 provides a general overview of the consumption of oil and coal in Slovenia compared to other shares of energy sources in gross inland consumption and based on electricity production. Chapter 1 also describes the energy policy on petrol and coal in Slovenia. Considering all aspects of the energy policy, reference is also made to Part I, Chapter 1 §1 Electricity Sector in the Republic of Slovenia and Part II, Chapter 1 §2 Slovenia's Natural Gas Sector Policy. The relevant regulations for the area of petrol and coal are included in individual chapters of this part.

414. Chapter 2 of this part merely points out the key issues related to petrol and coal in Slovenia in connection with the production of these two energy sources.

415. Chapter 3 merely refers to the relevant chapters of the monograph in which the topic is described.

416. Chapter 4 describes the method of transport and regulation of petrol and petroleum products in Slovenia. Regarding the transmission of electricity generated from coal, reference is made to the relevant part of the monograph in which the topic is discussed.

417. Chapter 5 describes the method of petrol distribution in Slovenia and the pricing of petroleum products. Regarding the distribution of electricity generated from coal, reference is made to the relevant part of the monograph in Part I.

418. Chapter 6 describes the method of providing the minimum reserves of petrol and petroleum products in Slovenia to prevent shortages. Regarding the use of electricity generated from coal, reference is made to the relevant part of the monograph in Part I.

Chapter 1. General Introduction

419. This chapter provides a general overview of the consumption of oil and coal in Slovenia compared to other shares of energy sources in gross inland consumption. Chapter 1 also describes the energy policy on petrol and coal. Considering all aspects of the energy policy, reference is also made to Part I, Chapter 1 §1 Electricity Sector in the Republic of Slovenia and Part II, Chapter 1 §2 Slovenia's Natural Gas Sector Policy. The relevant regulations for the area of petrol and coal are included in individual chapters and sections of this part.

420. As already pointed out, the share of petroleum products in the structure of final energy consumption stands out with a share of 46.6%, followed by electricity (23.5%), RES (12.6%), natural gas (11.9%), heat (3.6%), solid fuels (0.8%) and non-renewable industrial waste (1.0%).[500] Since Slovenia essentially depends on the import of petroleum products and natural gas,[501] whose share exceeds half of final energy consumption, it is only logical that the country depends on the import of energy. The country's energy import dependence in 2019 amounts 49.2%.[502,503] A comparison with the situation in 2012 reveals some changes, meaning that the above-mentioned structure is dynamic.[504]

500. *See* Energy Balance of the Republic of Slovenija for the year 2019 [Energetska bilanca Republike Slovenije za leto 2019], Republic of Slovenia, Ministry of Infrastructure, 2019, p. 7.
501. In 2019, almost all natural gas and petroleum products were imported; *see* Energy Balance of the Republic of Slovenija for the year 2019 [Energetska bilanca Republike Slovenije za leto 2019], Republic of Slovenia, Ministry of Infrastructure, 2019, p. 13.
502. *See* Energy Balance of the Republic of Slovenija for the year 2019 [Energetska bilanca Republike Slovenije za leto 2019], Republic of Slovenia, Ministry of Infrastructure, 2019, p. 12.
503. In order to get a broader picture about the Slovenia's dependence on imported energy, the following data shall be considered: 47% in 2018; 48% in 2017; 46% in 2016; 48% in 2015; 44% in 2014; 46.9% in 2013; 50.9% in 2012; 47.5% in 2011; 48.7% in 2010; 47.5% in 2009; 54.8% in 2008; 52.0% in 2007; 51.4% in 2006; 51.8% in 2005; 51.3% in 2004; 52.6% in 2003; 49.7 in 2002. Moreover, it shall be pointed out that oil (petroleum) was fully imported while almost all natural gas was imported.
504. The TPES – Total Primary Energy Supply or GIC – Gross Inland Consumption structure was dominated by the share of petroleum products (35.1%), followed by nuclear energy (20.7%), solid fuels (19.8%) and natural gas (10.2%) in Slovenia in 2012. Also in 2014, the share of petroleum products was the highest in the structure of FEC – Final Energy Consumption of the Energy Balance, namely 45.9%. The final consumption of petroleum products dropped by 3.6% compared to 2013; the bulk of petroleum products is consumed in the transport sector (83.8%). A total of 2,396 kt of petroleum products were needed in TPES of petroleum products in Slovenia in 2012, which was 2.1% less than in 2011; there was no domestic production. The final petroleum products consumption dropped by the same percentage in Slovenia in 2012. Final consumption dropped in all sectors but transport, where it increased by 1.1%. Nevertheless, a decrease was noted in the consumption of unleaded gas which was negative in the 2007–2013 period, dropping by the average of 3.2% per year. The consumption of diesel fuel has been on the increase since 2009. Its average growth in the transport sector in the 2007–2012 period was 4.1%. If we exclude the railway segment using electricity as the source of energy, the transport sector is fully dependent on imported petroleum products. In Slovenia, 40% of energy is used in the transport sector and practically the only source is imported petroleum products. With the new energy policy focusing on low-carbon society, the aim is to reduce the imports of fossil fuels and based on the new proposed Energy Concept from 2015, the goal is to halve the energy consumption of petroleum products by 2035 and to stop using fuel oil for heating, and then to stop using petroleum products for energy consumption in 2055. The

Chapter 2. Production

421. Chapter 2 of this part merely points out the key issues related to petrol and coal in Slovenia in connection with the production of these two energy sources. Energy infrastructure facilities in Slovenia used for petrol and coal extraction are principally categorized as mining facilities. It seems the construction of such facilities is not related to spatial planning of national significance any more. Namely, the repealed Siting of Spatial Arrangements of National Importance Act contained mining among spatial planning of national importance,[505] while the Spatial Planning Act in Article 50 does not include mining activities. Yet, this finding is relative since the said provision (paragraph 3) also leaves the door open for special acts (*lex specialis*), like, e.g., the ZRud-1 which, however, at the moment does not deal with this issue. Moreover, if mining is not included among spatial planning of national importance, it can be then considered as a spatial planning of local importance.

primary energy of solid fuels is being transformed into the secondary form of energy; electricity and heat in the energy converters, namely: power plants (production of electricity), power-heating plants (production of electricity and heat), heating plants (production of heat). The bulk of energy transformation is concentrated on electricity production with almost equal prevailing shares of solid and nuclear fuels used. The share of thermal power plants in electricity production dropped in 2014. The share of thermal power plants in the generation of electricity, which covered 98% of domestic demand, was 24.5%. In 2011 when the use of solid fuels still prevailed in the production of electricity available for consumption in Slovenia, as much as 33% of electricity was produced from this source. Of the nine companies on the Slovenian electricity production market in 2014 with production facilities of installed capacity above 10 MW, the Thermal Power Plant Šoštanj and the Thermal Power Plant Trbovlje generated electricity from coal (the latter was closed in September 2014 following the burning of the last stocks of coal), the Thermal Power Plant Brestanica generated electricity from liquid and gaseous fuels and the Public Utility Company Energetika Ljubljana produced heat and electricity in the cogeneration process, using coal. In the district heating production, the share of coal prevailed in 2014 (66.2%), while oil and petroleum products only accounted for 1.4%. In terms of final consumption, the consumption of solid fuels was only recorded in manufacturing and construction industries (in 2012, the share was 91%) and in non-energy consumption. According to the proposed Energy Concept striving for low-carbon society, the use of low-carbon sources of energy will be promoted in district heating systems. The use of the existing coal facilities in cogeneration of heat and electricity is no longer foreseen after 2035 or at the end of the useful life of the existing facilities, not even in highly efficient systems. Compare the following documents; RS, Ministry of Infrastructure, *Slovenia Energy 2012 in brief*, available at http://www.energetika-portal.si/fileadmin/dokumenti/publikacije/energija_slo/evs_2012_pb.pdf; the Energy Balance of the Republic of Slovenia for 2014, prepared by the Ministry of Infrastructure and Spatial Planning, 8; RS, Ministry of Infrastructure, Energy Directorate, Energy and Mining Department, Energy in Slovenia 2012, 22; Document for Public Debate, RS Ministry of Infrastructure, Proposed guidelines for the drafting of the energy concept of Slovenia, 2 Jun. 2015, 6–9; the document is available at https://www.energetika-portal.si/dokumenti/strateski-razvojni-dokumenti/; and the first edition of this monograph.

505. *See* Art. 2(2) of the Act regarding the setting of spatial arrangements of national significance in physical space (Official Gazette of the Republic of Slovenia No. 80/10, 106/10, 57/12 – ZUPUDPP).

§1. PETROL

422. It was described in Chapter 1 of this part that Slovenia is practically completely dependent on the import of petroleum products.[506] We have not had our own production and refinery facilities since Nafta Lendava stopped producing fuels years ago. In Slovenia, there is no political interest – considering the energy policy focused on low-carbon society, as described in Chapter 1 of this part – to continue researching the drills in Petišovci, Mura Depression, which supposedly has oil stocks; moreover, there is the issue of potential investors who would have to obtain the required environmental permit and consent that are subject to public approval, considering the fact that the local population is not particularly in favour of such activities. Pursuant to the Annex 1 to the Decree on the categories of activities for which an environmental impact assessment is mandatory,[507] the environmental impact assessment has to be always compiled for the facilities related to oil extraction,[508] refinery, storage[509] and transportation[510] (for more information on the procedures for obtaining the environmental approval (consent) and permit *see* Part IV, Chapter 2 Activities Affecting the Environment).

§2. COAL

423. In view of the weaknesses of coal as the source of energy, primarily the severe pollution of the environment with CO_2, the importance of coal is decreasing as a source of energy in Slovenia, as evident from the data specified in Chapter 1 of this part (regarding the regulatory framework concerning RES *see* Part IV, Chapter 3 §2 RES and Energy Efficiency).

424. The coal areas in Slovenia are: the Velenje basin, the Zasavje tertiary basin, the Krško-Brežice field and the north-eastern Slovenia. Before Slovenia became

506. Slovenia imports liquid fuels from many countries and we should be aware that the country of import is not necessarily the country of origin of the fuel, since it is subject to resale. In 2011 the bulk of liquid fuel was imported from Cyprus (34%), followed by Italy (18%) Austria (17%), Great Britain (13%), Hungary and Switzerland (4% each) and other countries with shares below 3% (*see* RS, Environmental Agency of the Ministry of the Environment and Spatial Planning Indicators of the Environment in Slovenia, EN25, Energy import dependency, available at http://kazalci.arso.gov.si/?data=indicator&ind_id=498).

507. Official Gazette of the Republic of Slovenia, Nos 51/2014, 57/15 and 26/17.

508. The environment impact assessment is always mandatory when extraction of petroleum (oil) does not exceed 500 t per day, while in case of smaller amount a preliminary procedure is needed in which a competent body checks if environment impact assessment is needed.

509. The environment impact assessment is always mandatory when the capacity of storage amounts 200,000 t while in case of smaller capacity, i.e. from 50,000 to 199,999 t, a preliminary procedure is needed in which a competent body checks if environment impact assessment is needed.

510. The environment impact assessment is always mandatory when the diameter of pipeline exceeds 800 mm and its length exceeds 40 km, while in case of shorter pipelines, i.e. from 1 km to 39.9 km, a preliminary procedure is needed in which a competent body checks if environment impact assessment is needed.

independent, it had several operational coal mines; after 1970, several medium-profitable coal mines have been closed. The biggest amount of brown coal and lignite was extracted in 1987, namely 6,846.400 t (75% of lignite and 25% of brown coal) in six coal mines. In addition to own production, we have also been importing lignite since 2006, but the figure is rather insignificant (2%) compared to own production.

425. The process of closing the coal mines has not yet been completed. The Trbovlje-Hrastnik Mine which has a 200-year tradition of coal extraction in Slovenia has been in the process of closure since 2000, based on the Act Regulating the Gradual Closure of the Trbovlje-Hrastnik Mine and the Economic Development Restructuring of the Region (ZPZRTH).[511] In 2014, the period of closure was extended until 2018, based on amended Act (it was originally planned to be closed by 2015), with the aim of lifting some burden from the annual national budget. In spite of that, the amount of closure works financing for the 2010–2018 period, i.e. the notified and approved amount of state aid totalling EUR 89,909,467, confirmed by the European Commission in the case 'State Aid N 175/2010 – Slovenia, Postponement of the closure of mine Trbovlje Hrastnik Ltd of 29/06/2011', will not change.[512] The law stipulates the closure works and the liquidation of the mine by the end of 2018. The new plan is to complete the closure of the mine facilities by the end of 2015 and to complete all the necessary works concerning the environmental and spatial rehabilitation of the surface, and resolve the issue of the remaining employees, in the 2016–2018 period.

426. After 2013, the only active coal producer in Slovenia has been the company Premogovnik Velenje, which is also scheduled to be gradually closed by 2054.[513] The new proposed Energy Concept foresees complete abolition of fossil fuels as a source of energy. In spite of that, it is still important to preserve the production of lignite in Premogovnik Velenje because of the diversification of energy sources, particularly for the production of electricity. The strategic reliability of energy supply is also important, above all due to extreme economic or political situation, since lignite, in addition to RES, is the only domestic source of energy (besides the insignificant production of gas). Premogovnik Velenje produces approx. 4,000 kt of coal per year. Premogovnik Velenje has not been selling coal for general consumption for a long time. In 2004, a long-term, ten-year agreement was signed with Holding Slovenske Elektrarne, and the sole buyer of lignite from Velenje is the thermal power plant Termoelektrarna Šoštanj which can use the coal in a relatively environmentally friendly manner for the production of electricity and heat. At this point, it is also worthy to point out the National Strategy for Decreased Use of Coal

511. Official Gazette of the Republic of Slovenia, No. 26/05 – official consolidated text, 43/10, 49/10 – amend., 40/12 – ZUJF, 25/14, 46/14 and 82/15.
512. The state aid was granted in accordance with the Council Decision of 10 Dec. 2010 on state aid to facilitate the closure of uncompetitive coal mines (2010/787/EU), OJ EU L 336/24, 21.12.2010.
513. *See* the Draft proposal of the National Energy Programme of the Republic of Slovenia for the period until 2030: 'Active Management of Energy', Ljubljana, 10 Jun. 2011, Jožef Stefan Institute, Energy Efficiency Centre (CEU), p. 105.

and for Restructuring of Coal Regions in Accordance with Principles of Fair Development. The preparation of the draft strategy is scheduled for September 2020, while the deadline for final version is still uncertain but it is reasonable to expect it in 2021.

Chapter 3. Exploitation

427. This chapter merely refers to the relevant chapters of the monograph in which the topic is described.

428. Petrol (crude petroleum, petroleum condensates) and coal (black, brown and lignite) are both categorized as mineral energy raw materials regulated by the ZRud-1, same as natural gas, which is why reference is made to Part II, Chapter 3 Exploitation for an explanation of conditions for potential obtaining of the concession for exploiting petrol and coal, the procedure for discontinuation of exploitation of each source and the permit for researching each energy source.

429. The data on consumption, quantity and future of these two resources in Slovenia is described in the previous two chapters (Chapter 1 and Chapter 2) of this part.

Chapter 4. Transport

430. This chapter describes the method of transport and regulation of petrol and petroleum products in Slovenia. Regarding the transmission of electricity generated from coal, reference is made to the relevant part of the monograph in which the topic is discussed.

§1. PETROL

431. As explained in the previous chapters of this part, Slovenia does not have its own facilities for petrol production and has to import it. It is therefore necessary to establish appropriate and safe regulation of transport through all lines (roads, railways and potential pipelines, should we ever decide to construct such facilities in Slovenia, which is doubtful in view of Slovenia's size and planned transition to the low-carbon society). Unless individual issues are otherwise regulated in specific laws, the provisions of the new EA-1 apply to petrol transport (*see* Article 6 EA-1). Pursuant to the new EA-1 (Item 40 of Article 159 EA-1), petrol production is categorized as upstream pipeline network, which means any pipeline or network of pipelines operated and/or constructed as part of an oil or gas production project. As the notion 'upstream pipeline network' explicitly includes nothing but 'petrol production' (in Slovenia, the only source of petrol is imported fuel), reference is made to the regulation according to EA-1, Part II, Chapter 3 Transport. While the gas pipeline system is being constantly upgraded in Slovenia and now covers almost 1,000 km, there is no oil pipeline (the construction of the Pan-European oil pipeline over the Karst to the sea was strongly opposed).

432. In Slovenia, the bulk of petrol and petroleum products is transported by road (supplying of service stations), railway and sea, which significantly increases the possibility of traffic accidents and natural disasters (spillage of hazardous materials into the underground water, destruction of material goods, etc.). Thus, all those involved in the transportation (sender, transporter and recipient) must be familiar with the legislation regulating the transportation of dangerous materials, which includes petrol transportation. This area is regulated by the Transport of Dangerous Goods Act (ZPNB)[514] which applies to all types of petrol transportation in Slovenia. The Act regulates the duties of the persons participating in the transportation, the conditions of packaging and vehicles, appointment of a security advisor, training of persons participating in the transportation, powers of national authorities and supervision over the implementation of the Act. This Act transposes the following directives of the European Communities into the legislation of the Republic of Slovenia: Directive 2008/68/EC of the European Parliament and of the Council of 24 September 2008 on the inland transport of dangerous goods[515] and Council Directive 95/50/EC of 6 October 1995 on uniform procedures for checks on the transport

---

514. Official Gazette of the Republic of Slovenia, No. 33/06 – official consolidated text, 41/09, 97/10 and 56/15.
515. Official Journal of the European Union, L 260, 30.9.2008, 13.

of dangerous goods by road as amended by Directive 2001/26/EC of the European Parliament and of the Council of 7 May 2001.[516]

433. Considering the absence of development of the oil pipeline network, Slovenia has not adopted any regulation on the safety of international, main and local transportation of petrol since gaining independence (including all liquid and gaseous hydrocarbons: crude oil, natural gas and products derived from them), which means that the laws from the former SFRY still apply. The law on the basic safety of oil and gas pipeline transmission[517] stipulates that oil pipelines must correspond to the technical standards and conditions stipulated by the technical regulations;[518] main pipelines must be equipped with appropriate communication network and facilities for safe and continuous transmission of messages regarding their maintenance and exploitation. There are also some limitations as to other facilities that can be constructed in their vicinity (electrical, telephone and other installations), as well limitations of access by unauthorized persons to the oil pipeline facilities and devices, and entry in the enclosed areas. Appropriate supervision must be ensured. In addition to technical regulations, safety during construction must also be considered by ensuring compliance with the relevant standards stipulated by the Explosive Substances, Flammable Fluids, Fumes and Other Dangerous Substances Act.[519]

434. Oil pipelines (and other pipelines with the diameter of at least 300 mm, if their total length is at least 1 km, with the relevant functional facilities; the storages of liquid fossil fuels with the capacity of 30,000 m^3 or more; the storages of LNG with the capacity of 10,000 m^3 or more)[520] and the construction of such facilities is considered spatial planning of national significance pursuant to the spatial legislation[521] (*see* the issues of all necessary permits related to spatial legislation for energy facilities, Part IV, Chapter 4 §1 Other Environmental Legislation Relevant

516. Official Journal of the European Union, L 168, 23.6.2001, 23.
517. Official Gazette of the SFRY, No. 67/73. This is an old Yugoslavian regulation which is still in use based on the Constitutional Act on Implementation of the Basic Constitutional Charter on the Independence and Sovereignty of the Republic of Slovenia (Official Gazette of the Republic of Slovenia, Nos 1/91-I, 45/94-I and 11/14 – amend.).
518. The Rules on the technical conditions and standards for safe transport of liquid and gaseous hydrocarbons through main oil and gas pipelines and international oil and gas pipelines (Official Gazette of the SFRY No. 26/85) and the Rules on specifications for the construction, operation and maintenance of pipelines of operating pressure over 16 bar (Official Gazette of the Republic of Slovenia Nos 60/01 and 26/02) must also be considered.
519. Official Gazette of the SRS, No. 18/77, Official Gazette of the Republic of Slovenia, No. 4/92, 96/02 – ZE, 101/05 – ZPNB-A and 83/12 – ZVPoz-D. This is an old Yugoslavian regulation which is still in use based on the Constitutional Act on Implementation of the Basic Constitutional Charter on the Independence and Sovereignty of the Republic of Slovenia (Official Gazette of the Republic of Slovenia, No. 1/91-I, 45/94-I and 11/14 – amend.).
520. Decree on the criteria and conditions for determining spatial arrangements of national significance (Official Gazette of the Republic of Slovenia, No. 103/2013).
521. *See* Art. 2(2) of the Act regarding the setting of spatial arrangements of national significance in physical space (Official Gazette of the Republic of Slovenia Nos 80/10, 106/10, 57/12 – ZUPUDPP).

to the Energy Sector in Slovenia), and they are subject to obtaining all other necessary permits, which is why references are included for individual permits and procedures for obtaining them in Part I, Chapter 2 §1 Permits and Consents System, Part II, Chapter 2 §2 System of Approvals or Consents and Permits for Gas Production and Part IV, Chapter 2 Activities Affecting the Environment.

§2. Coal

435. Coal is mainly transported by road and rail transport within Slovenia. Transmission of electricity generated from coal through the transmission grid or system is described in Part I, Chapter 3 Transport or Transmission of Electricity.

Chapter 5. Distribution

436. This chapter describes the method of petrol distribution in Slovenia and the pricing of petroleum products. Regarding the distribution of electricity generated from coal, reference is made to the relevant part of the monograph in Part I.

§1. Petrol

437. Distribution (and storage) of petrol in Slovenia is organized through the service stations operated by thirteen companies.[522]

438. The prices of petroleum products (motor gasoline, diesel fuel and extra light fuel oil) are determined on the basis of the provisions of the Decree setting prices for petroleum products.[523] In accordance with the Decree, the prices of petroleum products change every fourteen days.[524]

439. In accordance with the Decree, the retail price of each petroleum product is composed of the retail price without duties, environmental tax for polluting the air with carbon dioxide emissions (CO_2 tax), contribution for the increase of energy efficiency (EEU contribution), contribution for RES and high-efficiency cogeneration (RES+HECU contribution), excise duties and value added tax (VAT). For more information on excise duties and environmental tax *see* Part V Interaction Between Energy Law and Tax Law.

§2. Coal

440. The rules regarding the distribution of electricity produced from coal are explained in Part I, Chapter 4 Distribution of Electricity.

522. Petrol, OMV Slovenija, OMV Deutschland, AGIP, MOL, Nafta Lendava, Termoelektrarna Brestanica and Trbovlje, Shell, Vopak, Weser-Petrol, Oiltanking, Tanquid (information available at https://www.dbr.si/dejavnost/obvezne-rezerve/).
523. Official Gazette of the Republic of Slovenia, No. 39/20. This Decree entered into force on 1 Apr. 2020 and is valid for four months (as usual).
524. The changes in the prices are published on the Ministry's website https://www.energetika-portal.si/podrocja/energetika/cene-naftnih-derivatov/.

Chapter 6. Consumption

441. This chapter describes the method of providing the minimum reserves of petrol and petroleum products in Slovenia to prevent shortages. Regarding the use of electricity generated from coal, reference is made to the relevant part of the monograph in Part I.

§1. PETROL

442. Based on Slovenia's plans for the transition to low-carbon society, the consumption of petrol and petroleum products is planned to be reduced and the use of other alternative sources of energy in transportation is being promoted, also with appropriate tax incentives.

443. The Excise Duty Act[525] stipulates that excise duty shall be paid, *inter alia*, for energy products which are used as motor fuel or heating fuel. Biofuel (including bioethanol, biodiesel) can be considered as a motor fuel in case, in terms of physicochemical properties, they meet the conditions laid down in the applicable standards and are suitable for direct use for propulsion or as an additive to fossil fuels – for more information on excise duty *see* Part V, Chapter 2 Excise Duty.

444. However, until we stop using this energy product, Slovenia must, based on the principle of solidarity with other EU Member States, strive for the establishment of a system to improve the safety of petrol and petroleum products supply in the case of disturbances and instability on the market, with the focus on maintaining minimum reserves of petrol and petroleum products and the establishment of transparent mechanisms and methods of providing minimum reserves. For this reason, we must maintain sufficient physical reserves on our territory and broader, at all times, which can be activated in the event of a crisis, and we must have the appropriate intervention plans for releasing reserves in place.

445. Slovenia began establishing minimum reserves already in 1999. The area of commodity reserves is regulated by the Commodity Reserves Act (ZBR),[526] which was last amended in 2012 because of the alignment with the Council Directive 2009/119/EC of 14 September 2009 imposing an obligation on Member States to maintain minimum stocks of crude oil and/or petroleum products.[527] Following the German example, the Agency of the Republic of Slovenia for Compulsory Oil Stocks was established in 1999, which operates as a public agency. With gradual establishment of minimum reserves, Slovenia achieved the planned level already in 2005, with the higher of ninety-day minimum reserves of average net imports or

525. *See* Art. 54(3), point 10 of the Excise Duty Act (Official Gazette of the Republic of Slovenia, No. 47/16).
526. Official Gazette of the Republic of Slovenia, Nos 60/95, 50/04, 98/04, 86/09, 96/09 and 83/12.
527. Official Journal of the European Union, L 265, 9.10.2009, 9.

sixty-one-day average domestic consumption. Since then, Slovenia has always complied with the obligation regarding the minimum stocks of petrol and petroleum products pursuant to the provisions of the applicable Directive. The monitoring of reserve maintenance has been reinforced to enable the authorized representatives of the EU to check the status at any time. To this end, reports have to be sent to the Commission in the specified intervals.

446. Petrol reserves can be stored anywhere in the EU, with the only condition being that they are physically available in full. For this, the consent of the country storing the reserves and the country for which they are being stored must of course be obtained.

447. The Government of the Republic of Slovenia adopts five-year commodity reserves programmes.

448. The bulk of minimum reserves of petroleum products is in the form of physical stocks owned by the Agency and a small part in delegated stocks.

449. Complex logistic operations have to be in place for the maintenance of minimum reserves, such as lease and optimization of the storage facilities at home and abroad, purchase, sale and exchange of fuel, lease of delegated quantities and fuel transportation. Fuel quality control comprising the analysis of the quality of fuel, forecasting the ageing of fuel and cooperation in the acceptance of new fuel for storage is also extremely important. All activities related to quality control also dictate the activities related to the exchange of fuels and storage.

§2. Coal

450. The rules regarding the consumption of electricity produced from coal are explained in Part I, Chapter 5 Consumption of Electricity.

451. Putting aside the consumption of coal in other industries (e.g., pharmacy, transportation, paper industry), the biggest consumer of energy in Slovenia for energy purposes is the thermal power plant Termoelektrarna Šoštanj which uses coal (lignite) from Premogovnik Velenje.

Part IV. Interaction Between Energy Law and Environmental Law

452. Part IV of this monograph discusses the interaction between energy law and environmental law, but does not focus on Slovenian environmental law as a whole entity.

453. Chapter 1 (General Introduction) introduces the definition and basic principles of environmental law relative to energy law. It further discusses the basic acts in environmental law, which are relevant to energy law.

454. Chapter 2 discusses the extremely important procedures for assessing certain environmental impacts since all energy developments (constructing buildings, modifying installations, maintenance works) represent a certain activity affecting the environment.

455. Chapter 3 discusses the most important regulations for the energy sector governing trading with GHG emission rights, as well as issues of energy efficiency and RES related to climate change, all of which is regulated (through the relevant incentives) in the EA-1. However, they are also (predominantly) linked to environmental aspects as emphasis is given to their origin from natural processes and maintaining the natural balance between them.

456. In Chapter 4, we draw attention to other environmental legislation, which is relevant to the energy sector, as well as to the liability for violations of environmental laws borne by energy sector companies.

Chapter 1. General Introduction

457. Chapter 1 (General Introduction) introduces the definition and basic principles of environmental law relative to energy law. It further discusses the basic acts in environmental law, which are relevant to energy law.

§1. Definition of Environmental Law and Relevant Legislation

458. Slovenia set the course of environmental law with the adoption of the Slovenian Constitution in 1991, stipulating in Article 72 that everyone has the right to a healthy living environment and that the state shall promote a healthy living environment. It is further provided for in the Constitution that to this end, the conditions and manner in which economic and other activities are pursued shall be established by law.[528] Also, the law shall establish under which conditions and to what extent a person who has damaged the living environment is obliged to provide compensation.[529]

459. Environmental protection in Slovenia was first regulated with the EPA-1, which was adopted in 1993.[530] The respective Act regulated the protection of living environment and natural environment, which are two inseparable notions, as well as laid down the general conditions regarding the use of natural resources. Furthermore, it provided the foundation for contemporary environmental protection in the Republic of Slovenia. It unified the environmental protection principles and transformed the environmental protection from a conventional means of tackling increasing environmental issues, focused on the use of technical solutions targeted at limiting pollution, to an instrument ensuring a sustainable development. It already incorporated several principles and institutes of international environmental protection agreements and declarations, such as the UN Rio Declaration on Environment

528. It is also worthy to point out Art. 67(1) of the Constitution of the Republic of Slovenia according to which the manner in which property is acquired and enjoyed shall be established by law so as to ensure its economic, social, and environmental function. In other words, the owner which uses or organizes its property in order to carry out economic or non-economic activity is limited due to environmental concerns.

529. *See* paras 1–3 of Art. 72 of the Constitution of the Republic of Slovenia, Official Gazette of the Republic of Slovenia No. 33/91-I, Official Gazette of the Republic of Slovenia, No. 42/97 – Constitutional Act amending Art. 68 of the Constitution (UZS68), Official Gazette of the Republic of Slovenia, No. 66/00 – Constitutional Act amending Art. 80 (UZ80), Official Gazette of the Republic of Slovenia, No. 24/03 – Constitutional Act amending Arts 3a, 47 and 68 (UZ3a, 47, 68), Official Gazette of the Republic of Slovenia, No. 69/04 – Constitutional Act amending Art. 14 (UZ14), Official Gazette of the Republic of Slovenia, No. 69/04 – Constitutional Act amending Art. 43 (UZ43), Official Gazette of the Republic of Slovenia, No. 69/04 – Constitutional Act amending Art. 50 (UZ50), Official Gazette of the Republic of Slovenia, No. 68/06 – Constitutional Act amending Arts 121, 140, and 143 (UZ121, 140, 143), Official Gazette of the Republic of Slovenia, No. 47/13 – Constitutional Act amending Art. 148 (UZ148), and Official Gazette of the Republic of Slovenia, No. 47/13 – Constitutional Act amending Arts 90, 97, and 99 (UZ90, 97, 99).

530. Official Gazette of the Republic of Slovenia, No. 39/06 – official consolidated version, 49/06 – ZMetD, 66/06 – odl. US, 33/07 – ZPNačrt, 57/08 – ZFO-1A, 70/08, 108/09, 108/09 – ZPNačrt-A, 48/12, 57/12, 92/13, 56/15, 102/15, 30/16, 61/17 – GZ, 21/18 – ZNOrg and 84/18 – ZIURKOE.

and Development (1992), the Basel Convention on the Control of Transboundary Movements of Hazardous Wastes, the UN Framework Convention on Climate Change, and the Biodiversity Convention. In addition, the Act incorporated some fundamental principles and requirements of EU legislation, though not to the fullest extent but rather as guidelines. The compliance with all the EU legislation as a legal commitment occurred at a later stage, as the Republic of Slovenia decided to join the EU by becoming its Member State. However, the first EPA-1 already included some elements of the directives on environmental impact assessment and free access to environmental data sets, and naturally the fundamental 'polluter pays' principle incorporated in European agreements, defined within Recommendation 436/75/Euratom/CECA/CEE, and used in a number of directives and other legal acts of the EU which regulate environmental protection.

460. The adoption of the first EPA-1 was followed by the adoption and implementation of some fundamental international instruments regulating environmental protection. This refers in particular to the implementation of the Framework Convention on Climate Change through the adoption and ratification of the Kyoto Protocol and signing of the Aarhus Convention on access to information, public participation in decision-making, and access to justice in environmental matters, the ratification procedure of which has already begun.

461. Within a decade from the enactment of Slovenia's first EPA-1, several acts came into force which, referring to the basic principles of the EPA-1, regulated sustainable use of natural resources (e.g., Forest Act, ZRud-1, WA), protection of biodiversity, and conservation of valuable natural features (e.g., Nature Conservation Act – i.e., NCA).

462. For all of the above-stated reasons, Slovenia adopted a new EPA-1[531] in 2004, which is an umbrella act within environmental law, similar to what the Energy Act of 2014 (EA-1) is to energy law.

463. The term environment is defined as that part of nature which is or could be affected by human activity. Humans are an integral part of nature which is defined as the whole of the material world and the structure of interdependent elements and processes interlinked according to natural laws. The components of the environment include soil, mineral resources, water, air, and flora and fauna including their genetic material.[532]

464. Based on the subject matter of the EPA-1 we can derive a definition of the term environmental law, which is a set of rules of law and legal principles that govern the protection of the environment against burdens, which is a basic condition

531. Environmental Protection Act (EPA-1), Official Gazette of the RS No. 41/04, 20/06, 39/06 – official consolidated text, 49/06 – Meteorological Activities Act (ZMetD), 66/06 – Constitutional Court's Decision, 33/07 – Spatial Planning Act (ZPNačrt), 57/08 – Financing of Municipalities Act (ZFO-1A), 70/08, 108/09 – Spatial Planning Act (ZPNačrt-A), 48/12, 57/12, 92/13, 56/15, 102/15, 30/16, 61/17 – GZ, 21/18 – ZNOrg and 84/18 – ZIURKOE.

532. *See* Art. 3 EPA-1.

for sustainable development. Comparing that to the definition of energy law (Cf. Part I, Chapter 2 §1 Basic Features of Slovenian Energy Law) we can see that both legal spheres cover an overlapping section, as one as well as the other regulate the management of natural (energy) resources.

465. The purpose of the EPA-1 is to promote and direct such social development that ensures long-term conditions for human health, well-being and quality of life, and conservation of biological diversity.[533]

466. The objectives of the EPA-1 are as follows:

- to prevent and reduce environmental burdens;
- to conserve and improve the quality of the environment;
- to use natural resources in a sustainable way;
- to reduce the use of energy and increase the use of RES;
- to remedy the consequences of environmental burdens, to improve the disrupted natural equilibrium and recover its regeneration capacity;
- to increase material efficiency of production and consumption; and
- to abandon and substitute hazardous substances.[534]

467. It follows from the above-stated purpose and objectives that environmental law is intended to regulate proper use and exploitation of the environment (prevention against environmental burdens and pollution), as well as to eliminate the consequences of environmental burden due to pollution (curative measures).[535] Proper use and pollution of the environment in Slovenia, however, is not regulated only by the EPA-1, but also and in more detail by sector-specific instruments for individual environmental compartments (*see* further section of Part IV, Chapter 4 §1 Other Environmental Legislation Relevant to the Energy Sector in Slovenia). The sector-specific acts which are important also in respect of energy law are as follows:

- Waters Act (ZV-1).[536]
- Forest Act (ZG).[537]

533. *See* Art. 2(1) EPA-1.
534. *See* Art. 2(2) EPA-1.
535. The term used as a synonym for environmental law, which is based on legal institutes aimed at establishing an integrated code of conduct in relation to other biotic communities (the objective of which is then the formation of systemic ecocentrism rather than just limit pollution) is ecological law (according to D. Pichler, et al., *Komentar Zakona o varstvu okolja (Commentary on Environmental Protection Act)*, Inštitut za javno upravo pri Pravni fakulteti v Ljubljani, 2010, 95 and S. Pličanič, *Temelji ekološkega prava (Foundations of Ecological Law)*, Scientia Iustitia, Ljubljana, Cankarjeva založba, 2003, 113).
536. Official Gazette of the Republic of Slovenia, Nos 67/02, 2/04 – Health Inspection Act (ZZdrl-A), 41/04 – Environmental Protection Act (ZVO-1), 57/08, 57/12, 100/13, 40/14, 56/15 and 65/20.
537. Official Gazette of the Republic of Slovenia, Nos 30/93, 56/99 – Nature Conservation Act (ZON), 67/02, 110/02 – Construction Act (ZGO-1), 115/06 – Authentic Interpretation of Art. 40(1) of the Forest Act (ORZG40), 110/07, 106/10, 63/13, 101/13 – Real Property Tax Act (ZDavNepr), 17/14, 24/15, 9/16 and 77/16.

- Mining Act (ZRud-1).[538]
- Nature Conservation Act (ZON).[539]
- Ionising Radiation Protection and Nuclear Safety Act (ZVISJV).[540]
- Spatial Planning Act (ZPNačrt).[541]
- Spatial Management Act (ZUreP-1).[542]
- Building Act (ZGO-1).[543]
- Agricultural Land Act (ZKZ).[544]

468. In any case we should not forget that Slovenia has been compliant with acquis communautaire since May 2004,[545] which means that in the field of environmental protection also, founding contracts, secondary rules, and case law of the European Court of Justice and other legal sources constitute a special sui generis legal system, governed by the principles of autonomy, primacy, and direct effect. Therefore, the powers of the Republic of Slovenia or their extent in the field of environmental protection rely on the question whether EU legal acts cover individual fields or not and on the legal nature and contents of the respective acts. Given the broadly defined objectives of the environmental policy in Article 191 of the Treaty on the Functioning of the EU, hardly any of the issues concerning environmental protection is left within the sole province of the Member States.

469. Slovenian environmental protection policies are developed, in line with the EPA-1, largely through the environmental platform which constitutes a mandatory basis that anyone drawing up particular plans, programmes, or other arrangements must take into consideration. The policies are adopted by the Government. So far, the integral political documents constituting the environmental platform include the National Environmental Action Programme[546] and the Operational Environmental Action Programme. Environmental policymaking takes place at a local level, through municipal environmental protection programmes, which naturally cannot be in conflict with the national and the operational programmes. The National Environmental Action Programme containing long-term objectives, guidelines, and tasks

538. Official Gazette of the Republic of Slovenia, No. 14/14 – official consolidated text and 61/17.
539. Official Gazette of the Republic of Slovenia, No. 96/04 – official consolidated text, 61/06 – Societies Act (ZDru-1), 8/10 – National Farmland and Forest Fund Act (ZSKZ-B), 46/14, 21/18, 31/18 and 82/20.
540. Official Gazette of the Republic of Slovenia, Nos 76/17 and 26/19.
541. Official Gazette of the Republic of Slovenia, Nos 33/07, 70/08 – ZVO-1B, 108/09, 80/10 – Siting of Spatial Arrangements of National Importance Act (ZUPUDPP), 43/11 – Agricultural Land Act (ZKZ-C), 57/12, 57/12 – Siting of Spatial Arrangements of National Importance Act (ZUPUDPP-A) (109/12), 76/14 – Constitutional Court's Decision, 14/15 – Act Regulating Measures Aimed at Fiscal Balance of Municipalities (ZUUJFO) and 61/16.
542. Official Gazette of the Republic of Slovenia, No. 61/17.
543. Official Gazette of the Republic of Slovenia, Nos 61/17, 72/17 and 65/20.
544. Official Gazette of the Republic of Slovenia, No. 71/11 – official consolidated text, 58/12, 27/16, 27/17 – ZKme-1D and 79/17.
545. In fact even earlier, since even before the country joined the EU it was necessary to adjust its political, socio-economic and legal system.
546. National Environmental Action Programme (Official Gazette of the RS Nos 83/99 and 41/04 – Environmental Protection Act (ZVO-1)) and the Resolution on the National Environmental Action Plan 2005–2012 (Official Gazette of the Republic of Slovenia, No. 2/2006).

regarding environmental protection is adopted by the National Assembly of the Republic of Slovenia at the proposal of the Government.[547] For the implementation of the National Environmental Action Programme, or for the fulfilment of the obligations arising from the ratified and published international treaties, strategies, programmes, and EU regulations relative to the formulation of programmes concerning environmental protection, the relevant ministry shall draw up operational action programmes for the environment to be adopted by the Government.[548] The operational programme, on the other hand, contains a breakdown of objectives, guidelines, and tasks, normally for a period of four years. Moreover, both documents were adopted on the basis of the National Programme on Environmental Protection 2005–2012 which was in 'use' after its original temporal framework. This clearly shows it was about time to modernize the described policy framework. Just recently, i.e. on 20 March 2020, the National Assembly of the Republic of Slovenia adopted the Resolution on National Programme of Environmental Protection 2020–2030.[549] The new Programme is an umbrella strategic document in the fields of environmental protection, nature conservation and water management in Slovenia.[550] As such it clearly affects also the field of energy.

§2. Principles of Environmental Law Relevant to Energy Law

470. There are in all thirteen basic principles in the EPA-1 (*See* Articles 4–16 of the EPA-1), most of which are relevant also in terms of energy law.

471. The issues concerning environmental law (e.g., use of RES, climate improvement, conservation of species and preservation of natural balance) are closely related to the issues governed by energy law (management of energy sources).

472. Along with the principle of sustainable development which is considered fundamental as it drives the economic development towards long-term preservation of the environment and which is also one of the basic principles of energy law (Article 19 of EA-1), this section focuses in particular on those principles of environmental law that are most relevant also in terms of energy law, namely, the principle of integration, the principle of cooperation, the principle of prevention, the precautionary principle, the principle of responsibility of the person responsible for burden, and the principle of payment for burden.

---

547. *See* Art. 35(1) EPA-1.
548. *See* Art. 36(1) EPA-1.
549. This resolution was adopted on the basis of Art. 35 EPA-1 in connection with Art. 94 NCA, and on the basis of Art. 54 WA.
550. Since the Programme was adopted just recently there are no further documents but of course we can reasonably anticipate its concretization by action plans and operational plans and, at the end of the day, also a modification of legislative acts and other general legal acts in Slovenia.

473. The entities to whom the rules of law apply must observe the respective principles of the EPA-1 towards proper interpretation and application of the environmental law rules. This involves the principles that need to be considered in light of achieving the objectives regarding environmental law and in implementing environmental policy measures. At the same time, the respective principles largely affect also relevant energy policy and measures.

474. The principle of integration – as is evident from its name – is about providing integrated environmental protection, and is therefore binding upon national as well as municipal authorities at all levels of their operations. Environmental impact needs to be considered when adopting environmental policies, laws, and general legal acts and in dealing with other issues within their competencies (adoption of specific legal acts).[551]

475. Furthermore, it needs to be underlined that the principle of cooperation is also relevant with regard to energy law, stipulating that the state and the municipalities need to include all stakeholders (entities responsible for environmental burdens, providers of public services in environmental protection, and the general public) in their decision-making process regarding environmental policy and drawing up of general legal acts.[552]

476. The precautionary principle has developed from the principle of prevention, the key goal of which is to prevent or minimize the activities affecting the environment as soon as they emerge. However, the precautionary principle derives from the knowledge acquired based on the effects of introducing certain products or technologies, which, at a later stage, resulted in major environmental issues, due to the fact that at the time of their implementation it was impossible to make a critical assessment, in particular of their long-term impact. For this reason, the introduction of new technologies, production processes, and products shall only be permissible when no unforeseeable detrimental effects on the environment or human health could be expected, taking into account the state of science and technology and potential protective measures.

477. Article 9 of the EPA-1 defines the principle of responsibility of the person responsible for burden. This principle stipulates that the person responsible for a burden shall be held responsible (criminally responsible and liable for damages):

- for the elimination of the source and consequences of the excessive burden;
- for the prevention and remediation of environmental damage; and
- for such burden even in the case of liquidation or bankruptcy;
- the principle itself is operationalized in the Criminal Code and the Code of Obligations, while the provisions relating to the elimination of the sources and consequences and bankruptcy or liquidation are subject to the EPA-1.

551. *See* Art. 5 EPA-1.
552. *See* Art. 6 EPA-1.

478. Along with the principle of sustainable development, the precautionary principle, and the principle of prevention, the principle of responsibility of the person responsible for burden is also based on international legal acts, declarations, and EU documents.[553]

479. The principle of payment for burden provided for in Article 10 of the EPA-1 transposes some basic principles of contemporary environmental protection policies, such as the 'polluter pays' principle. This provision defines, at principle level, the obligations of the entity responsible for burden for the payment of costs of environmental burdens caused. The enforcement of this principle is reflected in those provisions of the law that govern the limit values of the emissions as well as rules of conduct or other obligations of the polluter to reduce its burdening, as it is the polluter who shall bear the cost of fulfilling statutory obligations. This principle is enforced also in the section of the law which governs economic and financial instruments of environmental protection.

553. *See*, e.g., Art. 191(2) of the TFEU which stipulates that the Union policy on the environment shall aim at a high level of protection taking into account the diversity of situations in the various regions of the Union. It shall be based on the precautionary principle and on the principles that preventive action should be taken, that environmental damage should as a priority be rectified at source and that the polluter should pay.

Chapter 2. Activities Affecting the Environment

480. Since all energy developments (constructing buildings, modifying installations, maintenance works) represent a certain activity affecting the environment, this chapter discusses the extremely important procedures for assessing certain environmental impacts.

481. The EPA-1 lays down the cases where an environmental consent and/or permit must be obtained for an activity affecting the environment.[554]

§1. Environmental Impact Assessments and Environmental Consents

482. One of the fundamental principles of the EPA-1 is that an activity affecting the environment shall only be admissible if it does not cause an excessive burden (Article 15 of the Environmental Protection Act). An excessive environmental burden is a burden that exceeds the limit values for emissions, environmental quality standards, rules of conduct or the permitted use of a natural good.[555]

483. The EPA-1 transposes fifteen directives of the EU,[556] including Directive 2011/92/EU of the European Parliament and of the Council of 13 December 2011 on the assessment of the effects of certain public and private projects on the environment into the Slovenian legal system. Directive 2011/92/EU is an important horizontal European directive contributing to more sustainable projects and the inclusion of environmental aspects in the drafting of implementation projects before their approval. At this point in time, Slovenia has not yet transposed Directive 2011/92/EU with Directive 2014/52/EU of the European Parliament and of the Council of 16 April 2014 amending Directive 2011/92/EU on the assessment of the effects of certain public and private projects on the environment.[557]

554. Specific use of environmental goods is subject to obtaining a licence in accordance with the relevant legislation governing such use (e.g., concession for exploitation of mineral raw materials pursuant to the Mining Act (ZRud) – *see* Part II, Chapter 3 §1 Granting the Concession to Extract Natural Gas).
555. Point 6.1. of Art. 3 of the Environmental Protection Act.
556. Most recently, i.e. on 20 Apr. 2016, Directive 2012/18/EU of the European Parliament and of the Council of 4 Jul. 2012 on the control of major-accident hazards involving dangerous substances, amending and subsequently repealing Council Directive 96/82/EC (Official Journal of the European Union, L 197, 24.7.2012, 1) was transposed in the Slovenian legal system through the amendment of Environmental Protection Act.
557. UL L 124, 25 Apr. 2014. The newly amended Environmental Impact Assessment (EIA) Directive (2014/52/EU) entered into force on 15 May 2014 to simplify the rules for assessing the potential effects of projects on the environment. It is in line with the drive for smarter regulation and thus aims to reduce the administrative burden. It also strives to improve the level of environmental protection, with a view to making business decisions on public and private investments more sound, more predictable and sustainable in the longer term.
Member States have to apply these rules as of 16 May 2017 at the latest (for more information, *see* http://ec.europa.eu/environment/eia/review.htm).

484. Pursuant to paragraph 3 of Article 51 of the EPA-1, in 2014 the Government issued a new Decree on environmental encroachments that require environmental impact assessments (hereinafter 'Decree on environmental encroachments'),[558] which defines the following in accordance with Directive 2011/92/EU of the European Parliament and of the Council of 13 December 2011 on the assessment of the effects of certain public and private projects on the environment:[559]

- Types of interventions in the environment for which an environmental impact assessment is mandatory.
- Types of interventions in the environment for which an environmental impact assessment is mandatory if it is determined in the preliminary procedure that they could have significant effects on the environment.
- Mandatory detailed criteria based on which the pre-litigation procedure determines whether an environmental impact assessment should be carried out for the planned activity affecting the environment.

485. An environmental impact assessment should be carried out and environmental consent obtained for the construction of a facility (as well as changes made to it or its or maintenance) that could have a significant effect on the environment.

486. An environmental consent must be obtained in all cases where it is necessary to carry out an environmental impact assessment.

I. Obligation to Assess the Environmental Impacts of Activities Affecting the Environment in the Field of Energy and Preliminary Proceedings

487. Prior to the implementation of the planned activity in the energy sector, which could have significant effects on the environment, it is necessary to assess its

558. Official Gazette of the Republic of Slovenia, Nos 51/2014, 57/15 and 26/17. The Decree replaced the old Decree on the categories of activities for which an environmental impact assessment is mandatory. In relation to the preliminary regulation in the pre-litigation procedure against the Republic of Slovenia No. 2012/2162, the European Commission concluded that it is not fully compliant with all the provisions of Directive 2011/92/EU and Annexes I, II and III of this Directive and the relevant case law because it failed to implement a pre-litigation procedure and the thresholds were too high. The Decree eliminates the infringement established by the European Commission and represents the last measure for the complete transfer of the provisions of Directive 2011/92/EU. At the same time it is important for reduction of the environmental load and environmental integration in various development areas: agriculture, mining, manufacturing, energy, environmental infrastructure, transport infrastructure, urban planning and construction, tourism, sport and recreation. By adopting the Decree on 4 Jul. 2014, the Government eliminated the infringement alleged by the European Commission and prevented new violations from occurring, while facilitating project applicants to the European structural and investment funds, which will perform an environmental impact assessment or preliminary procedure, and ensuring easier drawing of European funds, as this is a prerequisite for the drawing of European funds in the new Financial Perspective (*ex ante* conditionality).

559. Official Journal of the European Union, L 26, 28.1.2012, 1.

impacts.[560] The environmental impact assessment procedure shall identify, describe and estimate the long-term, short-term, indirect or direct impacts of a project affecting the environment on human beings, soil, water, air, biodiversity and natural values, climate and landscape, material assets and cultural heritage, and on their interaction.[561]

488. The assessment is always required for certain types of intervention in the environment, while for other types of environmental interventions the necessity of an impact assessment is determined in the so-called preliminary proceedings.[562] The Government is obliged to define criteria for both groups of interventions, i.e. interventions which automatically demand the environment impact assessment and interventions which can demand such assessment (or not) depending on findings in the preliminary proceedings. This obligation is fulfilled with the adoption of the Decree on environmental encroachments that require environmental impact assessments.[563]

489. Hence, the Decree on environmental encroachments in its Article 2 in combination with Appendix I of the discussed decree and relevant provisions of the EPA-1 provides for which encroachments the impacts assessment is always necessary as a precondition to final decision concerning environmental approval or consent, while Article 3 in combination with the aforementioned appendix and relevant legislative provisions[564] provides for which encroachments the developer of a project affecting the environment must request that the ministry establish whether an environmental impact assessment is required and an environmental consent is to be obtained for the project.[565] The ministry responsible for environmental protection may also commence the preliminary assessment procedure ex officio.[566]

490. A preliminary procedure is a special procedure in which it is established whether an impact assessment is required for certain activities and whether an environmental consent needs to be obtained. This is established on the basis of certain criteria as stipulated by the aforementioned Decree on environmental encroachments that require environmental impact assessments. It is conducted for certain types of activity affecting the environment in which significant impacts on the environment can be expected owing to the characteristics of the project or its location. Again, the relevant encroachments are defined by the aforementioned Decree.

491. The developer of a project affecting the environment must enclose with the request for a preliminary procedure a description of the project, the environment or elements thereof which the project is likely to affect, and a description of the possible significant impacts of the project on the environment or elements thereof.

560. *See* Art. 50 EPA-1.
561. *See* Art. 51(1) EPA-1.
562. *See* Art. 51(2) and (3) EPA-1.
563. Official Gazette of the Republic of Slovenia, Nos 51/14, 57/15 and 26/17.
564. *See* in particular Art. 51 a of the Environmental Protection Act.
565. Criteria which are used in the preliminary proceedings are defined in Appendix II of the discussed decree.
566. *See* Art. 8 of the Decree on environmental encroachments.

492. The request may also include a request for preliminary information.[567]

493. After receipt of the complete request, the ministry responsible for the environment issues a decision establishing whether an environmental impact assessment is required and an environmental consent is to be obtained for the anticipated encroachment. In establishing whether an environmental impact assessment is required, the criteria relating to the characteristics of the project affecting the environment, its location and the characteristics of its possible impacts on the environment shall be considered.

494. As part of a preliminary procedure, the ministry responsible for environmental protection can request ministries and other organizations that are with regard to the planned activity responsible for particular environmental protection matters or for the protection or use of natural assets or protection of cultural heritage or protection of human health provide their opinions on the planned activity. Such organizations shall provide their opinion within fifteen days.

495. Where a construction permit has to be obtained in accordance with the regulations on construction for the implementation of a project affecting the environment subject to a preliminary procedure and the developer of the project does not enclose an environmental consent for the project with the application for the construction permit, the competent administrative body must, prior to the granting of the construction permit, establish whether the ministry has issued a decision to the effect that an environmental impact assessment is not required for the project. Where the competent administrative body establishes that the ministry has not issued a decision regarding a project affecting the environment to the effect that an environmental impact assessment is not required, it shall be deemed, during the procedure for the granting of the construction permit, that an environmental consent has not been granted and the application for the construction permit shall be rejected.[568]

496. Notwithstanding the need for preliminary proceedings, the entity responsible for the planned activity shall file an application for the environmental consent accompanied by a project of the planned activity and an environmental impact report. If it is determined that an environmental impact assessment should be carried out and an environmental consent is required, the ministry responsible for the environment will instigate an environmental impact assessment.

567. *See* Art. 52 EPA-1 which provides for the possibility of the investor of an intervention, for which an environmental impact assessment is required, to obtain preliminary information on the scope and content of the environmental impact report. This is in the investor's favour as it ensures that based on additional proposals of the Ministry and other competent authorities responsible for the environment, the investor will produce a report that will be able to be the subject of an environmental impact assessment. The ministry should provide this information to the investor in writing within thirty days of its request, otherwise it is considered that the competent authorities have no additional requirements regarding the content of the report.

568. *See* Art. 51a(7) EPA-1.

497. In procedures for drawing up national spatial plans in accordance with the regulations on the physical placement of spatial plans of national importance,[569] the preliminary procedure shall be conducted at the stage and during the period in which the ministry decides, in accordance with Article 46 of the EPA-1, whether the environmental impacts of the plan are acceptable.

498. An environmental impact assessment is mandatory for the following facilities or activities in the environment relating to energy (point DI) and mining (point B):[570]

- Crude oil refineries (except installations for the production of lubricants from crude oil).
- Installations for gasification or liquefaction of 500 t or more of coal or bituminous shale per day.
- Storage areas for petroleum and petrochemical products (except for industrial plants for the production of paper, paperboard and cardboard with production capacity of at least 200 t per day). with a capacity of 200,000 t or more.
- Above-ground storage areas of liquefied petroleum gas, natural gas and other flammable gasses and terminals for LNG with a capacity of at least 25,000 t.
- Thermal power stations and other combustion plants with a minimum thermal output of 300 MW.
- CO_2 geological storage areas.
- Installations for the capture of CO_2 streams for the purposes of geological storage from all the foregoing devices (as well as from other devices listed in Annex 1 of the Decree on environmental encroachments, which are specially designated, e.g. nuclear power plants, pipelines for the transport of natural gas, oil and oil derivatives with a diameter above 800 mm and over 40 km in length), or where the total annual capture of CO_2 is 1.5 Mt or more and pipelines with a diameter of more than 800 mm and a length of over 40 km for transport of CO_2 streams for the purposes of geological storage, including the associated booster stations.
- Nuclear power plants and other nuclear reactors.
- Nuclear devices for research with the power above 1 KW of constant heat burden.
- Devices for production or enrichment of nuclear fuel.
- Devices for processing radioactive nuclear fuel or highly radioactive nuclear waste or reprocessing of nuclear fuel.
- Permanent (long-term) storages of used nuclear fuel or exclusively nuclear waste.
- Wind power plants with 20 or more wind turbines (devices) whose height is 30 m or more.

---

569. This issue is no longer stipulated by the Siting of Spatial Arrangements of National Importance Act since the latter was derogated by the Spatial Planning Act (ZUreP-2) as of 1 Jun. 2018. The latter now covers this issue in Art. 50.

570. *See* Annex 1 of the Decree on environmental encroachments.

- Hydro power plants whose capacity is at least 2 MW or is connected with certain dams.
- Pipelines for transport of natural gas, oil or oil derivatives whose diameter exceeds 800 mm and whose length exceeds 40 km.
- Above-ground power lines with electrical voltage 220 kV or more whose length exceeds 15 km.
- Exploration of hydrocarbons, provided at least 1,000 m^3 of water is planned to be injected into the well at the fracking stage or at least 7,500 m^3 of water per well in the whole fracking process.
- Exploitation of nuclear mineral raw materials.
- Oil and natural gas extraction where the extracted amount exceeds 500 t per day in the case of oil and 500,000 standard cubic metres (sm^3) per day in the case of gas.
- Quarries and opencast mining where the surface of the site exceeds 25 hectares, or peat extraction, where the surface of the site exceeds 150 hectares.

499. Preliminary proceedings to determine whether facilities (and/or activities in the environment) relating to energy (point D) and mining (point B) are subject to environmental impact assessment are mandatory for the following:

- Installations for gasification or liquefaction of less than 500 t coal or bituminous shale.
- Installations for the production of industrial charcoal.
- Installations for the production of coke (dry coal distillation).
- Storage areas for petroleum and petrochemical products and other fossil fuels except for gasses with a production capacity of at least 50,000 t and less than 200,000 t.
- Underground and above-ground storage areas for liquefied petroleum gas, natural gas and other flammable gasses and other gas terminals with a capacity of at least 150 t and less than 25,000 t.
- Industrial equipment for briquetting of coal and lignite.
- Thermal power plants and combustion plants for the production of electricity, steam and hot water with a rated thermal input of a minimum 50 MW and less than 300 MW.
- Other devices for the capture or transport of CO_2 streams for the purposes of geological storage.
- Nuclear devices for research with the power below 1 KW of constant heat burden.
- Deep drilling for storages of nuclear waste.
- Wind power plants with three (but less than twenty) wind turbines (devices) whose height is 30 m or more, or with one device whose power exceeds 1 MW.
- Hydro power plants whose capacity is between 0.5 MW and 2 MW.
- Stand-alone devices for exploitation of sun energy with a capacity of at least 250 KW or standing on the surface of at least 0.5 ha.
- Wood biomass boilers with a heat output of at least 20 MW.
- Biogas plant, other than E.1.5, or treatment of crude biogas with a production capacity of at least 1 million sm3 gas per year.

- Installations for the production of biofuels with chemical processes with a capacity of at least 50 t per year.
- Geothermal drilling and other installations for the exploitation of geothermal energy sources, excluding shallow geothermal systems.
- Pipelines for the transport of natural gas, oil and petroleum products, except connections to public infrastructure facilities, over 1 km.
- Industrial installations for the transmission of gas, steam or hot water with a pipeline of more than 1 km or more than 100 mm in diameter.
- District heating systems with a capacity of at least 1MW, except for the construction of individual connections.
- High-voltage lines for overhead or underground transmission of electricity and high-voltage transformer stations which do not fall in the previous group as explained in paragraph 497 of this monograph.
- Exploration of hydrocarbons and of other mineral resources with deep drilling which do not fall in the previous group as explained in paragraph 497 of this monograph.
- Oil and natural gas extraction which do not fall in the previous group as explained in paragraph 497 of this monograph.
- Quarries and opencast mining where the surface of the site exceeds 5 hectares (or even less in the case when explosive is used).
- Exploitation of mineral resources except those described in B2, B3 and B4.
- Mining objects and infrastructure.
- Processing or disposal of waste arising from the exploration, extraction, enrichment or storage of mineral resources and the operation of quarries.

II. Procedure for Obtaining Environmental Consent

500. Let us point out again, before starting the implementation of an intervention or encroachment that may have a significant impact on the environment, an assessment of its impact on the environment must be carried out and the environmental consent of the ministry must be obtained. Holder of the planned action must submit a request on the ministry together with a project of intended intervention in the environment (as defined in Article 53 of the Environmental Protection Act) and report on the impact of the planned intervention on the environment (as defined in Article 54 of the Environmental Protection Act). The aforementioned holder is a party of the procedure; however, under certain conditions also other persons can participate in the procedure as side parties of the procedure, including NGOs.[571] Such participation in the procedure shall not be, however, equated with the right of the other ministries (and competent organ of other Member States in which planned intervention may cause significant effects) to issue an opinion in the matter.

501. The said procedure shall be transparent. Among other measures to ensure transparency, the Environmental Protection Act demands that the request is publicly available, meaning that interested public can read the request and its appendencies.

571. *See* Art. 64 of the Environmental Protection Act.

Moreover, even the draft decision regarding the environmental consent must be available to the interested public. The latter can even give opinions and observations as to the aforementioned documents, including draft decision. Moreover, in the case of cross-border effects, i.e. in case the planned intervention could significantly impact the environment in other Member States, the ministry informs the competent organs of the relevant Member State. The latter can decide to be involved in the procedure in the sense of Article 59 of the Environmental Protection Act.[572] Similarly, as already said, also certain ministries can issue an opinion in the matter.

502. The procedure shall last up to three months.[573] In case the ministry finds out that the planned intervention manifestly runs contra laws and regulations on environment protection, nature conservation, water management or cultural heritage protection and, as a consequence, the planned intervention shall not be carried out, it issued a negative decision which means it refuses to issue environmental consent.[574] If, however, there no grounds to refuse the environmental consent, the ministry issued a positive decision which can contain some conditions or limitations in order to prevent, reduce or remove the detrimental effect on environment. The decision must be announced to public.

§2. Environmental Permits

503. The concept of environmental permit was included in the EPA-1 already due to the need to transpose Directive 2008/1/ESC (the IPPC (Integrated Pollution Prevention and Control) Directive),[575] subsequently recast with the IED Directive 2010/75/EU[576] (Industrial Emissions Directive) as well as due to certain other directives that define other rules of conduct, including those related to waste (including Directive 2008/98/EC on waste and the repeal of certain other Directives)[577] and Directive 96/82/EC[578] (the SEVESO Directive). The rights of the public are considered in the process of obtaining an environmental permit in accordance with the requirements of the Aarhus Convention and Directive 2003/35/EEC.[579]

572. The same logic applies in the opposite direction; *see* Art. 60 of the Environmental Protection Act.
573. However, this time limit seems to be instructive only.
574. *See* Art. 57 of the Environmental Protection Act.
575. Directive 2008/1/EC of the European Parliament and of the Council of 15 Jan. 2008 concerning integrated pollution prevention and control (Official Journal of the European Union, L 24, 29.1.2008) aims to ensure that plant operators fulfil the conditions that will allow pollution prevention and environmental pollution as a whole.
576. Directive 2010/75/EU of the European Parliament and of the Council of 24 Nov. 2010 on industrial emissions (integrated pollution prevention and control), Official Journal of the European Union, L 334, 17.12.2010, 17.
577. Directive 2008/98/EC of the European Parliament and of the Council of 19 Nov. 2008 on waste and repealing certain Directives (Official Journal of the European Union, L 312, 22.11.2008, 3).
578. Council Directive 96/82/EC of 9 Dec. 1996 on the control of major-accident hazards involving dangerous substances (Official Journal of the European Union, L 10, 14.1.1997, 13).
579. Directive 2003/35/EC of the European Parliament and of the Council of 26 May 2003 providing for public participation in respect of the drawing up of certain plans and programmes relating to

504. Due to different levels of environmental pollution and due to the different requirements of the directives, the EPA-1 governs different types of environmental permits as follows:

- for operation of installations (devices) which could cause large-scale pollution (referred to in the IPPC Directive); *see* Articles 68–81;
- for operation of other types of installations (devices) and activities (referred to in directives governing emissions and waste management); *see* Articles 82–85;
- for operation of facilities (referred to in the SEVESO Directive); *see* Articles 86–91 c.

505. The difference between them is in particular in the extent of the requirements that must be fulfilled for the permit to be issued within the period of the authorization and the public participation. The public has an enhanced role in issuing environmental permits for installations that can cause large-scale pollution in accordance with the requirements of the Directive.

506. An installation is a fixed or mobile technological unit which is determined as being capable of causing environmental burden for the reason that one or more specified technological processes are conducted within it and that other directly associated technological processes are conducted in the same place which could cause an environmental burden (IPPC installations).[580]

I. Environmental Permits for the Operation of Installations That Could Cause Large-Scale Pollution (IPPC Installations)

507. In accordance with Article 68 of the EPA-1, an environmental permit must be obtained for the operation of installations (devices) in which activities will be conducted that could cause large-scale environmental pollution. Environmental permit may be granted for one or more installations or parts thereof which are at the same location and have the same operator, where the environmental permit must include the conditions that each installation or part thereof is obligated to meet.[581] Moreover, it may also be issued for one or more installations or parts thereof located on the same site and operated by different operators, provided that the environmental permit contains the conditions to be met by each installation or part thereof and the obligations of each operator.[582]

508. The procedure is triggered by the request of with all necessary appendencies.[583] The request is submitted by the operator of the installation. The operator is

---

the environment and amending with regard to public participation and access to justice Council Directives 85/337/EEC and 96/61/EC (Official Journal of the European Union, L 156, 25.6.2003, p. 17).

580. *See* Point 8 of Art. 3 EPA-1.
581. *See* Art. 68(2) EPA-1.
582. *See* Art. 68(3) EPA-1.
583. *See* Art. 70 EPA-1.

a party of the procedure in question. In addition, the other person may participate in the procedure in case they prove legal interest, including NGOs.[584] The procedure shall be transparent which includes, *inter alia*, access of the interested public to the request with appendencies and to draft decision. The interested public can give opinions and observations which must be considered by the competent authority.[585] The procedure shall be carried out in six months but this time limit seems to be instructive only. After the decision is adopted, it must be publicly announced.

509. Activity can be carried out only after the decision becomes definitive.[586]

510. The operation of the energy installation is by its very nature a long-term activity; it is only logical that there can be changes or modifications of the installation and, of course, that the activity will not last forever. Not surprisingly, the EPA-1 regulates both, change of the environmental permit (Articles 77 and 78) and its end (Articles 79–81).

II. Environmental Permits for Operation of Other Installations and Activities

511. Environmental permit must be acquired also for the operation of other installations which do not fall under the aforementioned (IPPC) installations and activities for which legislative acts explicitly demand such permit. The procedure is triggered by the request with appendencies and shall be finished in three months.[587] The request shall be lodged by the operator of the installation. The latter is a party in the procedure. In addition, also in this procedure there is a space for other participants which prove legal interest.

III. Environmental Permit for Facilities

512. Environmental permit for facilities is also triggered by request with appendencies[588] lodged by the operator of the facility. The procedure must be transparent[589] and must be finished in three months.[590] Since the operation of the facility indicates long-term activity, it is only logical that the discussed legislative act regulates modifications (Article 90) as well as the end of the validity of the permit (Article 91–91 c). Several aspects of the procedure are not explicitly regulated;

584. *See* Art. 73 EPA-1.
585. *See* Art. 71 EPA-1.
586. Moreover, when operation or change of operation of the installation demands construction or building according to the laws and regulations on construction, one can begin with construction only after the decision becomes definitive; *see* Art. 69 f EPA-1.
587. Also this time limit seems to be instructive only.
588. *See* Art. 87 EPA-1.
589. In this regard it is also important to underline the access of the interested public to documentation and to draft decision; *see* Art. 88 EPA-1.
590. Also this time limit seems to be instructive only.

instead references to similar procedures are used, e.g. for public participation (Article 88), modification of the environmental permit (Article 90), start of operation of the facility (Article 91), and end of validity of environmental permit (Article 91). At this point, it is also worth to mention a possibility to merge procedures. In case a facility or its part is also considered as an installation, the investor or operator can request that the conditions relating facility can be checked in the procedure which relates the installation.

Chapter 3. Combating Climate Change and Reducing CO_2 Emissions

513. This chapter discusses the most important regulations for the energy sector governing trading with GHG emission rights, as well as issues of energy efficiency and RES related to climate change, all of which is regulated (through the relevant incentives) in the EA-1. However, they are also (predominantly) linked to environmental aspects as emphasis is given to their origin from natural processes and maintaining the natural balance between them.

§1. GHG Emissions Trading

514. In Slovenia, the second EPA-1 (for more information on regulations governing environmental protection, *see* Chapter 1 §1 Definition of Environmental Law and Relevant Legislation) established in 2004 a legal basis for the implementation of the Kyoto Protocol requirements[591] and the requirements of Directive 2003/87/EC[592] establishing a scheme for GHG emission allowance trading (hereinafter 'GHG'). Before the Act was adopted, in July 2013, the Government of the Republic of Slovenia adopted the Operational programme of reducing GHG emissions, which defined the main measures per individual sector and estimated the potential reduction in GHG emissions.[593]

I. GHG Emissions Permit

515. Every operator of an installation in which activities are conducted that generate GHG emissions requires a GHG emissions permit.[594]

516. The ministry responsible for the environment is also responsible for issuing the permit, as well as for keeping a list of such permits and reporting to the European Commission.

591. Slovenia signed the Kyoto Protocol in October 1998, and ratified it in July 2002 with the Act Ratifying the Kyoto Protocol to the United Nations Framework Convention on Climate Change (Official Gazette of the Republic of Slovenia, No. 60/02, MP, 17/02). As a result, Slovenia undertook to reduce GHG emissions by 8% in the first target period (2008–2012) compared to the initial year 1986. In 1986, Slovenia recorded GHG emissions of 20.60 million tons of carbon dioxide equivalents, while an 8% reduction would mean that Slovenia cannot exceed annual emissions of 18.95 million tons of carbon dioxide equivalents.
592. Subsequent amendments of the Environmental Protection Act transposed into the Slovenian legal system subsequent amendments of this Directive in the form of Directives 2008/101/EC and 2009/29/EC.
593. For example, paying environmental fees for CO2 emissions, encouraging increased use of renewable sources, energy labelling of household appliances, encouraging the construction of buildings with methods and construction materials that result in a 30% reduction in CO2 emissions (by 60,000 t a year).
594. *See* Art. 118(1) EPA-1.

517. With the Decree on GHGs, activities and installations for which a GHG emissions permit is required or monitoring of GHG emissions must be implemented (hereinafter 'the GHG Decree'),[595] the Government defined GHG, as well as activities and types of installations for which a GHG emissions permit must be obtained in accordance with the EPA-1. In terms of the energy sector, the list provided in Annex 1 to the GHG Decree also includes mineral oil refineries and coke production, as well as combustion of fuels in installations with a total rated thermal input power of over 20 MW.

518. The GHG Decree defines the following as GHG: carbon dioxide (CO_2), methane (CH_4), nitrous oxide (N_2O), hydrofluorocarbons (HFC), perfluorinated hydrocarbons (PFC), sulphur hexafluoride (SF_6) and other natural and anthropogenic gaseous components of the atmosphere that absorb and re-emit infrared radiation.

519. In addition to the installations, activities and GHG specified in the GHG Decree, the ministry may also include other installations, activities and GHGs in the trading scheme, either at its own initiative or at the request of the operator of an installation. For their inclusion in the GHG emissions trading system, the Government of the Republic of Slovenia shall obtain the favourable opinion of the European Commission.[596]

520. We would like to highlight that the ministry shall grant a GHG emissions permit for an installation or part thereof if it establishes that the operator is capable of providing monitoring and reporting on GHG emissions in accordance with the EPA-1.[597] The permit may be granted for one or more installations or parts thereof if they are at the same location and operated by the same operator. In addition, paragraph 3 of Article 119 of the EPA-1 defines the mandatory components of the permit.

521. The operator shall inform the ministry of any changes to and of the cessation of operations of the installation. In both cases, the ministry shall act accordingly and issue new decisions (on the modification or termination of the GHG permit, respectively). The ministry shall withdraw the GHG emissions permit ex officio when the operator fails to fulfil the GHG emission monitoring requirements or has carried out a change in the installation and has not informed the ministry thereof.[598]

595. Official Gazette of the Republic of Slovenia, Nos 55/11 and 1/13.
596. Article 126 b EPA-1.
597. *See* Art. 119(1) EPA-1.
598. *See* Art. 122(1) EPA-1.

II. GHG Emissions Allowance and Emission Coupons

522. In accordance with the Slovenian EPA-1, GHG emissions allowance is a right of an installation operator which has the right to emit GHG (as well as the right of an operator of an aircraft with the relevant permit)[599] to emit GHG in the scope of emission coupons obtained for the installation in accordance with the EPA-1.[600]

523. An emission allowance is the right to GHG emissions expressed in tonnes of CO_2 equivalent.[601]

524. However, it should be noted that in line with paragraph 2 of Article 125 of the EPA-1, other rights granted by other Member States for the purpose of GHG emissions trading in their territory shall be equivalent to emission allowances, as shall those rights which, in the event of the conclusion of an appropriate international treaty and for the purpose of GHG emissions trading, are granted in their territory by signatory states of the Kyoto Protocol.

525. Since its introduction in 2004 with the entry into force of the EPA-1, the GHG emissions rights trading system as one of the fundamental economic instruments for controlling climate change has changed considerably, especially through the gradual introduction of public auctions of emission coupons, which is expected to entirely replace their free-of-charge distribution by 2027.

526. Slovenska izvozna in razvojna banka, d.d. Ljubljana (SID Banka) shall be the official auctioneer selling emission allowances at auction in the name and on behalf of the Republic of Slovenia.[602]

527. The sale of emission coupons takes place at public auctions in accordance with the method and conditions defined by Commission Regulation No. 1031/2010/EU,[603] which was issued pursuant to Directive 2009/29/EC. Together with twenty-four other Member States, Slovenia has opted to join a common auctioning system which is performed by the EEX stock market in Leipzig, Germany, in the name of the relevant Member States.

---

599. This refers to an aircraft operator in accordance with Art. 139.a EPA-1. However, since such operators belong to the transport rather than the energy sector, they are not discussed below.
600. *See* Art. 124 EPA-1.
601. A tonne of carbon dioxide equivalent means one metric tonne of carbon dioxide or the corresponding quantity of another greenhouse gas with the same potential to cause global warming of the atmosphere (Art. 125(1) EPA-1).
602. *See* Art. 127 EPA-1.
603. Commission Regulation (EC) No. 1031/2010 of 12 Nov. 2010 on the timing, administration and other aspects of auctioning of greenhouse gas emission allowances pursuant to Directive 2003/87/EC of the European Parliament and of the Council establishing a scheme for greenhouse gas emission allowances trading within the Community (Official Journal of the European Union, L 302, 18.11.2010, 19), last amended by Commission Regulation (EU) No. 176/2014 of 25 Feb. 2014 amending Regulation (EU) No. 1031/2010 especially due to the determination of the quantity of greenhouse gasses emission rights subject to auction between 2013 and 2020 (Official Journal of the European Union, L 56, 26.2.2014, 1).

528. The sale of emission coupons has been carried out as described since November 2012. At this point in time it is very difficult to give a more detailed estimate of the revenue gained from emission coupon sales as their price is still very volatile.

529. As early as in 2013, electricity-generating installations and CO_2 capturing, transmission and storing units had to purchase all emission coupons.[604]

§2. RES and Energy Efficiency

530. RES, namely their effective and efficient use, and energy efficiency in general are fundamental pillars in combating climate change as well as in achieving genuine energy aims.[605] Not surprisingly, the EA-1 deals with both issues (*see* fifth part of the EA-1; Articles 312–382 a). But before we discuss some relevant provisions of the EA-1, we have to point out, for practical reasons, that the new energy legislative package of the EU, i.e. the Clean Energy for all Europeans package, put much attention to these two issues. In fact, three legislative acts deal with them (Directive (EU) 2018/2001 of the European Parliament and of the Council of 11 December 2018 on the promotion of the use of energy from renewable sources,[606] Directive (EU) 2018/2002 of the European Parliament and of the Council of 11 December 2018 amending Directive 2012/27/EU on energy efficiency,[607] and Directive (EU) 2018/844 of the European Parliament and of the Council of 30 May 2018 amending Directive 2010/31/EU on the energy performance of buildings and Directive 2012/27/EU on energy efficiency).[608] Let us point out that so far, i.e. until mid-2020, the aforementioned legislative acts were not transposed in the Slovenian legal system. Therefore, the EA-1 is discussed regarding the present situation. Moreover, it is anticipated that after the new legislative package will be transposed in the Slovenian law (but the exact time is uncertain, in particular in case we recall the huge delay when transposing the third legislative package), the EA-1 will be substituted by several legislative acts.

531. As already said, also in Slovenia, green energy represents a source of various legal questions – in addition to environmental protection issues, also questions concerning the energy sector and state aid. In order to enhance Slovenia's competitiveness and make the gradual shift to a low-carbon society, both energy efficiency (hereinafter 'EEU') and RES are important in addition to developing active electricity distribution networks.

532. One of the goals of the EA-1, which implemented Directive 2009/28/EC of the European Parliament and of the Council of 23 April 2009 on the promotion of

604. *See* Art. 126(1) EPA-1.
605. Of course, in addition to decrease in use of fossil fuels.
606. Official Journal of the European Union, L 328, 21.12.2018, 82.
607. Official Journal of the European Union, L 328, 21.12.2018, 210.
608. Official Journal of the European Union, L 156, 19.6.2018, 75.

the use of energy from renewable sources and amending and subsequently repealing Directives 2001/77/EC and 2003/30/EC (hereinafter 'Directive 2009/28/EC'),[609] includes increasing the production and use of RES.

533. In accordance with Article 28 EA-1, the Government shall, at the proposal of the ministry responsible for energy, adopt a RES Action Plan (AN OVE) by 2020 and forward it to the European Commission.

534. The Government of the Republic of Slovenia adopted the AN OVE by 2020 before the adoption of the EA-1 in accordance with Directive 2009/28/EC, which provides that every Member State must adopt a national AN OVE for the 2010–2020 period.[610] These plans should also define the national goals of Member States concerning the shares of RES in gross final energy used for heating and cooling, as well as for use of electricity in transport in 2020, and be forwarded to the European Commission by 30 June 2010.

535. In accordance with the action plan, Slovenian energy policy has the following goals: ensuring a 25% share of RES in final energy consumption and a 10% share of RES in transport by 2020, stopping the growth in final energy consumption, enforcing EEU and RES as priorities of economic development, and increasing the share of RES in final energy consumption in the long-term until 2030 and onwards.

536. The industry goals of the AN OVE by 2020 include the following target shares of RES expressed in the gross final energy use: 30.8% of RES for heating and cooling, 39.3% of RES for electricity and 10.5% of RES in transport. But not to forget, we are already in 2020. Therefore we have to point out a new document, i.e. the National Energy and Climate Plan of the Republic of Slovenia for the time period 2020–2030.[611] Its key targets are as follows: (a) reduction of total GHG emissions by 36%; (b) at least 35% improvement in energy efficiency, which is higher than the target set at EU level (32.5%); (c) at least 27% of RES, where Slovenia had to agree to a lower target than the target at EU level due to relevant national circumstances (32%), but with efforts to increase ambition in the next update of the NEPN (2023/24); and (d) 3% of GDP in R&D, of which 1% of GDP is public funding. Fulfilling NEPN leads us to reduce our dependence on fossil fuels, and at the same time we support sustainable solutions in transport, buildings and industry, together with NEPN. Among other things, the NEPN also sets targets for reducing and phasing out the use of coal, by 2030 by 30%.

537. In accordance with Article 315 EA, the promotion of measures to improve EEU and the use of RES shall be implemented with a view to decreasing the use of

---

609. Official Gazette of the Republic of Slovenia, No. 140 dated 5 Jun. 2009, 16.
610. Akcijski načrt za OVE za obdobje 2010–2020 Slovenija, Ljubljana, July 2010; the English language version is also accessible at https://www.energetika-portal.si/dokumenti/strateski-razvojni-dokumenti/akcijski-nacrt-za-obnovljivo-energijo/.
611. *See* para. 135 of this monograph.

energy, increasing the quantity and share of RES, improving the security of the energy supply, reducing dependence on energy imports and other energy reasons laid down in the energy concept of Slovenia.

538. As already said, Part 5 of the EA-1, namely Articles 312 through 382, are dedicated to RES and EEU. In addition to the EA-1, 13 regulations also govern this field.[612] As a result, in this section, we can only highlight certain characteristics of the Slovenian system.

539. The promotion of measures to improve EEU and the use of RES is performed through programmes aimed at educating, informing and raising the awareness of the public, through energy advice, encouraging energy audits, drafting regulations, financial incentives and through other support mechanisms.[613]

I. Energy Efficiency

540. Energy efficiency (which means less energy consumption due to less or more rational use of energy as well as due to use of devices which demand less energy for the same or even better function)[614] is exceptionally important because

612. The following regulations are relevant:

- Decree on the method of determining and charging the contribution for providing support to the high-efficiency generation of electricity through cogeneration and from renewable energy sources (Official Gazette of the Republic of Slovenia, Nos 46/15 and 76/17).
- Decree on guaranteeing end-use energy savings (Official Gazette of the Republic of Slovenia, No. 96/14).
- Act on the use of the register of guarantees of origin of electricity and the method of reporting information on electricity production (Official Gazette of the Republic of Slovenia, No. 33/09).
- Rules of operation of the support centre (Official Gazette of the Republic of Slovenia, No. 88/16).
- Rules on the promotion of efficient energy use and the use of renewable energy sources (Official Gazette of the Republic of Slovenia, Ns. 89/08, 25/09, 58/12 and 17/14 – EA-1).
- Decision on the harmonization of the premiums for the purchase of electricity from hydropower plants for year 2010 (Official Gazette of the Republic of Slovenia, No. 106/10).
- Decree on determination of the amount of electricity from the high-efficiency cogeneration of heat and electricity and determination of the efficiency of the conversion of energy from biomass (Official Gazette of the Republic of Slovenia, Nos 37/09 and 17/14 – EA-1).
- Decree on the issuing of declarations for generating installations and guarantees of origin (Official Gazette of the Republic of Slovenia, Nos 8/09, 22/10 – EA-D, 45/12 and 17/14 – EA-1).
- Decree on the compulsory measurements for generating installations that receive a guarantee of origin and support for the electricity produced (Official Gazette of the Republic of Slovenia, Nos 21/09, 33/10, 45/12 and 17/14 – EA-1).
- Decree on the self-supply of electricity from renewable energy sources (Official Gazette of the Republic of Slovenia, No. 17/19).

613. *See* Art. 314(1) EA-1.

614. The former is closely connected with the users' behaviour, while the latter demands technical or technological innovations.

it ensures other energy policy targets as well as the wider development goals of the state, especially given the potential for improving the competitiveness of society, green growth and employment potential. EEU makes a major contribution to ensuring the strategic reliability of supply by reducing dependence on imported fossil fuels. Energy efficiency is one of the most cost-effective measures for achieving the goals of reducing GHG emissions and achieving the 25% target share of RES in the consumption balance of gross final energy consumed by 2020. Energy efficiency is also vital for households in controlling costs, boosting their purchasing power and improving their standard of living, particularly in the context of adapting to climate change.

541. We would like to highlight that at its 37th regular session on 21 May 2015, the Government of the Republic of Slovenia adopted the National Energy Efficiency Action Plan 2014–2020 (hereinafter 'AN-URE 2020').[615]

542. With AN-URE 2020, in accordance with Article 3 of Directive 2012/27/EU on energy efficiency, Slovenia[616] set itself the national goal of achieving a 20% improvement of energy efficiency by 2020. The goal is to ensure that primary energy consumption in 2020 does not exceed 7.125 million tons (82.86 TWh). This means that it will not increase by more than 2% compared to 2012.

543. The AN-URE 2020 action plan contains measures aimed at households, the public sector, industry and transport. Most measures already exist, are being implemented and have resulted in the interim goals being reached so far. The new action plan brings some new measures, especially to the public sector, as every year 3% of surfaces of public buildings need to be renovated. The state's aim is to ensure that all new buildings owned and used by the public sector starting in 2018 will be almost zero-energy, and in other sectors starting in 2020. Additional measures are envisaged for industry since EEU is an increasingly important factor of improving the industry's competitive position.

544. The existing range of buildings represents a sector with the greatest potential for achieving energy savings. In order to achieve the goal, one fourth will need to be refurbished by 2020, which represents approximately 22 million m^2 of building surfaces. As a result, use of energy in buildings will fall by nearly 10%. In addition, these measures will also accelerate economic growth as they will result in

615. The document is available on the following website https://www.energetika-portal.si/dokumenti/strateski-razvojni-dokumenti/akcijski-nacrt-za-energetsko-ucinkovitost/.

616. Article 24 of Directive 2012/27/EU on energy efficiency (hereinafter 'Directive 2012/27/EU') provides that by 30 Apr. 2014, and every three years thereafter, Member States shall submit National Energy Efficiency Action Plans. These plans should define the measures aimed at significantly improving energy efficiency and ensuring the relevant energy savings are made in order to achieve the energy efficiency targets referred to in Art. 3 of the Directive. In accordance with Art. 24(2) of the Directive, the European Commission has provided a template as guidance for the National Energy Efficiency Action Plans, which contains a list of the mandatory contents of such plans. AN-URE 2020 has been drawn up entirely in accordance with the relevant template and fulfils all the requirements outlined in the Directive.

annual investments of EUR 500 million. In addition to high energy costs savings and the resulting smaller energy imports, these investments are also expected to impact employment and provide 10,000 jobs.

545. In order to ensure the implementation of existing and new measures, the relevant funds must be ensured, namely funds collected from the contribution for effective energy use, select fund funding and funds provided by the Climate fund.

546. The AN-URE 2020 relies significantly upon established instruments and upgrades them in accordance with the requirements outlined in the EA-1 and Directive 2012/27/EU. Since the time frame of the AN-URE 2020 indicates its expiration, we have to rely on the aforementioned National Energy and Climate Plan which is relevant, *inter alia*, from the energy efficiency perspective. One of its targets is to improve energy efficiency for at least 35%, which is higher than the target set at EU level (32.5%).

547. The EA-1 retains and enhances the successful schemes for reaching the national energy efficiency targets, such as the contribution for improving energy efficiency. Now, the funds will be earmarked entirely for measures aimed at increasing the energy efficiency of households and multi-dwelling buildings, which are implemented by the Eco Fund.

548. The EA-1 provides that the state shall stimulate measures for energy efficiency and for use of renewable sources of energy,[617] e.g. with education, informing, consulting, inspections, regulations, subsidies, etc.[618] The Eco Fund shall draw up and implement the programme for improving energy efficiency at the national level, on the basis of which the Eco Fund shall also provide financial incentives for investments in EEU measures.[619] Measures and mechanisms for energy efficiency and for use of renewable resources of energy shall be concretized by action plans. No building permit is required for the installation of devices for the production of

617. The EA-1B explicitly regulates that the self-supply or self-sufficiency in electricity from renewable energy sources is the production of electricity from renewable energy sources to fully or partially cover the needs of the final customer with a self-supply device. Electricity produced in self-sufficient appliances is used for individual self-sufficiency or for community self-sufficiency. Community self-sufficiency shall be provided to all final customers who consume electricity through metering points: (a) the same multi-apartment, business-residential, residential-business or business buildings with business premises having their own metering points, or other buildings with several metering points, connected to the common internal low-voltage installation of this building; or (b) which are connected to the low-voltage network of the same transformer station as the self-supply device. The final customers shall be connected to the Community self-supply on the basis of a contract regulating their mutual relations, in particular agreeing on the key of sharing the produced electricity in the self-supply device belonging to each end customer in the Community self-supply. The final customer with individual or community self-sufficiency concludes a self-sufficiency contract with the supplier. The self-supply contract and the key for the division of the produced electricity are registered with the distribution operator. *See* Art. 315a EA-1.

618. Beneficiaries of the subsidies can be natural and legal persons of private law as well as legal person of public law except direct users of the state budget; *see* Art. 316 EA-1.

619. The programme also defines the funds necessary for programme implementation, which are provided through a contribution on energy use aimed at enhancing energy efficiency.

electricity from RES or high-efficiency cogeneration that are installed on, in or next to an existing building or civil engineering structure constructed in accordance with the regulations governing the construction of facilities. The Government shall, by a decree, determine the types, size and conditions for the installation and connection of devices for the production of electricity from RES or by high-efficiency cogeneration for which a building permit is not required.[620] The promotion of measures for energy efficiency and use of RES shall be carried out with the aim of reducing energy consumption, increasing the amount and share of RES, increasing security of energy supply, reducing import dependence on energy supply and other energy reasons set out in the energy concept of Slovenia.

549. The EA-1 prescribes fines for obligated parties that have failed to achieve savings or have failed to contribute to the Energy Fund funds for implementing the energy efficiency improvement programme.

550. The EA-1 also envisages fines for obligated parties that have failed to report to the Energy Agency in accordance with the Act.[621] Since the fines are defined in the relevant ranges, they can be imposed with regard to the severity of the offence. The first report on scheme implementation will be drawn up in 2016 when data will become available on any violations recorded until then.

551. In accordance with Article 318(1) EA-1, suppliers of electricity and heat and suppliers of solid, liquid or gaseous fuels to final customers shall be designated as obligated parties to ensure the achievement of energy savings among final customers.[622]

552. However, the obligated parties may, instead of achieving the actual energy savings among final customers, fulfil their obligation by making a payment to the Eco Fund. The amount to be paid shall be equal to the product of the energy savings that the obligated parties were required to achieve among final customers and the specific costs of achieving the savings by the Eco Fund.[623]

---

620. *See* Art. 314 EA-1.
621. *See* Arts 427 and 428 EA-1.
622. Since the market shares of suppliers change, and since new stakeholders enter the market:

> The savings to be achieved by individual obligated parties, expressed as a share of energy sold in the previous year. The savings to be achieved by individual obligated parties thus amount to:
>
> - 0.25% in 2015.
> - 0.50% in 2016 and 2017.
> - 0.75% in 2018 and 2020.
> - 0.25% every year in the sale of car petrol and diesel fuel for use in transport (AN URE 2020, p. 23).

623. *See* Art. 318(2) EA-1. The manner of financing measures implemented by the relevant obligated persons is not defined (incentives, loans, financing provided by a third party, etc.). The measures implemented by obligated persons will be implemented in all sectors included in the emission trading system (the ETS sector), including transport and the industry.

553. The EA-1 provides[624] that the Government shall determine the following by means of a decree:

- The period and level of end-use energy savings that the obligated parties have to achieve over the period.
- The method of calculating the level of savings.
- The distribution of savings by individual years of the set period.
- The method and deadlines for the fulfilment of obligations by the obligated parties.

554. In accordance with Article 319 EA, the types of energy services and energy efficiency improvement measures to achieve energy savings include the following:

- Measures for EEU and greater use of RES in heat generation in the public and service sectors and in industry and households.
- EEU measures in buildings.
- EEU measures in transport.
- Measures to increase the efficiency of district heating systems.
- Energy audit programmes.

555. Article 324 EA-1 regulates, in detail, the introduction of energy management systems, while Article 354 EA-1 regulates energy audits.

556. The EA-1 also contains the legal basis for measuring and charging for energy in accordance with the relevant EU directives, as well as the awareness-raising and training and general information aimed at various target groups provided by the Centre for RES/CHP Support.

557. Consumer awareness-raising also includes energy rating and environmentally adequate design of products relating to energy use.

II. Renewable Energy Sources

558. Wood biomass is the most important RES in Slovenia, followed by water energy, while in recent years, we have seen dynamic growth in harnessing solar energy and biogas.[625]

559. The EA-1 contains a support scheme which authorizes the Government of the Republic of Slovenia to decide on the anticipated growth in investments in RES generating units and heat and electricity coproducing units (hereinafter 'HECU') for future periods in light of the fulfilment of interim goals contained in renewable energy and AN-UREs, taking into consideration the possibility to increase contributions and the availability of other sources for the support scheme envisaged by

624. *See* Art. 318(3) EA-1.
625. AN OVE, 3.

the EA-1. The support scheme supporting the production of electricity from RES and high-efficiency HECU is the most important instrument aimed at achieving Slovenia's international obligations in the field of electricity. The new scheme came into force in 2009 as an improvement of the 'feed in' system introduced in 2002. The new scheme sees increased incentives in order to achieve more rapid development in the fields of RES and HECU.

560. The 2014 revision EA-1 brought a complete overhaul of the support scheme aimed at RES and HECU electricity, this time aimed at controlling the costs spent on the support scheme. The European Commission was notified of the scheme as a permitted form of state aid aimed at environmental protection.[626]

561. In order to prevent the excessively rapid growth of the support scheme in the future, compared to the old EA, the new EA-1 contains lower power thresholds for the producing units eligible for incentives: the threshold for RES producing units has fallen from 125 MW to 10 MW, with the exception of wind, where the threshold is 50 MW, and from 200 MW to 20 MW for HECU producing units.[627] This was decided since in the 2009–2013 period, no new producing unit was established with a power exceeding the threshold contained in the new EA-1.

562. Although the EA-1 scheme was revised in 2014, the legal bases applicable to installations already included in the scheme remain unchanged. However, in 2015, the procedures and conditions for new installations to enter the scheme changed significantly. Quotas have now been imposed and the best bidders are selected through a public tender, which also serves as the basis for determining the amount of the incentive.[628]

563. In 2014, electricity generation from RES accounted for approximately 70% of the entire electricity generated under the scheme. In 2014, most electricity under the scheme was generated from natural gas (29.6%), followed by solar energy (27%), hydro energy (17.3%), biogas (11.7%) and wood biomass (11.0%). Of these, in the 2011–2014 period, generation of electricity from solar energy is up the most

---

626. *See* Poročilo o doseganju nacionalnih ciljev na področju OVE in SPTE za obdobje 2012–2014, 3 Apr. 2015 (accessible at https://www.agen-rs.si/izvajalci/ove-ure/obnovljivi-viri-in-soproizvodnja/porocilo-o-doseganju-nacionalnih-ciljev-na-podrocju-ove-in-spte). Incentives for technologies reducing the environmental impact are still needed due to the market imperfections resulting in prices of fossil fuels and electricity failing to reflect all costs resulting from environmental pollution. This is similar to how incentives were needed when new technologies appeared on the market. Increased incentives for technologies in the early commercialization phase are also justified due to the development benefits (for more on the issue of state aid, *see* A. Ferčič & N. Samec, *European Union State Aid Law and Policy, and Local Public Services*, *Lex Localis*, 12(2) J. Local Self -Government 267–287 (April 2014)).

627. *See* Art. 372(2) EA-1.

628. For more information on the topic of contributions for supporting electricity production, *see* A. Ferčič, Pravnopolitični vidiki določanja prispevkov za zagotavljanje podpor proizvodnji električne energije iz obnovljivih virov energije, Pravna praksa, No. 11-12/2015, 28 (the same article is also freely available at the following website https://jm-excellence.pf.um.si/wp-content/uploads/2013/10/WP-12-April-2015Ales-Fercic-Pravnopoliti%C4%8Dni-vidiki-dolo%C4%8Danja-prispevkov-proizvodnji-elektri%C4%8Dne-energije-iz-OVE.pdf).

(by 165 GWh or 392%), followed by natural gas (by 85 GWh or 46%), hydro energy (by 63 GWh or 68%) and wood biomass (by 62 GWh or 165%).[629]

564. At this point we would like to mention that in year-on-year terms, the costs of supporting electricity generation from RES and high-efficiency HECU as a proportion of GDP has been on the rise; in 2014, the value of support reached 0.33% of GDP.[630]

565. In accordance with the EA-1, every year the Energy Agency must organize a public call for RES and HECU installations wanting to join the support scheme. In classifying the proposed projects, the Agency shall consider the conditions defined by the Government (through defining the scope of new investments and considering the adopted action plans for the relevant period), as well as other criteria outlined in Article 373(2) EA-1 (the provision of part of the relevant funds from tenders held by European funds and the prices offered for the electricity generated).

566. The other EA-1 provisions that define other sources the Government can use to provide funding for support schemes and thus reduce the pressure on final customers are also important.

567. At the same time, in its concern for the competitiveness of energy-intensive industry, the Government may reallocate the burdening represented by the contribution between user groups unless such conduct would be contrary to the rules governing state aid.

568. Financial incentives are intended to promote innovative systems based chiefly on high-efficiency energy conversion technologies and the exploitation of RES.

569. The ministry responsible for the energy sector is drafting a National Action Plan for Promoting Almost Zero-Energy Buildings (Article 331 EA-1). The measures are to be divided into systemic and incentivizing measures to increase the proportion of almost zero-energy buildings. Targets and measures are set separately for the public sector.

570. Article 361 EA-1 provides that the Energy Agency shall, every two years, publish a report analysing the level of success in achieving the adopted national framework objectives set for electricity generated from high-efficiency cogeneration and RES. The report shall also consider climatic factors which might affect the achievement of the adopted objectives and shall establish the extent to which the

629. Taken from the Poročilo o doseganju nacionalnih ciljev na področju OVE in SPTE za obdobje 2012–2014, 5 Apr. 2015 (accessible at https://www.agen-rs.si/izvajalci/ove-ure/obnovljivi-viri-in-soproizvodnja/porocilo-o-doseganju-nacionalnih-ciljev-na-podrocju-ove-in-spte).

630. Poročilo o doseganju nacionalnih ciljev na področju OVE in SPTE za obdobje 2012–2014, 9 Apr. 2015 (accessible at https://www.agen-rs.si/izvajalci/ove-ure/obnovljivi-viri-in-soproizvodnja/porocilo-o-doseganju-nacionalnih-ciljev-na-podrocju-ove-in-spte).

measures adopted comply with the national commitments in relation to climatic changes. The report shall include all measures adopted to ensure the reliability of the guarantee system so that guarantees of origin are accurate and reliable.

571. We would also like to outline the significance of the following EA-1 provisions governing RES:

- Guarantees of origin (paragraph 9 of Article 372 EA-1 and Articles 365 through 368).
- The Rules on efficient use of energy in buildings[631] prescribe that new buildings and major building renovations must consider a minimum 25% share of thermal power from RES (*see* Articles 330 through 350 of EA-1).
- The obligatory share of biofuels in fuels for transport on the market[632] is the most important mechanism in the transport sector (*see* Articles 380 through 382a EA-1).
- Encouraging the use of RES as part of energy management systems in the public sector (Article 324 EA-1).
- Obligatory efficient use in district heating and cooling systems; obligatory minimum share of RES, cogeneration and surplus energy in district heating systems or a combination thereof (Article 360 EA-1).

572. We would also like to mention the following steering mechanisms for EEU and RES:

- Encouraging EEU and RES as part of green public procurement (Decree on green public procurement,[633] AN-URE 2015–2020).
- Steering towards using EEU as part of local energy concepts (Article 326 EA-1; AN OVE 2010–2020).

573. Educating, informing and encouraging the awareness of citizens according to the EA-1 also has an important role, namely through: networks of energy advice services for citizens, single information points (Borzen), and local energy agencies which perform various activities including advice and expert support to local communities (*see* Articles 351 through 359 EA-1).

---

631. Official Gazette of the Republic of Slovenia, No. 52/2010.
632. *See also* the Decree on Promotion of the Use of Biofuels and Other Renewable Fuels for the Propulsion of Motor Vehicles (Official Gazette of the Republic of Slovenia, Nos 103/07, 92/10 and 74/11).
633. Official Gazette of the Republic of Slovenia, Nos 102/11, 18/12, 24/12, 64/12, 2/13 and 89/14.

Chapter 4. Other Environmental Legislation Relevant to the Energy Sector and Liability for Violations of Environmental Laws

574. In this chapter we draw attention to other environmental legislation, which is relevant to the energy sector, as well as to the liability for violations of environmental laws borne by energy sector companies.

§1. Other Environmental Legislation Relevant to the Energy Sector in Slovenia

575. Energy sector companies in Slovenia must also be aware of the requirements imposed by environmental legislation in the broader sense, particularly in terms of the required additional conditions to obtain special permits and approvals (consents), namely the following:

– Spatial Planning Act (ZPNačrt).[634]
– Spatial Management Act (ZUreP-2).[635]
– Building Act (BA).[636]
– Waters Act (ZV-1).[637]
– Forest Act (ZG).[638]
– Mining Act (ZRud-1).[639]
– Nature Conservation Act (ZON).[640]
– Ionising Radiation Protection and Nuclear Safety Act (ZVISJV-1).[641]
– Agricultural Land Act (ZKZ).[642]
– Cultural Heritage Protection Act (ZVKD-1).[643]

634. Official Gazette of the Republic of Slovenia, Nos 33/07, 70/08 – ZVO-1B, 108/09, 80/10 – ZUPUDPP, 43/11 – ZKZ-C, 57/12, 57/12 – ZUPUDPP-A (109/12), 76/14 – odl. US, 14/15 – ZUUJFO and 61/17.
635. Official Gazette of the Republic of Slovenia, No. 61/17.
636. Official Gazette of the Republic of Slovenia, Nos 61/17, 72/17 and 65/20.
637. Official Gazette of the Republic of Slovenia, Nos 67/02, 2/04 – ZZdrl-A, 41/04 – ZVO-1, 57/08, 57/12, 100/13, 40/14, 56/15 and 65/20.
638. Official Gazette of the Republic of Slovenia, Nos 30/93, 56/99 – ZON, 67/02, 110/02 – ZGO-1, 115/06 – ORZG40, 110/07, 106/10, 63/13, 101/13 – ZDavNepr, 17/14, 24/15, 9/16 and 77/16.
639. Official Gazette of the Republic of Slovenia, No. 14/14 – official consolidated text and 61/17.
640. Official Gazette of the Republic of Slovenia, No. 96/04 – official consolidated text, 61/06 – ZDru-1, 8/10 – ZSKZ-B, 46/14, 21/18, 31/18 and 82/20.
641. Official Gazette of the Republic of Slovenia, Nos 76/17 and 26/19.
642. Official Gazette of the Republic of Slovenia, No. 71/11 – official consolidated text, 58/12, 27/16, 27/17 – ZKme-1D and 79/17.
643. Official Gazette of the Republic of Slovenia, Nos 16/08, 123/08, 8/11 – ORZVKD39, 90/12, 111/13, 32/16 and 21/18 – ZNOrg.

§2. The Responsibility for Violations of Environmental Law Borne by Energy Sector Companies

576. It is already clear from the preceding chapters of this monograph that energy sector companies must be aware of a number of rules also in the field of environmental protection that restrict their behaviour and business plans (*see* Chapter 2 Activities Affecting the Environment and Chapter 3 Combating Climate Change and Reducing CO_2 Emissions).

577. An energy sector company (i.e., a polluter) carrying on an activity for which an environmental permit must be obtained in accordance with environmental regulations (*see* Chapter 2 §2 Environmental Permits of this part), is subject to strict liability for hazards caused that could result in damage to the environment or for the damage itself.[644] As a result, all polluters defined as such in the IPPC Directive (installations that can cause large-scale pollution) and in the SEVESO Directive (plant operators) must appoint an environmental protection commissioner, which should – in light of their competencies set out in paragraph 2 of Article 30 of the EPA-1 – contribute to controlling and reducing environmental costs through preventive (and any required curative) action.

578. The arrangements concerning environmental damage in Slovenia are based on the principle outlined in Article 10 of the EPA-1, namely that the 'polluter pays'.

579. Environmental damage borne by energy sector companies is a concept used by the Slovenian EPA-1 and derived from Directive 2004/35/EC of the European Parliament and of the Council of 21 April 2004 on environmental liability with regard to the prevention and remedying of environmental damage.[645] Several articles of the EPA-1 also refer directly to the arrangements in Directive 2004/35/EC and its Annexes (*see*, e.g., Articles 110.b, 110.c and 110.e).

580. We would like to emphasize that the term environmental damage represents a specific concept of environmental law, which refers to significant damage

644. *See also* Art. 110.a(2) EPA-1, which provides an exhaustive list of activities for which the polluter is objectively liable (strict liability) for preventing an imminent threat of emergence and for preventing and remedying any environmental damage (without regard to their actual fault). For other activities (not related to water of the ground), culpable liability is provided for a lower level of environmental damage (*see* Art. 110(39) EPA-1).

645. Official Journal of the European Union, L 143, 30.4.2004, 56. The deadline for the transposition of the Directive into national law was 30 Apr. 2007. Since Slovenia was rather late in implementing the requirements of the Directive, the Commission brought an action before the court, which on 12 Mar. 2009 established an infringement of Slovenia in Case C-402/08. Most of the requirements of the Directive, with the exception of Annex I and II, were transposed into Slovenian legislation by the Act Amending the Environmental Protection Act (Official Gazette of the Republic of Slovenia, No. 70/08; ZVO-1B). Annex I was transposed with the Rules on the content defining environmental damage (Official Gazette of the Republic of Slovenia, No. 46/09), while Annex II was transposed with the Decree on types of measures for remediation of environmental damage (Official Gazette of the Republic of Slovenia, No. 55/09).

caused to specific parts of the environment.[646] Such damages do not have a victim in the 'traditional' sense. The environment alone cannot protect its rights as a subject of law.[647]

581. The concept of environmental damage is different (narrower) than the Slovenian civil law concept of damage as defined in the Code of Obligations.[648]

582. Not all (legally recognized pecuniary and non-pecuniary) damage is considered environmental damage; this concept only applies to damage that was caused to protected species, their habitats and habitat types and that has a significant adverse effect on reaching or maintaining their favourable state according to nature conservation regulations.[649] In addition, a polluter is responsible for environmental damage to water and environmental damage to the soil.[650]

583. Damage caused by adverse effects on protected species, their habitats or habitat types, which, although established, is permitted or prescribed pursuant to the acceptability assessment procedure of plans and activities affecting nature or due to the implementation of derogations from the strict protection of protected species according to nature conservation regulations, shall not be deemed environmental damage.

584. It should be noted that the polluter is not liable for the occurrence of hazards or environmental damage in all cases. The polluter shall have no liability if certain exhaustively listed circumstances exist. *Inter alia*, this includes cases that can be defined as force majeure and exclusions in accordance with international conventions governing pollution and cases of nuclear accidents; as well as diffuse pollution (all examples have been taken from the EPA-1, and are derived from Article 4 of Directive 2004/35/EC). In addition, in certain cases, the polluter can itself limit its liability in accordance with the provision of paragraph 3 of Article 4 of Directive 2004/35/EC.

585. The liability of the polluter to provide compensation for environmental damage is also excluded (which means that in these cases no obligation to bear the cost of preventive or remedial measures exists, or that the polluter will have recourse against the person responsible) when the polluter can demonstrate:

---

646. Point 6.8.2. of Art. 3 EPA-1.

647. *See*: R. Knez, *Vpliv pravil o varovanju okolja na poslovanje podjetij*. V: Ramšak, Franci (ed.). *Gospodarski subjekti na trgu – novosti in aktualna vprašanja gospodarskega prava: (pravo gospodarskih družb, pogodbeno pravo, evropsko pravo, delovno pravo, davčno pravo)*. Maribor; Pravna fakulteta: Inštitut za gospodarsko pravo, 2011, 153–164. Also available at https://jm-excellence.pf.um.si/wp-content/uploads/2013/10/WP-4-Decemebr-2013-Rajko-Knez-VPLIV-PRAVIL-O-VAROVANJU-OKOLJA-NA-POSLOVANJE-PODJETIJ.pdf.

648. The Code of Obligations (Official Gazette of the Republic of Slovenia, No. 97/2007 – official consolidated text) is the fundamental civil legal act governing general questions of liability for damages in Slovenia.

649. Whether this involves a major adverse impact on the subject of damage is determined on the basis of the criteria laid down in the Rules on the content defining environmental damage.

650. *See* Art. 110.b(3) and (4) EPA-1.

- that the imminent threat of environmental damage or environmental damage was caused by a third party, while the damage occurred despite the fact that appropriate protection measures had been taken;
- that the direct threat of environmental damage or environmental damage resulted from compliance with a compulsory order or instructions of state or municipal authorities or entities holding public authority, unless such an order was issued subsequently to the emission or incident caused by the polluter's activity.[651]

586. When there are several agents of environmental damage and it is impossible to ascertain the responsibility of each individual agent, such agents shall be jointly and severally liable.[652]

587. Polluters must implement all preventive and remedial measures and bear the costs thereof. These measures aim to 'remedy' the damage caused to the environment. The ministry responsible for the environment may also impose such measures by way of a decision; the ministry is also responsible for supervising any such measures. The polluter can initiate an administrative dispute against decisions issued by the ministry.[653]

588. Affected third parties and certain non-governmental organizations can also file an application requesting the ministry's action in the case of environmental damage.[654]

589. It should be further pointed out that in accordance with the rules of the Code of Obligations, the polluter remains liable to any third parties[655] who have suffered either pecuniary or non-pecuniary damage due to the polluter's conduct. That said, 'traditional' victims will of course have the burden of proving the assumptions of liability for damages, which is somewhat easier when the polluter is objectively liable (strict liability) in accordance with Article 149 of the Code of Obligations.[656]

590. In addition to all the above-mentioned, the polluter may also face potential individual *actio negatoria* claims of third parties provided for by civil legislation due to the impacts caused by its activities or operations.[657]

---

651. *See* Art. 110f(6) EPA-1.
652. *See* Art. 110a(5) EPA-1. This provision also differs from the general scheme under which several polluters bear joint and several liability in any case (Art. 186(1) of the Code of Obligations), meaning independently of the possibility of ascertaining the contribution of each agent.
653. *See* Art. 110d(4) and (5) of Art. 110.e EPA-1.
654. *See* Art. 110g EPA-1.
655. *See also* Art. 110(6) EPA-1.
656. For more on the issues concerning the demarcation of the administrative and civil regime for environmental damages, *see* M. Juhart, *Okoljska odgovornost – med javnim in zasebnim pravom*, Zbornik znanstvenih razprav Pravne fakultete v Ljubljani, 2008, 109; D. Jadek Pensa, *Pravica do zdravega življenjskega okolja in denarna odškodnina za nepremoženjsko škodo*, Podjetje in delo, No. 6-7/2009, 1320.
657. For further reading, *see* M. Juhart, *Zahtevki za opravljanje splošno koristne dejavnosti*, Podjetje in delo, No. 6-7/2009, 1302–1311.

591. Due to the specific characteristics of environmental damages (which can be caused, e.g., by a long-term energy activity), the relevant statute of limitations period is thirty years from the date of the cause of occurrence, provided no proceedings are initiated against the polluter under the EPA-1 during this period.[658]

592. Any polluter (being a legal[659] or natural person) can also be held criminally liable for illegal activities concerning the environment. We highlight in particular the criminal offences of failing to prevent a threat (Article 321 of the Criminal Code)[660], burdening and polluting the environment (Article 332 of the Criminal Code), marine pollution from vessels (Article 333 of the Criminal Code) and unlawful handling of nuclear and other hazardous radioactive substances (Article 334 of the Criminal Code).

658. Article 110i EPA-1.
659. In Slovenia, legal entities are liable for criminal offences in the field of environmental damage in accordance with items 14 and 15 of Art. 25 of the Liability of Legal Persons for Criminal Offences Act (Official Gazette of the Republic of Slovenia, No. 98/04 – official consolidated text; 65/08 and 57/12).
660. Official Gazette of the Republic of Slovenia, No. 50/12 – official consolidated text, 6/16 – popr., 54/15, 38/16, 27/17, 23/20 and 91/20.

Part V. Interaction Between Energy Law and Tax Law

593. The fifth part of this monograph briefly deals with the general aspects of the interaction between energy law and tax law. It consists of four chapters, as follows.

594. Chapter 1 (Introduction) discusses the interaction between the energy policy and other public policies, with emphasis on the interaction between energy and tax policy.

595. Chapter 2 (Excise Duties) discusses the valid regulation of excise duties on electricity and energy sources in the Republic of Slovenia.

596. Chapter 3 (VAT) discusses the valid manner of regulating VAT in supplies of electricity and certain other energy sources.

597. Chapter 4 (Special Environmental Taxes) discusses the current regulations governing the environmental tax for CO_2 atmospheric pollution, the environmental tax on energy consumption aimed to enhance energy efficiency, and the environmental tax providing funding for the support scheme for generating electricity from RES and high-efficiency cogeneration.

Chapter 1. Introduction

598. The interaction between energy law and tax law is first and foremost a result of the interaction between energy and tax policy, while at the same time it is also a result of the interaction with various other public policies. No policy is adopted in isolation, and every policy is in constant interaction with various other public policies. In this regard, it should be specifically mentioned, e.g., that nowadays, energy and environmental policy go hand in hand, as do environmental and tax policy, etc.[661]

599. When discussing the aforementioned public policies, the supranational dimension should also be considered. As a member of the EU, the Republic of Slovenia must also consider the EU measures adopted in accordance with the powers held by the EU in the field of energy and fiscal policies and more generally in terms of the internal market policy and individual public policies that are important for this part of the monograph.

600. Since the interaction between energy and environmental policies, which is largely determined by the pursuit of environmental protection, has already been discussed in Part IV of this monograph, for the sake of transparency we briefly point out that taxes and public levies can pursue regulatory objectives, namely by directing taxpayers from undesirable behaviour (environmentally unfriendly practices) to desirable behaviour (environmentally friendly practices, such as the enhancing of energy efficiency, encouraging the production and use of renewable energies and the internalization of negative externalities). In addition, taxes and other public levies, by their very nature, pursue fiscal goals, namely filing the public coffers. Since energy products are consumer goods, we focus on excise duties and VAT, which represent a major part of the budgetary revenue of the Republic of Slovenia, while some attention is also paid to state aid in the meaning of Article 107(1) of the TFEU granted in the form of tax credits and so-called green incentives.

661. The relationship between energy policy and competition is discussed in Part VI of this monograph. At the same time, for the sake of completeness, we also highlight (without discussing in depth) that energy policy also has close ties to economic and social policy.

Chapter 2. Excise Duties

601. This chapter discusses the valid regulation of excise duties on electricity and energy products in the Republic of Slovenia. First, we briefly present the concept of excise duties, including the applicable regulations; then we separately present the main features of the applicable Slovenian regulations governing excise duties on electricity and natural gas.

§1. General

602. Excise duty is a form of tax on consumption, which aims to particularly tax specific products or groups of products, among which the Republic of Slovenia also includes electricity and various energy products.

603. In the Republic of Slovenia, the excise duty system began to be implemented in 1999. However, since Slovenia joined the EU in 2004, the excise duty system is subject to the harmonized excise legislation of the EU, which is in the context of the topic means especially Directive 2003/96/EC.[662] This Directive requires thorough renovation (which, despite some attempts, has not yet occurred),[663] as it is more or less limited to measures that serve the integration of the internal market and in this context the prevention of distortion of competition and trade between EU Member States due to an excessive gap between taxes and the prices of electricity and energy products in the EU (level playing field), and is not a sufficiently effective tool for addressing issues that fall within the sphere of energy and environmental policy.

604. The fundamental law governing the system of excise duties and the liability to pay excise duties on certain products (including electricity and various energy products) released onto the market in the Republic of Slovenia is the Excise Duty Act.[664] This Act is then fleshed out by several regulations, the most important from the point of view of the topics discussed being the following:

- Regulation determining the amount of excise duty on electricity.
- Decree determining the amount of excise duty on energy products.[665]
- Rules on the implementation of the Excise Duty Act.[666]
- Rules on the method for repaying excise duty for fuel used for agricultural and forestry machinery.[667]

---

662. The Slovenian Excise Duty Act transposes eight EU directives and it goes in line with three EU regulations.
663. For more information, *see*: http://ec.europa.eu/taxation_customs/taxation/excise_duties/energy_products/energy_tax_proposal/index_en.htm.
664. Official Gazette of the Republic of Slovenia, No. 47/16.
665. Official Gazette of the Republic of Slovenia, Nos 34/18, 45/20, 55/20, 62/20, 72/20, 81/20, 87/20, 92/20, 99/20 and 105/20.
666. Official Gazette of the Republic of Slovenia, Nos 62/16, 67/16 – popr., 62/18 and 13/19.
667. Official Gazette of the Republic of Slovenia, Nos 70/17 and 8/18.

- Rules on the conditions and procedures for excise duty exemptions for energy-intensive companies.[668]
- Rules on the maximum permissible shortage of excise products.[669]
- Rules on the method of repaying excise duty for fuel used for industrial and commercial purposes and for commercial transport.[670]
- Order on the conversion of the amount of excise duty on natural gas.[671]

605. The Excise Duty Act governs excise duty on electricity and certain energy products in a special chapter (Articles 88–100), which contains special provisions governing the burdening of electricity (Article 90) and natural gas (Article 91) with excise duty.[672]

606. Generally speaking, excise duty is charged on electricity and certain energy products used as propulsion fuel[673]or as heating fuel.[674] That said, the Act does introduce some exceptions, such as the refund of excise duty paid for industrial and commercial purposes (Article 93), the refund of excise duty paid on agricultural and forestry machinery (Article 94), the refund of excise duty paid on commercial transport (Article 95), the exclusion or refund of excise duty for energy-intensive companies and also explicitly defines certain uses of electricity and certain energy products which are not subject to excise duty (Article 97).

§2. Excise Duty on Electricity

607. Excise duty on electricity is governed by the general rules of the Excise Duty Act and the special rules contained in Article 90 of the Excise Duty Act, and regulations governing excise duty in general.

608. Article 90 of the Excise Duty Act defines the concept of persons liable to excise duty by determining the following persons liable:

---

668. Official Gazette of the Republic of Slovenia, No. 83/16.
669. Official Gazette of the Republic of Slovenia, No. 50/17.
670. Official Gazette of the Republic of Slovenia, No. 70/17.
671. Official Gazette of the Republic of Slovenia, No. 81/16.
672. In order to ensure transparency, these two special provisions are presented below, each within its own section.
673. Biofuels shall be considered motor fuels if their physical and chemical properties meet the requirements of applicable standards and if they are adequate for direct use as motor fuels or fossil fuels additives.
674. The type of energy product and electricity shall be determined on the basis of its classification within a particular tariff code of the Combined Nomenclature of the Customs Tariff or depending on the characteristics of each individual product. The EA-1 contains a list of energy products subject to excise duty. For practical reasons, we would like to highlight that for excise duty purposes, energy products shall include also any other hydrocarbons for sale or to be used or intended as heating fuel, other than peat or biomass (defined as the biodegradable fraction of products, waste and residues from agriculture, including organic matter of vegetable and animal origin, forestry and related industries, as well as the biodegradable fraction of industrial and municipal waste).

- suppliers of electricity to end users in[675] Slovenia;
- a final customer or end user who, in the course of performing his activities, obtains electricity for his final use in another Member State or imports it from third countries or supplies it to a supplier who is not established in Slovenia;
- a producer who produces electricity to cover his own needs or supplies it to another person for its final use.[676]

609. Another important aspect, which does not follow the general rule as defined in Article 6 of the Excise Duties Act, is the moment when occurs the obligation to calculate excise duty. According to Article 90(4) of the said act, the obligation to calculate excise duty occurs when: electricity from the electricity transmission or distribution network is supplied by the supplier to the final customer at the point of consumption;[677] the final customer enters or imports electricity into Slovenia or is supplied to the point of consumption by a supplier not established in Slovenia;[678] or when the producer uses the produced electricity to cover its own needs or supplies it to another person for its final use.[679]

610. Moreover, the Excise Duty Act stipulates specifically for electricity that the electricity supplier charges excise duty on the amount of electricity supplied to end customers during the tax period. The electricity supplier may charge excise duty on the basis of the estimated monthly supply for those customers to whom the metering devices do not read during the tax period. For subsequently determined quantities of electricity actually supplied, which relate to previous tax periods, the electricity supplier shall settle the excise duty in the monthly excise tax return for the month in which it determines the quantities of electricity actually supplied.[680]

675. End consumers of electricity shall mean end users of electricity equipped with measuring devices installed at the termination for measuring consumption of electricity in accordance with energy legislation.
676. However, there is no obligation to calculate the excise duty for producers who produce electricity in a small hydropower plant or from another type of renewable energy of non-fossil or nuclear origin, with a capacity not exceeding 2 MW, and consumed by the producer for his own consumption. The same is true for electricity produced in the household or on appliances used for own consumption or for temporary electricity supply in the event of a failure or disruption of the normal electricity supply, provided that the excise duty on energy used in the household or in appliances, used for temporary electricity supply, paid.
677. However, the obligation to calculate excise duty for the holder of a self-supply electricity device, determined by a regulation governing the self-supply of electricity from renewable energy sources, occurs for the amount of electricity determined by the difference between the electricity supplied by the supplier and the delivered electricity from a self-supply device with electricity read at the same metering point; *see* Art. 90(6) of the Excise Duty Act.
678. It is considered that the final customer 'inserted' or imported electricity into Slovenia when he has took it from the electricity network; *see* Art. 90(7) of the Excise Duty Act.
679. The obligation to calculate excise duty arises on the last day of the month in which the producer used the produced electricity to cover his own needs or supplied it to another person for its final use.
680. *See* Art. 90(9) of the Excise Duty Act.

§3. Excise Duty on Natural Gas

611. Excise duty on natural gas is governed by the general rules of the Excise Duty Act and the special rules contained in Article 91 of the Excise Duty Act, regulations governing excise duty in general, as well as the special order on the conversion of the amount of excise duty on natural gas.[681] As with the excise duty on electricity, the Excise Duty Act also in case of natural gas defines the concept of obligated persons and the moment the obligation arises to calculate excise duty on natural gas.

612. Article 91(1) of the Excise Duty Act addresses the following persons:

- a supplier of natural gas based in Slovenia from the network to end customers in Slovenia;
- a final customer who, in the course of performing his activities, obtains natural gas from the network for his final use in another Member State or imports it from third countries or supplies it to a supplier who is not established in Slovenia; and
- a producer who uses the produced natural gas to cover his own needs or supplies it to another person for its final use.

613. Article 91(3) of the Excise Duty Act provides that the liability to calculate excise duty arises when:[682]

- natural gas from the natural gas transmission or distribution network is delivered to the final customer at the point of consumption;
- the final customer enters or imports natural gas into Slovenia or is supplied to it at the point of consumption by a supplier who is not established in Slovenia;[683]
  the producer uses the produced natural gas to cover his own needs or supplies it to another person for its final use.[684]

614. The natural gas supplier charges excise duty on the quantity of natural gas supplied to final customers during the tax period. The supplier of natural gas may charge excise duty on the basis of the estimated monthly supply for those customers to whom the metering devices do not read during the tax period. For subsequently determined quantities of natural gas actually supplied, which relate to previous tax periods, the natural gas supplier shall settle the excise duty in the monthly excise tax return for the month in which it determines the actually supplied quantities of natural gas.[685]

---

681. Official Gazette of the Republic of Slovenia, No. 81/16.
682. Also in this case the discussed act departs from its general regime as stipulated in Art. 6 of that act.
683. It is considered that the final customer entered or imported natural gas into Slovenia when he took it from the natural gas network at the point of consumption.
684. The obligation to calculate excise duty arises on the last day of the month in which the producer used the produced natural gas to cover his own needs or sold it to a person for its final use.
685. *See* Art. 91(7) of the Excise Duty Act.

§4. Excise Duty on Liquid Fuel

615. Excise duty on liquid fuel is subject to the general provisions of the Excise Duty Act which were presented in the introduction above. These provisions of law are fleshed out by both general and specialized regulations, including the regulation determining the amount of excise duty on energy products. This regulation is changed very frequently, mainly due to fiscal reasons and frequent changes in the excise duty policy relating to liquid fuels.

Chapter 3. Value Added Tax

616. This chapter discusses the valid manner of regulating VAT in supplies of electricity and certain other energy products. The VAT Act[686] is the fundamental act which is fleshed out by the following regulations:

- Rules on the implementation of the VAT Act.[687]
- Rules on the terms and methods of tax exemptions for diplomatic missions, consular posts and international organizations in compliance with international agreements binding on the Republic of Slovenia.[688]

617. The VAT Act defines several types of taxable transactions, where supplies of goods are relevant to the topic of this monograph since electricity, (natural) gas,[689] and cooling and heating energy (and similar) are deemed goods.[690]

618. Regardless of the aforementioned, according to Article 50(1)(11) of the VAT Act, the importation of gas through the natural gas distribution system or any network connected with such system, or the supply of gas to the natural gas distribution system from a ship designed to transport gas, or through an upstream gas distribution network, or electricity or energy for heating or cooling through district heating or cooling networks, shall be deemed exempt from VAT.

---

686. Official Gazette of the Republic of Slovenia, No. 13/11 – official consolidated version, 18/11, 78/11, 38/12, 83/12, 86/14, 90/15, 77/18, 59/19 and 72/19.
687. Official Gazette of the Republic of Slovenia, Nos 141/06, 52/07, 120/07, 21/08, 123/08, 105/09, 27/10, 104/10, 110/10, 82/11, 106/11, 108/11, 102/12, 54/13, 85/14, 95/14, 39/16, 45/16, 86/16, 50/17, 84/18 and 77/19.
688. Official Gazette of the Republic of Slovenia, Nos 141/06, 117/08, 68/09, 82/11 and 109/13.
689. As shown below, a special regime applies to gas supplied through a natural gas distribution system established in the territory of the EU or through any network connected with such system.
690. The transfer by a taxable person of goods forming part of his business assets to another Member State shall be treated as a supply of goods for consideration. A transfer of goods to another Member State shall be deemed to have been made if a taxable person or another person acting on his behalf dispatches or transports the goods for the purposes of his business to another Member State, except for the (*inter alia*) supplies of gas through the natural gas distribution system established in the territory of the Union or through any network connected with such system, supplies of electricity or energy for heating or cooling through district heating or cooling networks. Article 22 of the VAT Act specifically deals with the place of supply in the supply of gas through the natural gas distribution system, the supply of electricity or energy for heating or cooling through district heating or cooling networks. In such cases, the place of delivery to a taxable dealer shall be considered to be the place where the taxable dealer has established his business or has a fixed establishment for which the goods are supplied, or, in the absence of such a place of business or fixed establishment, the place where he has his permanent address or usually resides. If the case does not concern the case described above, the place of supply shall be deemed to be the place where the customer effectively uses and consumes gas, electricity or energy for heating or cooling. Any non-consumed goods shall be deemed to have been used and consumed at the place where the customer has established his business or has a fixed establishment for which the goods are supplied. In the absence of such a place of business or fixed establishment, the customer shall be deemed to have used and consumed the goods at the place where he has his permanent address or usually resides. For interaction the sake of completeness, we should mention that Art. 30.d provides special place of supply rules for the supply of services to non-taxable persons established outside the Union.

619. The general VAT rate (continues to be)[691] 22%.[692]

691. The so-called anti-crisis act increased the general VAT rate from 20% to 22%.
692. The VAT Act defines also lower rates, namely 9.5% and 5%, but none of them seems to be applicable for the energy and energy-related services.

Chapter 4. Special Environmental Levies

620. This chapter discusses the current regulations governing the environmental tax for CO_2 atmospheric pollution, the environmental tax on energy consumption aimed to enhance energy efficiency, and the environmental tax providing funding for the support scheme for generating electricity from RES and high-efficiency cogeneration.

§1. Environmental Tax on CO_2 Emissions

621. The basic regulation governing environmental tax on CO_2 emissions is the EPA-1, which is fleshed out by many implementing regulations, the most important from the point of view of this topic being the Decree on the environmental tax on pollution caused by CO_2 emissions.[693]

§2. Environmental Tax on Energy Consumption Aimed to Enhance Energy Efficiency

622. The basic regulation governing environmental tax on energy consumption aimed at enhancing energy efficiency is the EA-1, which is fleshed out by many implementing regulations, the most important from the point of view of this topic being the regulation on energy savings requirements.

623. Article 317 (funds for providing programmes of the Eco Fund with the help of tax on energy consumption to increase energy efficiency) and Article 318 (energy savings by end users and the alternative option of paying a contribution to the Eco Fund) of the EA-1 provide the basis for the environmental tax on energy consumption to increase energy efficiency. The legislator has given the Government the power to flesh out these provisions, which has to this end adopted the regulation on energy savings requirements, which, *inter alia* (in addition to the period and the size of energy savings, the method of calculating the energy savings, the distribution of energy savings per each year of the specified period, the ways and deadlines for fulfilling the obligation to achieve energy savings and the types of energy services and measures to achieve energy savings) sets the amount of the contribution on the use of energy to increase energy efficiency earmarked for the implementation of the Eco Fund's programmes, i.e. the Slovenian Environmental Public Fund.

693. Official Gazette of the Republic of Slovenia, No. 48/18.

§3. Environmental Tax Providing Funding for the Support Scheme for Generating Electricity from RES and High-Efficiency Cogeneration

624. The basic regulation governing the environmental tax providing funding for the support scheme for generating electricity from RES and high-efficiency cogeneration is the EA-1, which is fleshed out by many implementing regulations, the most important from the point of view of this topic being the following:

- Rules on support for electricity generated from RES and from high-efficiency cogeneration.[694]
- Act on the contribution for ensuring support for the production of electricity from high-efficiency cogeneration and RES.[695]

625. Article 378 EA-1 provides the basis for defining the aforementioned public levy. However, the Government is authorized to flesh out this provision, and to this end it has defined a system marked by a general levy and exemptions and lower contributions that are deemed state aid in the sense of Article 107(1) of the TFEU. The Government has exercised some options provided for in the Communication from the Commission – Guidelines on state aid for environmental protection and energy 2014–2020. Thus businesses, which would otherwise be excessively burdened to the extent that they would be uncompetitive in international markets, or even forced into failure (and of course in order to prevent so-called carbon leakage), taking into account their specific activity, which is characterized by high electricity intensity and exposure to international trade, are subject to a reduced charge.[696] 626

694. Official Gazette of the Republic of Slovenia, Nos 74/14 and 74/20.
695. Official Gazette of the Republic of Slovenia, No. 56/15.
696. For more information, *see* A. Ferčič, *Pravnopolitični vidiki določanja prispevkov za zagotavljanje podpor proizvodnji električne energije iz obnovljivih virov energije*, Pravna praksa, No. 11-12/ 2015, 28 and subsequent.

Part VI. Interaction Between Energy Law and Competition Law

626. The sixth part of this monograph deals with the relationship between energy law and competition law. It consists of four chapters, as follows.

627. Chapter 1 (Introduction) examines the concept of competition law, EU competition law, the development of Slovenian competition law, the interaction between competition and energy law, and the competent authorities in this legal field.

628. Chapter 2 (The Slovenian Law Against Unfair Competition) covers the legal regulation of unfair competition and unfair market practices.

629. Chapter 3 (The Slovenian Law Against Restricted Competition) discusses the basic acts that may restrict competition, namely restrictive coordination, abuse of a dominant position, market concentration and restriction of competition by regulatory instruments.

630. Chapter 4 (Use of Competition Law in the Slovenian Energy Sector) provides insight into the activities of the Slovenian competition ombudsman in the energy sector. Examples of restrictive practices and market concentrations are given separately.

Chapter 1. Introduction

631. This chapter examines the concept of competition law, EU competition law, the development of Slovenian competition law, the interaction between competition and energy law, and the competent authorities in this legal field.

§1. The Concept of Competition Law

632. In the broadest sense, competition law is a system of legal principles and rules governing the establishment and protection of market competition. At the most basic level, it can be divided into two parts depending on whether it prevents:

- unfair competition and unfair market practices by undertakings;
- (illegal) restriction of competition or restrictive actions by undertakings or public authorities.

633. Undertakings restrict competition through:

- illegal restrictive coordination of undertakings (agreements, decisions of associations of undertakings or concerted practices);
- abuse of a dominant position made by one or more undertakings;
- illegal market concentration.

634. Public authorities restrict competition through:

- illegal state aid;
- illegal restrictive market regulation.

§2. EU Competition Law

635. EU competition law forms part of the internal market law,[697] whereby it should be noted that it is chiefly related to preventing illegal restrictions of competition. However, the EU does not have a systemic framework in place for the prevention of unfair competition. As a result, regulation of this sub-field is mainly left to the discretion of individual Member States.[698]

636. On the other hand, EU law contains an extensive corpus of detailed rules preventing illegal restrictions of competition by undertakings and authorities. Due to practical reasons and the fact that this monograph focuses on genuine national

697. The Protocol (No. 27) on the internal market and competition (OJ C 115, 9.5.2008, 309) provides, among other things, that the internal market as set out in Art. 3 of the TFEU includes a system ensuring that competition is not distorted.
698. Unfair commercial practices are mainly prevented in the context of EU consumer protection legislation, which governs the relationships between undertakings and consumers, i.e. B2C.

rules, we only discuss the fundamental legal resources. It should be emphasized that a vast corpus of regulations, directives and soft law also exists in addition to EU Commission decisions and EU Court of Justice rulings.

637. Illegal restrictive coordination of undertakings is regulated by the first paragraph of Article 101 of the TFEU, which (relatively) prohibits such practices with cross-border implications and labels them as incompatible with the internal market. The second paragraph of this provision provides for one of the consequences of infringement, i.e. nullity of the Act which was used for the contested coordination. The third paragraph of the same provision sets out the conditions for exceptions to the principled prohibition of restriction of competition, which means that certain practices that may restrict competition and have an impact on cross-border trade are compatible with the internal market and thus admissible (provided they bring more benefits than harm).

638. Abuse of a dominant position made by one or more undertakings is regulated by Article 102 of the TFEU. A dominant position is not prohibited in itself, but it gives the holder a certain responsibility in accessing the market. Generally permitted practices may be considered as abuse if carried out by an undertaking holding a dominant position on the market. Abuse of a dominant position is absolutely prohibited, without exception. However, if a certain practice is objectively justified, it does not constitute abuse.

639. Illegal market concentrations are not directly regulated by the TFEU, but rather by Council Regulation (EC) No. 139/2004 of 20 January 2004 on the control of concentrations between undertakings (Official Journal of the European Union, L 24, 29. 1. 2004, pp. 1–22).

640. Illegal state aids are regulated by Articles 107–109 of the TFEU. In principle, they are construed as incompatible with the internal market, unless explicitly specified by the TFEU. In this respect, it is important to point to a number of provisions containing exceptions to the principled prohibition.

§3. Development of Slovenian Competition Law

641. Slovenian competition law in the true sense of the word has only existed since the country's independence in the 1990s. The establishment of the state also kick-started a complex process of economic transformation from an administrative-command planned economy, where market competition was not important or did not even exist in the real sense,[699] into a (social) market economy, where generally

699. Note that almost all the companies were public and for decades none of them collapsed for being uncompetitive.

undistorted market competition is a prerequisite for normal functioning of the market and thus for achieving certain public goals.[700]

642. From the formal legal perspective, the aforementioned process began upon the adoption of the new Slovenian Constitution, which introduced all the classical postulates of the market-oriented economy, including the principle of protecting market competition, into the Slovenian legal system. This constitutional amendment was gradually followed by amendments to laws and other regulations at the lowest level, which led to a new economic and legal regulation. Furthermore, from the constitutional point of view, it is important to note that a special provision was inserted into Slovenia's Constitution after its accession to the EU, i.e. Article 3a. The provision explicitly stipulates that, put simply, legal acts and decisions adopted within the framework of the EU are applied in the Republic of Slovenia in accordance with the EU legal system. As the principle of primacy of the EU law forms part of this legal regulation, Slovenia needs to follow it as well. As far as competition law is concerned, this principle implies that all EU rules have primacy over (the remaining) Slovenian rules, should there be a conflict of rules. In the absence of a special regulation,[701] the relationship between those rules is determined according to this general principle. In this respect, the EU has exclusive competence to establish competition rules necessary for the functioning of the internal market.[702] EU law refers solely to the cases in which anticompetitive practices may have an influence on the internal market or trade between two or more Member States.

643. In 1993, the Protection of Competition Act (hereinafter 'the PCA') was adopted as the first systemic regulation governing all practices of undertakings and public authorities that may restrict competition as well as unfair competition practices (in addition to illicit speculation, dumped and subsidized imports).[703]

644. In the context of EU accession, the Prevention of Restriction of Competition Act (hereinafter 'the PRCA') was adopted in 1999. It repealed those provisions of the PCA which governed the practices of undertakings and public authorities that may restrict competition and re-regulated that area. However, it was superseded in 2008 by the new PRCA-1, which has been amended several times but is currently in force.[704]

---

700. Market competition is not supposed to be a means in itself, but rather a means of achieving certain goals while taking into account the limits of both the market and market competition.
701. This is the case of Council Regulation (EC) No. 1/2003 of 16 Dec. 2002 on the implementation of the rules on competition laid down in Arts 81 and 82 of the Treaty (Official Journal of the European Union, L 1, 4.1.2003, 1–25) and Council Regulation (EC) No. 139/2004 of 20 Jan. 2004 on the control of concentrations between undertakings (Official Journal of the European Union, L 24, 29.1.2004, 1–22).
702. *See* indent b of the Art. 3(1) TFEU.
703. Subsequent amendments to the PCA repealed the majority of its provisions. Today, the PCA is only relevant in terms of unfair competition practices, and even as such it requires thorough amendments.
704. Official Gazette of the Republic of Slovenia, Nos 36/08, 40/09, 26/11, 87/11, 57/12, 39/13 – odl. US, 63/13 – ZS-K, 33/14, 76/15 and 23/17.

645. Other regulations from the same area are also important, such as state aid monitoring, consumer protection, telecommunications, postal services, transport, media and, of course, energy. Leaving aside some of the issues with the implementation of EU directives pertaining to individual economic sectors, including the energy sector, we can conclude that the Slovenian legal system in terms of market competition legislation is more or less substantively adequate and consistent with the standards of EU (competition) law.

646. Nevertheless, the adoption of new legislation adapted to the social market economy is (was) only one part of the task. The implementation of adopted regulations in day-to-day practice proved to be quite problematic, although specialized bodies were established for the needs of public enforcement of competition law in the widest sense.[705] The bodies in combination with other (generally) competent administrative authorities and courts were supposed to be enforcing competition law in day-to-day practice. Public implementation of competition law in Slovenia today is relatively well developed. Conversely, private implementation of competition law is still in its infancy, although visible progress has been made in recent years. Overall, the awareness of the existence and significance of competition law is increasing.

§4. Interplay Between (Slovenian) Competition Law and Energy Law

647. Competition law is not an isolated system; it interacts with other legal fields, including energy law.

648. The two systems are quite different. However, competition law is multisectoral. As a rule, it is designed for *ex post* interventions and focuses on the goals of market competition. On the other hand, energy law is sectoral. As a rule, it is designed for *ex ante* interventions and focuses on energy-related goals. In practice, however, the systems share some common points, which is increasingly the case. This is understandable, considering that energy markets of the Member States[706] have undergone a liberalization process and witnessed the establishment of a comprehensive internal energy market. This means that energy-related activities should be conducted in competitive open markets as much as possible. The new Slovenian EA-1 thus sets out certain goals with competitive potential. However, in different places it refers expressly to competition law.

---

705. Competition law in the broadest sense regulates unfair commercial practices or unfair competition on the market exclusively in relationships between two or more undertakings, and practices limiting market competition in a manner contrary to the law in relationships between two or more undertakings (restrictive coordination, abuse of dominant position, market concentrations) or between two or more undertakings and public authorities (state aid and restrictive market regulation).

706. Only the UK is slightly different in this respect.

649. The aforementioned clearly indicates that the two systems share some common points. This raises another question as to whether sectoral (energy) competition law should be introduced alongside general competition law, thus taking into account the specific characteristics of the energy sector. There is no general answer to this question, which is why the advantages and disadvantages need to be considered. The number of supranational rules superseding national rules is rising owing to the complexity of the relationship between competition law and energy law.

650. In addition to the above challenge, numerous outstanding issues can be identified in the institutional area. This is a question of the relationship between the competition ombudsman and the sectoral regulator. In this regard, attention should be drawn to the case law of the EU Court of Justice which, in contrast to the US Supreme Court, decided that compliance of a certain practice with the framework of a sectoral regulator does not ensure that the same practice is not contrary to competition law.

651. This is particularly relevant in the light of more recent practices of the European Commission. After holding a sector enquiry, the EU Commission has often resorted to the tools provided for in competition law (particularly Article 102 of the TFEU) to achieve liberalization objectives in the field of energy. As already mentioned, the EU has the exclusive right to establish competition rules necessary for normal functioning of the internal market. However, its competence in the field of energy is currently much more limited. Another reason may be that there is less need for *ex ante* regulation when the level of competition in the observed market is rising. If we look at the telecommunications sector, which, in our opinion, has progressed more significantly in the liberalization process than the energy sector, we can envisage that the aforementioned practice will continue and competition law in the energy sector will be used more extensively in the future. This trend can also be observed at the national level in terms of the practice of the competition ombudsman in the energy sector (*see infra*, Part VI, Chapter 4).

§5. Competent Slovenian Public Authorities

652. Although the legislative and judicial branches of power are involved in formulating the Slovenian competition policy, this monograph is limited to discussing the most typical actors from the executive branch of power and their role in the competition policy. These chiefly include the competition ombudsman, sectoral regulators, inspection services and specialized units within individual ministries.

653. The function of a horizontal or multisectoral competition ombudsman is (currently) held by the Slovenian Competition Protection Agency. The Agency is a legal entity under public law which is fully competent for supervising the implementation of the PRCA-1. It is also competent for supervising the implementation of[707] Articles 101 and 102 of the TFEU. However, these provisions fail to regulate all the actions that may distort competition on the Slovenian market.[708] The Competition Protection Agency deals with the actions of undertakings that may unlawfully restrict competition on the Slovenian market, i.e., through restrictive coordination of undertakings, abuse of a dominant position and market concentration.[709]To this end, it monitors and analyses the situation on the market where this is significant to the development of effective competition; it conducts proceedings[710] and issues rulings[711] (and resolutions) in accordance with the law and provides opinions on general issues within its competence to the National Assembly and to the Government. In the event of a breach of the aforementioned competition rules, it acts as an offences authority, which empowers it to impose a fine on the offender amounting to 10% of their annual turnover in the previous financial year. It can also lodge a suit before the competent court under statutory conditions to establish the nullity of an unlawful restrictive agreement or unlawful market concentration.

654. As the name suggests, sectoral regulators are only responsible for one or more (similar) sectors rather than for all sectors, which is the case of the competition ombudsman (the Competition Protection Agency). Here the emphasis is on the sectoral regulator responsible for energy, i.e. the Energy Agency.[712] One of the most important tasks of the sectoral regulator is to establish (effective) market competition, mainly by ensuring actual access to the network and determining adequate prices for its use. To do so, *ex ante* regulation is necessary; it is characterized by a more intensive intervention in the market or market relationships than *ex post* interventions by the Competition Protection Agency. To this end, special attention should be devoted to proportionality and other principles of the rule of law, although the EU is mainly responsible for this regulative framework. However, the EU deviates from its general orientation in the field of sectoral regulators as it gives the Member States freedom to organize their public administration. As far as the sectors that are

707. Considering the framework set out in Council Regulation (EC) No. 1/2003 of 16 Dec. 2002 on the implementation of the rules on competition laid down in Arts 81 and 82 of the TFEU (Official Journal of the European Union, L 1, 4.1.2003, 1).
708. For instance, the Competition Protection Agency is not competent to supervise neither the implementation of the PCA nor state aid in the sense of the Art. 107(1) TFEU.
709. Moreover, it only has limited powers (providing opinions) regarding regulatory instruments and acts restricting the (Slovenian) market.
710. The procedure in matters pertaining to competition law is a special administrative procedure.
711. No appeal may be lodged against the Agency's decisions.
712. The Energy Agency performs the function of the Slovenian energy regulator. It is publicly authorized to perform administrative and other tasks provided for in the EA-1, EU regulations defining the competences of national energy regulators and general acts adopted under the law. Its tasks also involve taking measures to establish (and maintain) market competition (with regard to the latter, it should be noted that its scope of powers has been extended to market-based activities). As part of the legal framework, the Energy Agency adopts general acts, conducts procedures and issues decisions and other individual acts, but with significant deviations from the act regulating the general administrative procedure. In principle, its decisions and individual acts are final. It is possible to initiate an administrative dispute against them. In certain cases, the dispute is considered as urgent. Independence in this case is not absolute, but the Energy Agency has primacy over substantive decision-making (taking into account judicial controls over its work).

subject to liberalization are concerned, EU law obliges the Member States[713] to establish highly specialized and independent regulatory bodies, which should be able to effectively transform uncompetitive markets into (more) competitive ones within a cogent framework. The fact that EU law grants the Member States organizational autonomy clearly shows the significance of sectoral regulators.

655. The Market Inspectorate of the Republic of Slovenia is a constituent body of the ministry responsible for economic development and technology. It conducts (horizontal) inspection and supervision of the implementation of laws and other regulations pertaining to economic activities, trade, crafts, pricing, criteria, quality of goods, consumer protection and fair competition, unless otherwise provided by law. It transpires that the protection against unfair competition is merely one of the tasks of the Market Inspectorate,[714] which is not an issue in itself. However, it is appropriate to ask whether better solutions are available. It is absolutely necessary to ensure that unfair competition practices are being prevented despite limited human resources and an overwhelming number of tasks to be performed.

656. The State Aid Monitoring Department is an organizational unit of the Public Property Directorate at the Ministry of Finance of the Republic of Slovenia. It is, among other things, responsible for the implementation of the Monitoring of State Aids Act, which delegates it the following tasks: process, evaluate and forward notifications for state aid to the EU Commission, if necessary;[715] process, evaluate and provide opinions regarding the conditions for a general block exemption and *de minimis* aid; select, process and monitor data about state aid and *de minimis* aid and keep records; prepare an annual report; provide advice to state aid administrators. The main idea here is 'control' aiming to prevent illegal state aid and ensure that the Republic of Slovenia generally fulfils the obligations imposed by EU rules on state aid. Very few national rules deal with state aid; they are mainly a result of the implementation of obligations arising from EU membership.

---

713. *See* Directive 2009/72/EC […] and Directive 2009/73/EC […].

714. The inspection procedure is a special administrative procedure governed by the Inspection Act or some other relevant act, with subsidiary application of the act regulating the general administrative procedure. An appeal is allowed, but it does not delay its enforcement, unless otherwise determined by a separate act. Final inspection decisions are, of course, made subject to deliberation in an administrative dispute.

715. Considering the Art. 108(3) TFEU.

Chapter 2. Slovenian Law Against Unfair Competition

657. Unfair competition was first regulated by Article 13 of the PCA (certain provisions are contained in sectoral regulations),[716] however, now the said provision is repealed and its content is simply (using copy-paste operation) incorporated into Articles 63 a and 63 b of the PRCA-1 (this is, according to our opinion, 'unlucky' legislative measure not only because the aforementioned provision should be modified but also because the concept of unfair competition is now regulated in the Act which is dedicated to the concept of restricted competition).

658. The first paragraph of Article 63 a of the PRCA-1 stipulates that unfair competition is prohibited, without exception. Absolute prohibition of unfair competition practices is understandable considering the aforementioned framework of constitutional law. It would be unconstitutional if the legislator of the PRCA-1 specified otherwise.

659. The second paragraph of Article 63 a of the PRCA-1 provides that unfair competition is an act of an undertaking in accessing the market which is contrary to good business practices and causes or may cause damage to other market participants. In this sense, this is a general clause involving a personal (undertaking, market participants), local (the market), damage-related (potential or actual damage) and moral (good business practices) component.

660. The third paragraph of Article 63 a of the PRCA-1 specifies that unfair competition referred to in the preceding paragraph denotes:

- advertising or offering goods or services by stating false information or information and expressions that create or may create confusion on the market, or abusing the lack of knowledge or credulity of consumers;
- advertising or offering goods and services or disparaging another undertaking on the basis of their nationality, race, political affiliation or religious beliefs;
- disclosing information about another undertaking if the information damages or may damage their reputation and business;
- selling goods with labels or information that cause or may cause confusion regarding the origin, method of production, quantity, quality or other characteristics of goods;
- concealing defects in goods or services or misleading consumers in a different way;
- acts aiming to terminate a business relationship between other undertakings or preclude or obstruct such relationships;
- unjustified non-compliance with or termination of a contract with an undertaking in order to conclude an identical or similar contract with another undertaking;

716. Let us point out that the rules on the protection of consumers against unfair commercial practices also have an impact on the protection against unfair competition. However, we only mention them to provide a more general framework.

- advertising an apparent sale or apparent price reductions and similar acts misleading consumers about prices;
- unjustified use of the name, company name, brand or any other indication of another undertaking, regardless of whether the other undertaking approved it, if it creates or may create confusion on the market;
- giving or promising gifts, material or other benefits to another undertaking, their employee or person working for another undertaking so the donor can benefit to the detriment of another undertaking or consumers;
- unauthorized use of services of a travelling salesperson, sales representative or a representative of another undertaking;
- acquiring buyers of goods or using services by giving or promising awards or any other material benefits or bonuses that are worth considerably more than the goods and services which give the buyer the opportunity to win the award;
- unlawful acquisition of business secrets of another undertaking or unjustified exploitation of an entrusted business secret of another undertaking.

661. The above indicates that Article 63 a of the PRCA-1 is defined by the system of supremacy of the general clause.[717] In each individual case, it is necessary to verify whether the conditions provided for in the general clause have been met. For instance, if a certain business practice is (abstractly) contained in the list of typical acts of unfair competition in the third paragraph of Article 63 a of the PRCA-1,[718] it does not necessarily constitute unfair competition. Such cases still need to be considered from the perspective of the general clause provided for in the second paragraph of Article 63 a of the PRCA-1.

662. The implementation of the PRCA-1 in the public interest is the responsibility of the Market Inspectorate of the Republic of Slovenia. As for the affected individuals, they can bring their compensation claims before general courts to protect their private interest.

The PRCA-1 also regulated rights of the person who is harmed by the illegal anti-competition behaviour. The issue in question is covered by Article 63 b of the PRCA-1 as follows. In case the damage is done by illegal anti-competition behaviour to an individual, the latter may demand compensation in accordance with the rules of the law of obligations. The affected participant in the trade of goods or services on the market may, by means of an action in civil proceedings, request the prohibition of further acts of unfair competition, the destruction of objects with which the act of unfair competition was committed and the restoration of the previous situation, if possible. If the act of unfair competition was committed by the

717. This means that the PRCA-1 does not contain the system of:

- secondary implications of the general clause, where the general clause is added to definitions of individual acts of unfair competition as a kind of a safety net in order to catch the acts of unfair competition that have not been explicitly stated by the legislator;
- enumerations in the absence of a general clause which serve only as a list of individual acts of unfair competition and their definitions.

718. In this case, this is not a final list (*numerus clausus*).

media or in a similar way (e.g., by leaflets, signs in public places) or affected many participants, the affected participant may also request the publication of the judgment in the media.

Chapter 3. Slovenian Law Against Restricted Competition

663. This chapter discusses the basic acts that may restrict competition, namely restrictive coordination, abuse of a dominant position, market concentration and restriction of competition by regulatory instruments.

§1. Cartels and Other Forms of Restrictive Business Coordination

664. This chapter deals with the principled prohibition of cartels and other forms of coordination of undertakings and touches on the exceptions to the prohibition. It also discusses general clauses and typical examples of coordination of undertakings as stipulated in the PRCA.[719]

I. Relative Prohibition and Exceptions

665. The first paragraph of Article 6 of the PRCA-1 provides that agreements between undertakings, decisions by associations of undertakings and concerted practices of undertakings, which have as their object or effect the prevention, restriction or distortion of competition on the territory of the Republic of Slovenia, are prohibited, null and void. However, this prohibition is not absolute. The legislator exercised the option provided for in the Constitution and laid down exceptions to the prohibition.

666. In this respect, it is sensible to highlight the *de minimis* rule,[720] which is specified in Article 7 of the PRCA-1. Agreements of minor importance are agreements between the undertakings whose aggregate market share on any of the relevant markets on the territory of the Republic of Slovenia to which the agreement pertains, does not exceed: 10% in the case of undertakings operating at the same level of production or trade ('horizontal agreements'); 15% in the case of undertakings operating at different levels of production or trade ('vertical agreements'); 10% in the case of mixed horizontal-vertical agreements or where it is difficult to determine whether an agreement is horizontal or vertical. If competition on a relevant market is restricted by the cumulative effects of parallel or similar agreements between other undertakings, the market share thresholds referred to in the preceding paragraph decrease by 5%. However, the *de minimis* rule does not apply to: horizontal agreements having as their object the fixing of prices, the limiting of production or sales, or the sharing of markets or sources of supply; and to vertical agreements having as their object the fixing of resale prices, or granting territorial protection to the participating undertakings or to third persons.

719. For clarity, it should be noted that in addition to the PRCA-1, which is applicable horizontally, certain area laws contain special sectoral provisions.

720. In simple terms, those acts under this rule that do not restrict competition to a sufficient extent are not considered restrictive practices in the sense of the Art. 6(1) of the PRCA-1.

667. The exemptions to the aforementioned relative prohibition as stipulated in the first paragraph of Article 6 of the PRCA-1 are regulated by the third and fourth paragraphs of Article 6 and by Article 8 of the PRCA-1. In accordance with these provisions, the prohibition from the first paragraph of Article 6 of the PRCA-1 is inapplicable if the agreements contribute to improving the production or distribution of goods or to promoting technical and economic progress, while allowing consumers a fair share of the resulting benefit. However, those agreements may not impose on the concerned undertakings restrictions which are not indispensable to the attainment of these objectives and afford such undertakings the possibility of eliminating the competition in respect of a substantial part of the products or services that are the subject of the agreement.[721] An undertaking invoking the exemption bears the burden of proving that the conditions referred to in a specific case have been fulfilled.

II. General Clause

668. The first paragraph of Article 6 of the PRCA-1, which only provides for a relative prohibition of cartels and other forms of coordination of undertakings, also has the nature of a general clause. It stipulates that agreements between undertakings, decisions by associations of undertakings and concerted practices of undertakings, which have as their object or effect the prevention, restriction or distortion of competition on the territory of the Republic of Slovenia, are prohibited, null and void. From the above we can discern several elements of a general clause. This one determines the addressees of the relative prohibition (undertakings), relevant forms of prohibited restrictive practices (agreements between undertakings, decisions by associations of undertakings and concerted practices of undertakings), a relevant consequence (the object or effect is the prevention, restriction or distortion of competition) and a relevant area (the territory of the Republic of Slovenia).

669. Overall we can say that the elements of the general clause in the Slovenian competition law and relevant case law have the same content as the elements of the general clause from Article 101 of the TFEU as perceived by the EU Court of Justice and the EU Commission. Nonetheless, some of the elements of the PRCA-1 are expressly defined compared to the TFEU.[722]

---

721. Pursuant to Art. 8 of the PRCA-1, in cases of groups of agreements that meet the above conditions for exemption, the provisions of regulations of the EU Commission or the Council of the EU governing the use of the Art. 101(3) TFEU are applied *mutatis mutandis*, even when the influence on trade between EU Member State is not demonstrated. The Government may additionally specify by decree other categories of agreements that meet the aforementioned conditions for exemption (currently no Government decree is regulating additional block exemptions). The Competition Protection Agency may withdraw the benefit of the block exemption if it finds that a particular agreement has certain effects which are incompatible with the Art. 6(3) of the PRCA-1 or Art. 101(3) TFEU.
722. The PRCA defines the undertaking as an entity engaged in economic activities (activities performed on the market for payment), regardless of its legal and organizational form and ownership status. An undertaking may also be an association of undertakings that is not directly engaged in an economic activity, but affects or may affect the behaviour of undertakings on the market.

III. Typical Examples of Coordination Between Undertakings

670. The second paragraph of Article 6 of the PRCA lists some of the typical examples of coordination of undertakings,[723]as follows:

- directly or indirectly imposing purchase or selling prices, or other trading conditions;
- limiting and controlling production, sales, technical development or investment;
- applying dissimilar conditions to equivalent transactions with other trading parties, thereby placing them at a competitive disadvantage;
- making the conclusion of contracts subject to acceptance of supplementary obligations which, by their nature or according to commercial usage, have no connection with the subject of the contract;
- sharing of markets or sources of supply between participants.

671. In principle, these typical examples of coordination between undertakings fall within the category of the most severe practices harming the market and market competition (*hardcore* restrictive practices by undertakings). Such practices are typically dealt with very strictly.

§2. Abuse of a Dominant Position

672. This chapter deals with absolute prohibition of abuse of a dominant position, followed by a discussion about the general clause and typical examples of abuse of a dominant position as stipulated in the PRCA-1.[724]

I. Absolute Prohibition

673. The first paragraph of Article 9 of the PRCA-1 provides that abuse of a dominant position on the market by one or more undertakings on the territory of the Republic of Slovenia or on a substantial part thereof is prohibited.

674. Under this provision, an individual or collective dominant position is not prohibited in itself.[725] This is logical because the social market economy allows for free economic initiative, which may only be limited in the public interest. Nonetheless, superiority of undertakings acquired through fair market competition is a mere ideal.

723. As stated above, coordination between undertakings regarding individual market parameters is based on horizontal or vertical agreements between undertakings, decisions by associations of undertakings and concerted actions of undertakings.

724. For the purpose of clarity, it should be noted that in addition to the PRCA-1, which is applicable horizontally, certain area laws contain special sectoral provisions.

725. To clarify, by lawful acquisition of a dominant position we primarily mean the respect of the rules on market concentrations.

675. Yet an undertaking holding a dominant position has a special responsibility: it may not perform certain acts that are otherwise normal and permitted because it has an influence on the market. In other words: a dominant position enables the holder to adversely affect the market and cause damage. To this end, an undertaking holding a dominant position on a relevant market is scrutinized more carefully. In fact, identical acts which are usually not problematic may seem different, i.e. hostile towards the market and the competition, if performed by an undertaking holding a dominant position.

676. The first paragraph of Article 9 of the PRCA-1 does in no way prohibit a dominant position, but rather its abuse. However, the Act does not lay down any exceptions: abuse of a dominant position is absolutely prohibited.

677. The key element is the existence of abuse (of a dominant position). Another relevant question is whether the observed conduct of a dominant undertaking or undertakings in given circumstances is objectively justified. If it is, then it does not constitute abuse (of a dominant position).

II. General Clause

678. The first paragraph of Article 9 of the PRCA-1 does not merely provide for a prohibition of a dominant position; in combination with the second, third, fifth and sixth paragraphs of Article 9 of the same Act it also has the nature of a general clause.

679. It stipulates that abuse of a dominant position on the market by one or more undertakings on the territory of the Republic of Slovenia or on a substantial part thereof is prohibited. From the above we can discern several elements of a general clause. This one determines the addressees of the prohibition (undertakings), a qualifying circumstance (a dominant position), a relevant form of the prohibited restrictive conduct (abuse) and a relevant area (the territory of the Republic of Slovenia or a substantial part thereof).

680. Overall we can say that the elements of the general clause in the Slovenian competition law and relevant case law have the same content as the elements of the general clause from Article 102 of the TFEU as perceived by the EU Court of Justice and the EU Commission. Nonetheless, some of the elements of the PRCA-1 are expressly defined compared to the TFEU. The second paragraph of Article 9 of the PRCA-1 thus expressly provides that an undertaking or several undertakings are deemed to have a dominant position when they can, to a significant degree, act independently of competitors, clients or consumers. The third paragraph of Article 9 of the PRCA-1 states that in determining the dominant position, the Slovenian Competition Protection Agency takes into consideration particularly the market share, funding options, legal or actual entry barriers, access to suppliers or the market, and existing or potential competition. In terms of the market share, the fifth and sixth paragraphs of Article 9 of the PRCA further stipulate that an undertaking is deemed to have a dominant position if its share on the market of the Republic of Slovenia exceeds the 40% threshold; two or more undertakings are deemed to have a dominant position if their share on the market of the Republic of Slovenia exceeds 60%.[726]

III. Typical Examples of Abuse of a Dominant Position

681. The fourth paragraph of Article 9 of the PRCA-1 lists some of the typical examples of abuse of a dominant position, as follows:

- directly or indirectly imposing unfair purchase or selling prices or other unfair trading conditions;
- limiting production, markets or technical development to the prejudice of consumers;
- applying dissimilar conditions to equivalent transactions with other trading parties, thereby placing them at a competitive disadvantage;
- making the conclusion of contracts subject to acceptance of supplementary obligations which, by their nature or according to commercial usage, have no connection with the subject of the contract.

682. Abuses of a dominant position are categorized according to different criteria. The most common distinction is between exclusionary and exploitative abuses. A dominant position may be abused through active or passive acts.[727]

§3. Market Concentrations

683. This chapter examines the notification obligation for an intended market concentration and touches on the concept of market concentration and the assessment of market concentrations.

I. Notification Obligation for an Intended Market Concentration (Ex Ante Control)

684. The first paragraph of Article 42 of the PRCA-1 provides that a concentration must be notified to the Slovenian Competition Protection Agency if:

- the total annual turnover of the undertakings involved in a concentration, together with other undertakings in the group, on the market of the Republic of Slovenia in the preceding financial year exceeded EUR 35 million; and

726. Both cases are subject to a rebuttable presumption.
727. Typical examples of abuse of a dominant position with passive conduct are: unjustified refusal to supply or unjustified refusal to enter a legal transaction.

- the annual turnover of the acquired undertaking, together with other undertakings in the group, on the market of the Republic of Slovenia in the preceding financial year exceeded EUR 1 million; or if in the case referred to in the third indent of the first paragraph of Article 10 of this Act the annual turnover of at least two undertakings concerned in a concentration, together with other undertakings in the group in the preceding financial year exceeded EUR 1 million.

685. Irrespective of whether the above threshold has been achieved, concentrations need not be notified if they are to be appraised by the EU Commission in line with Regulation 139/2004/EC.

686. Even if the concentration does not reach the above thresholds, the Slovenian Competition Protection Agency may, no later than fifteen days following the date on which the undertakings involved in the concentration inform the Agency of its implementation, invite them to notify the concentration if they, together with other undertakings in the group, hold more than a 60% market share on the market of the Republic of Slovenia.

II. Notion of Market Concentration

687. The first paragraph of Article 10 of the PRCA-1 provides that a concentration is be deemed to arise where a change of control[728] on a lasting basis results from:

- the merger of two or more previously independent undertakings or parts of undertakings;
- the acquisition, by one or more natural persons already controlling at least one undertaking, or by one or more undertakings, whether by purchase of securities or assets, by contract or by any other means, of direct or indirect control of the whole or parts of one or more other undertakings; or
- the creation of a joint venture by two or more independent undertakings, performing on a lasting basis all the functions of an autonomous economic entity.

688. The Act thus recognizes that mergers and special operations (status transformations) allowed by company law are not the only way to change control on a lasting basis over one or more undertakings; certain contracts may produce the same effect. In view of this, the legislator selected a functionally more appropriate term, i.e. market concentration, instead of a merger.

728. Control of a whole undertaking or a part thereof is constituted by rights, contracts or any other means that, either separately or in combination and having regard to the considerations of facts or regulations involved, confer the possibility of exercising decisive influence on such an undertaking or part thereof, in particular: ownership or the right to use all or part of the assets of an undertaking; rights or contracts that confer a decisive influence on the composition, voting or orders of the bodies of an undertaking. Control is acquired by persons or undertakings that are holders of rights or entitled to rights under the contracts concerned or have the power to exercise the rights deriving from contracts while not being holders of such rights or entitled to rights under such contracts.

689. For clarity, the fourth paragraph of Article 10 of the PRCA-1 stipulates that a concentration is not deemed to arise when banks, insurance companies, savings institutions or other financial institutions, the normal activities of which include transactions and dealing in securities for their own account or for the account of others, hold on a temporary basis business assets that they have acquired in an undertaking with a view to reselling them, provided that they do not exercise voting rights in respect of those business assets with a view to determining the competitive behaviour of that undertaking or provided that they exercise such voting rights only with a view to preparing the disposal of these business assets and that any such disposal takes place within one year of the date of acquisition of these business assets.[729]

III. Appraisal of Market Concentration

690. The appraisal of market concentration is carried out on the basis of criteria set out specifically for this purpose in Article 11 of the PRCA-1. This provision prohibits concentrations that would significantly impede effective competition on the territory of the Republic of Slovenia or on a substantial part thereof, in particular as a result of the creation or strengthening of a dominant position. The Competition Protection Agency shall appraise concentrations primarily on the basis of the market position of the undertakings involved in the concentration, their financial options, market structure, alternatives available to suppliers and users, their access to sources of supply or markets, any legal or other barriers to entry, supply and demand trends for the relevant markets, the interests of intermediate and ultimate consumers and the development of technical and economic progress, provided that it is to consumers' advantage and does not form an obstacle to competition.

691. In terms of joint ventures, the PRCA-1 specifies that if the creation of a joint venture has as its object or effect the coordination of the competitive behaviour of undertakings that remain independent, such coordination shall be appraised in accordance with the criteria set out in Article 6 of this Act for such restrictive agreements. If the Competition Protection Agency finds that the conditions for principled exemption from the prohibition of restrictive agreements in a specific case are not met, it shall issue an order declaring the concentration incompatible with competition rules and prohibit the concentration.

§4. Restriction of Competition by Regulatory Instruments

692. The PRCA acknowledges that market competition may be restricted not only by the aforementioned acts of undertakings, but also by other acts of public authorities, which are prohibited in a separate part of this Act (Articles 64–72).

729. The period of one year may be extended by order of the Competition Protection Agency on request when the undertaking can show that the disposal was not reasonably possible within the prescribed period. No judicial protection is allowed against such an order.

693. The Government, state authorities, local community authorities and holders of public authority may not restrict the free performance of undertakings on the market. For the purposes of this Act, restriction of the free performance of undertakings on the market shall be deemed to be general (regulations)[730] and individual legal instruments[731] that, in contravention to the Constitution and the law, restrict free trade in goods and services, free entry into the market or free performance on the market, or that prevent competition in any other way. However, the Act fails to grant the Competition Protection Agency the necessary supervisory powers for effective prevention of the restriction of competition by public authorities. The Agency may only provide opinions, either when it deems necessary to consider a certain regulation of a competent body or upon request of the prime minister or other competent minister to submit an opinion on a draft act or regulation.

694. As with the prevention of restriction of market competition by undertakings, the Act provides for some exceptionally permitted restrictions that public authorities may apply. Article 67 of the PRCA-1 stipulates that if public interest cannot be protected with measures in undertakings, import or by current economic policy measures, the Government may introduce extreme measures, i.e. market restrictions, in the following cases: (a) if, as a result of a natural disaster, epidemics,

---

730. In case of regulatory restrictions on the free performance of undertakings, the protection of interests of undertakings shall be ensured in a procedure for appraising the compliance of regulations with the Constitution and law if such protection cannot be ensured in an administrative dispute. For the purposes of this Act, regulations that in accordance with the Constitution guarantee human rights and economic and social relations shall not be considered to restrict free performance of undertakings on the market, particularly regulations laying down:

- conditions for trade in goods and services specifying the properties of goods or the method of the provision of services for sanitary, veterinary, phytopathological, environmental protection, safety at work, technical and similar reasons;
- price control measures in accordance with a specific law;
- the method of operation of undertakings with a view to protecting customers in accordance with a specific law;
- obligatory standards;
- the obligation of legally specified undertakings to carry out their activity for users.

731. Restrictions on free performance by individual instruments and actions are mainly instruments and actions that:

- prevent an undertaking from carrying out its activity in a specific area or in respect of a specific activity, although the undertaking concerned complies with the legally specified conditions;
- delay without good cause the procedure for issuing a permit for an activity or other permits important for the performance of the undertaking on the market;
- indirectly or directly constitute discrimination among undertakings with respect to their registered offices;
- prohibit trade in goods and services outside the area of a local community;
- ensure a specific undertaking a privileged position in respect of operations on the market without good cause.

If legal remedies against instruments and actions are not ensured in an administrative procedure, the undertaking affected may initiate an administrative dispute.

state of emergency or similar circumstances, serious disturbances in the market and in supplies for the population, or disturbances in other fields if they pose a threat to the safety and health of the population, have occurred or may occur; (b) if significant disturbances on the market have occurred or may occur due to a lack of goods indispensable for production or processing, or for the everyday life of the population; (c) if there is a need to meet the demand for products, raw materials and reproduction materials, which are of specific or strategic importance for the defence of the Republic of Slovenia. In the above cases, the Government may prescribe: (a) a prohibition of trade in specific goods, restrictions in the trade in specific goods in terms of quantity and quality, or a determination of specific conditions for trade in specific goods or type of goods; (b) the obligation of specific undertakings to put into circulation specific quantities or types of goods, and to make them available or deliver them to specific users in accordance with a set order of priority; (c) the obligation of specific undertakings to create reserves, within which they must keep specific quantities and types of goods.[732] The Government is obliged to cancel a restriction immediately after the reasons for which the restriction was prescribed cease to exist, or when the situation can be eliminated by the introduction of other measures.[733]

695. Clearly, these measures represent a significant intervention in the market, which may cause damage to certain undertakings, particularly those directly affected by such measures. To this end, the PRCA-1 expressly provides that the competent national body must adopt measures for mitigating the damage in such a way that the consequences of the prescribed national measures for the undertaking are not substantially disproportionate in comparison with the consequences suffered by consumers, other undertakings, the state or the local community. Should one or several undertakings suffer substantially disproportionate damage in the absence of subsequent mitigating measures, the undertaking may claim for compensation of the damage from the Republic of Slovenia.

696. It should be noted that Slovenian authorities are also bound by EU rules (and national implementing provisions) on state aid as it may seriously restrict market competition.

732. Corresponding prohibitions or obligations may be prescribed for services.
733. If the Government fails to cancel the measures within six months of their adoption, it must notify the legislator of the measures and report to it on the effects of these measures.

Chapter 4. Use of Competition Law in Slovenian Energy Sector

697. This chapter examines the use of competition law by the national competition authority in the Slovenian energy sector. It covers the period from 2007 when the EU Commission carried out a sector enquiry in the internal market. Restrictive practices and market concentrations are dealt with separately.

§1. RESTRICTIVE PRACTICES

698. Since 2007, the Slovenian competition authority (Competition Protection Office) has applied competition law in the energy sector in the following cases:

- cartel agreements on the prices of five electricity distribution companies;[734]
- cartel agreements on the prices – energy holding company (production, trading and supply) and supplier;[735]
- abuse of a dominant position by the operator of an electricity distribution network;[736]
- cartel agreements and concerted practices on the prices between natural gas suppliers;[737]
- abuse of a dominant position by a natural gas trader.[738]

§2. MARKET CONCENTRATIONS

699. Since 2007, the Slovenian competition authority examined numerous market concentrations. None of them were prohibited, meaning that the authority either approved them[739] or found that notification was not necessary. The majority of concentrations were identified in the area of electrical energy and natural gas, as expected.

§3. OTHER INFORMATION

700. The Slovenian competition authority has not yet conducted a sector enquiry in the energy sector. Cooperation between the authority and the sectoral regulator has been established.[740] No conflicts have occurred thus far.

734. The Agency issued a decision in which it confirmed the allegations in 2008.
735. The Agency did not found evidences for alleged illegal behaviour and for this reason it stopped the procedure in 2016.
736. The Agency issued a decision in which it confirmed the allegations in 2012.
737. The Agency did not found evidences for alleged illegal behaviour and for this reason it stopped the procedure in 2014.
738. The undertaking which abused its dominant position proposed the commitments which the Agency has accepted in 2017.
739. In one case this approval was subject to certain conditions.
740. Their cooperation is stipulated in EA-1 and PRCA-1.

Selected Bibliography

Action plan for RES 2010–2020 Slovenia, Ljubljana, July 2010; the English language version is also accessible at http://www.energetika-portal.si/dokumenti/strateski-razvojni-dokumenti/akcijski-nacrt-za-obnovljivo-energijo/.

Carsten, C. *Energy Law in Germany: And Its Foundations in International and European Law*. München: C. H. Beck, 2003.

Document for Public Debate, RS Ministry of Infrastructure, *Proposed Guidelines for the Drafting of the Energy Concept of Slovenia*, 2 June 2015. Available at http://www.energetika-portal.si/dokumenti/strateski-razvojni-dokumenti/energetski-koncept-slovenije/.

Document RS, Ministry of Infrastructure, Energy Directorate, Energy and Mining Department, *Energy in Slovenia 2012*. Available at http://www.energetika-portal.si/fileadmin/dokumenti/publikacije/energija_slo/evs_2012.pdf.

Document RS, Ministry of Infrastructure, *Slovenia Energy 2012 in Brief*. Available at http://www.energetika-portal.si/fileadmin/dokumenti/publikacije/energija_slo/evs_2012_pb.pdf.

Document RS, Environmental Agency of the Ministry of the Environment and Spatial Planning Indicators of the Environment in Slovenia, EN17, *Electricity Production by Fuel*. Available at http://kazalci.arso.gov.si/?data=indicator&ind_id=456.

Draft Proposal of the National Energy Programme of the Republic of Slovenia Until 2030: Active Energy Management [Osnutek predloga nacionalnega energetskega programa Republike Slovenije za obdobje do leta 2030: 'aktivno ravnanje z energijo'], June 2011.

Energy Balance of Republic of Slovenia [Energetska bilanca Republike Slovenije za leto 2014], Ministry for Infrastructure and the Environment, August 2014.

Erbguth, W. & Schlacke S. *Umweltrecht*. 5th ed. Baden-Baden: Nomos Verlagsgesellschaft, 2014.

Ferčič, A. *Public Services and Related Concepts in the European Union: Understanding European Union's Legal Framework for Services of General Economic Interest,* Nova Science Publishers, 2020.

Ferčič, A. & N. Samec. 'European Union State Aid Law and Policy, and Local Public Services.' *Lex Localis – Journal of Local Self-Government* 12, no. 2 (April 2014): 267–287.

Ferčič, A. & R. Knez. 'Organizational Challenges of the (local) Water Supply in the European Union Member States.' *Lex Localis – Journal of Local Self Government Annual Conference 2015 – Bled/Slovenia* (11 June–12 June 2015): special issue (*Lex Localis*, ISSN 1581-5374, 13, no. 3, July 2015). Maribor: Institute for Local Self-Government and Public Procurement, 2015, str. 765–787.

Ferčič, A. *Liberalisation in Slovenia: Past and Future Development*. V: KNEZ, Rajko (ur.), Rozehnalová, Naděžda (ur.), TÝČ, Vladimír (ur.). Five years of EU membership: case of Czech Republic and Slovenian law. Maribor: Pravna fakulteta: = Faculty of Law, 2009, str. 29–37.

Ferčič, A. *Einige institutionelle Aspekte der Liberalisierung in Slowenien: ein einzigartiges System oder déjà vu?*. WiRO, ISSN 0941-6293, 2010, let. 19, št. 7, str. 198–204.

Ferčič, A. *Geneza reguliranih sektorjev*. 1. izd. Maribor: Poslovna založba, 2015. 161 str.

Ferčič, A. *Državne pomoči podjetjem: teorija, praksa in predpisi*. 1. natis. Ljubljana: Uradni list Republike Slovenije, 2011. 405 str. I.

Ferčič, A. *Pravnopolitični vidiki določanja prispevkov za zagotavljanje podpor proizvodnji električne energije iz obnovljivih virov energije*, Pravna praksa, No. 11-12/2015, p. 28 (the same article is also freely available at the following website http://www.jm-excellence.si/wp-content/uploads/2013/10/Ales-Fercic-Pravnopoliti%C4%8Dni-vidiki-dolo%C4%8Danja-prispevkov-za-zagotavljanje-podpor-proizvodnji-elektri%C4%8Dne-energije-iz-OVE.pdf).

Gerland, G. & T. Helm. 'Übergang zum Übertragungsmodell (Ownership Unbundling) bei Energieversorgungsunternehmen – Wege aus dem Pachtmodell?'. *Betrebs-Berater* (2008): 192–196.

Heffron, R.J. *Energy Law: An Introduction*. Heidelberg, Germany: Springer, SpringerBriefs in Law, 2015.

Henneke, H. G. & K. Ritgen. *Kommunales Energierecht*. Wiesbaden: Kommunalund Schul-Verlag, 2010.

Johnston, A. C. & G. Block. *EU Energy Law*. Oxford: Oxford University Press, cop. 2012.

Jadek Pensa, D. *Pravica do zdravega življenjskega okolja in denarna odškodnina za nepremoženjsko škodo*, Podjetje in delo, No. 6-7/2009, 1320.

Juhart M. *Okoljska odgovornost – med javnim in zasebnim pravom*. Zbornik znanstvenih razprav Pravne fakultete v Ljubljani, 2008, 109.

Juhart, M. *Zahtevki za opravljanje splošno koristne dejavnosti*, Podjetje in delo, No. 6-7/2009, 1302–1311.

Knez R. *Vpliv pravil o varovanju okolja na poslovanje podjetij*. V: Ramšak, Franci (ed.). Gospodarski subjekti na trgu – novosti in aktualna vprašanja gospodarskega prava: (pravo gospodarskih družb, pogodbeno pravo, evropsko pravo, delovno pravo, davčno pravo). Maribor; Pravna fakulteta: Inštitut za gospodarsko pravo, 2011, 153–164. Also available at http://www.jm-excellence.si/wp-content/uploads/2013/10/Rajko-Knez-Vpliv-pravil-o-varovanju-okolja-na-poslovanje-podjetij-.pdf.

Landmann & Rohmer (ed). *Umweltrecht*. München: C. H. Beck, 71. Akt., 2014.

Lecheler, H. & J. Gundel. 'Ein weiterer Schritt zür Vollendung des EnergieBinnenmarktes: Die Beschlunigungs-Rechtsakte für den Binnenmarkt für Strom und Gas'. *Europäische Zeitschrift für Wirtschaftsrecht* (2003): 625.

Leidinger, T. *Energieanlagenrecht*. Stuttgart: Boorberg, 2007.

Lehnert, W. & J. Vollprecht. 'Neue Impulse von Europa: Die Erneuerbare-Energien Richtlinie der EU'. *ZUR* (2009): 307 et seq.

Lyster, R. & A. J. Bradbrook. *Energy, Law and the Environment*. Cambridge: Cambridge University, 2006.

Martin, B. 'Die Energieeffizienzrichtlinie'. *EnWZ* (2012): 62 et seq.

Massai, L. *European Climate and Clean Energy Law and Policy*. London; New York: Earthscan, 2012.

McHarg, A et al. (ed.).*Property and the Law in Energy and Natural Resources*. Oxford; New York: Oxford University Press, 2009.

Petersen, M. *Umweltschadensgesetz, Kommentar*. Köln: Carl Heymanns Verlag, 2013.

Petersen, M. Die *Umsetzung der Umwelthaftungsrichtlinie im Umweltschadesgesetz*. Köln: Carl Heymanns Verlag, 2008.

Petersen, M. 'The Environmental Liability Directive – Extending Nature Protection in Europe'. *Environmental Law Review* 11 (2009): 5.

Petrovič, T. & P. Zorin. 'Recent Developments in the Slovenian Energy Market'. *European Energy Review* 2011, 307–309.

Pichler, D et al. *Commentary on Environmental Protection Act [Komentar Zakona o varstvu okolja]*. Inštitut za javno upravo pri Pravni fakulteti v Ljubljani, 2010, 95.

Pličanič, S. *Foundations of Ecological Law*, [Temelji ekološkega prava]. Scientia Iustitia, Ljubljana, Cankarjeva založba, 2003.

Report of the Slovenian Energy Agency, Important Indicators of the Electricity and Natural Gas Supply in 2014 [Pomembnejši kazalniki na področju oskrbe z električno energijo in zemeljskim plinom za leto 2014], May 2015.

Report of the Slovenian Energy Agency on the Situation in the Slovenian Energy Sector in 2015 [Poročilo o stanju na področju energetike v Sloveniji v letu 2013], June 2014.

Report on Public Consultation of Draft Proposal of the National Energy Programme of the Republic of Slovenia, Part 1 [Poročilo o javni obravnavi predloga nacionalnega energetskega programa, 1. del], February 2012.

Roggenkamp, M. M et al. *Energy Law in Europe: National, EU, and International Law and Institutions*. New York: Oxford University Press, 2001.

Samec, N. & A. Ferčič. 'Die Problematik der Schadensersatzhaftung des öffentlichen Auftraggebers in Slowenien.' *WiRO*, ISSN 0941-6293, 2015, jhrg. 24, 1, str. 3–8.

Säcker, F. J. (ed.). *Berliner Kommentar zum Energierecht*. vol. 1, 2nd ed. Frankfurt am Main: Verlag Recht und Wirtschaft, 2010.

Schneider, J. P. & C. *Theobald. Recht der Energiewirtschaft*. 2nd ed. München: C. H. Beck, 2008 & 4th ed. 2013.

Schomerus, T. 'Die Umsetzung von Art. 7 Energieeffizienz-Richtlinie 2012/27/EU in nationales Recht'. *ER* 2013: 184 et seq.

Sellner, D., O. Reidt & M. J. Ohms. *Immissionsschutzrecht und Industrieanlagen*. 3rd ed. München: C. H. Beck, 2006.

Talus, K. *EU Energy Law and Policy: A Critical Account*. Oxford: Oxford University Press, 2013.

Tratnik, M. & A. Ferčič. *EU competition law* (POGESTEI editions). Belgrade: University, Faculty of Law; Niš: University, Faculty of Law; Novi Sad: University, Faculty of Law; Maribor: University, Faculty of Law, 2008.

Viler-Kovačič, A. 'Environmental permit [Okoljevarstveno dovoljenje]', *Pravna praksa* 2006, Nos 19–20, 6–9.

Viler-Kovačič, A. 'Environmental consent [Okoljevarstveno soglasje]', *Pravna praksa* 2004, No. 30, 15–18.

World Energy Trilemma – Time to get real – the case for sustainable energy investment, World Energy Council, 2013.

Zillman, D. N et al. (ed.). *Beyond the Carbon Economy: Energy Law in Transition.* Oxford; New York: Oxford University Press, 2008.

Index

The numbers here refer to paragraph numbers.

Index

www.ingramcontent.com/pod-product-compliance
Lightning Source LLC
Chambersburg PA
CBHW071434230926
51846CB00001B/227
9789403529943